Processes of Community Change and Social Action

THE CLAREMONT SYMPOSIUM
ON APPLIED SOCIAL PSYCHOLOGY

This series of volumes highlights important new developments on the leading edge of applied social psychology. Each volume focuses on one area in which social psychology knowledge is being applied to the resolution of social problems. Within that area, a distinguished group of authorities present chapters summarizing recent theoretical views and empirical findings, including the results of their own research and applied activities. An introductory chapter frames the material, pointing out common themes and varied areas of practical applications. Thus, each volume brings trenchant new social psychological ideas, research results, and fruitful applications bearing on an area of current social interest. The volumes will be of value not only to practitioners and researchers, but also to students and lay people interested in this vital and expanding area of psychology.

Series books published by Lawrence Erlbaum Associates:

- *Reducing Prejudice and Discrimination,* edited by Stuart Oskamp (2000).

- *Mass Media and Drug Prevention: Classic and Contemporary Theories and Research,* edited by William D. Crano and Michael Burgoon (2002).

- *Evaluating Social Programs and Problems: Visions for the New Millennium,* edited by Stewart I. Donaldson and Michael Scriven (2003).

- *Processes of Community Change and Social Action,* edited by Allen M. Omoto (2005).

- *Applications of Nonverbal Communication,* edited by Ronald E. Riggio and Robert S. Feldman (2005).

Processes of Community Change and Social Action

Edited by

Allen M. Omoto
Claremont Graduate University

The Claremont Symposium
on Applied Social Psychology

2005

LAWRENCE ERLBAUM ASSOCIATES, PUBLISHERS
Mahwah, New Jersey   London

Camera ready copy for this book was provided by the editor.

Lawrence Erlbaum Associates, Inc., Publishers
10 Industrial Avenue
Mahwah, New Jersey 07430
www.erlbaum.com

Cover design by Kathryn Houghtaling Lacey

Library of Congress Cataloging-in-Publication Data

Processes of community change and social action / edited by Allen
   M. Omoto.
      p. cm.
   Includes bibliographical references and index.
ISBN 0-8058-4393-0 (c. : alk. paper)
ISBN 0-8058-4394-9 (pbk. : alk. paper)
   1. Voluntarism. 2. Social action. 3. Political socialization.
   4. Civil society.   I. Omoto, Allen Martin.

HN49.V64P75 2004
302'.14—dc22   2004056396
                                                    CIP

Printed in the United States of America
10   9   8   7   6   5   4   3   2   1

TABLE OF CONTENTS

PREFACE

This volume, an outgrowth of the annual meeting of the Claremont Symposium on Applied Social Psychology, focuses on examples of social change and the processes at work in creating change. The Claremont Symposium on Applied Social Psychology has a long and distinguished history. Each year, scholars from around the world come together for a one-day meeting focused on a topic or set of issues in applied social psychology. The day is one full of presentations and intellectual exchange. In the case of the symposium that gave birth to this volume, titled "Processes of Community Change and Social Action," the presenters were stellar and provocative. It was a special treat, indeed, to be part of this symposium. The scholars who presented their research engaged each other and the audience in thinking about how best to create and sustain social change. In focusing on these topics, of course, lessons for the flip side—of how best to suppress, restrain, and prevent social change—were also discernable. This volume represents a product of their cumulative insight, research results, and perspectives; it includes chapters from each of the symposium presenters as well as a few select chapters from other scholars. The chapters, when taken as a whole, present findings from rigorous and provocative programs of research that offer illuminating lessons for anyone interested in community change, civic participation, and social action.

Overview of the Volume

Across the chapters, topics related to service learning, social movements, political socialization, civil society, and especially volunteerism, are addressed. It is an exciting and unique collection, with contributors from different disciplines and even different subdisciplines of psychology. Specifically, the research and thinking described in these pages has been conducted by sociologists, public health researchers, social psychologists, developmental psychologists, personality-oriented psychologists, and community psychologists. Thus, from a number of different perspectives and disciplinary traditions, all of the contributors have been attempting to understand processes of community change and the effects of such efforts on the individuals involved in creating them and on society at large.

Moreover, the contributors to this volume are all distinguished researchers and theorists, well known for their work on different aspects of processes of community change and social action. The reader will find, however, that these contributors do not necessarily have a shared vision of how to approach these issues. And, although outright disagreement is not clearly evident in the pages that follow, the chapters differ considerably in the constructs, explanatory mechanisms, outcomes, and units of analysis on which they focus. As a whole, then, the volume can most profitably be viewed as providing cutting-edge and complementary approaches to understanding the causes and effects of broad civic participation. Much can be learned and a number of viable approaches can be taken in deciphering the complexities in this area. For the receptive and perceptive reader, this volume will teach and also point to directions for important new theorizing and research.

Because this volume contains descriptions of contemporary research, scholars interested in processes of community change and social action will find a great deal of useful information in its pages. The volume could also be the focus of a seminar or ancillary reading material for advanced undergraduate and graduate courses. The chapters provide a snapshot of current research in this area and offer many themes and ideas for future work. Many of the authors have included explicit suggestions for future research and application in their chapters. Moreover, all of the chapters are presented in an accessible manner, even when highly technical and rigorous research methods are described. Thus, in addition to an academic audience, this volume should prove helpful, if not educational, for practitioners of social change. In fact, many of the chapters will be of special interest to individuals who work with or rely on volunteers to provide services or to assist with community education and change initiatives.

Acknowledgments

The Claremont Symposium on Applied Social Psychology and this volume would not have been possible without the hard work and efforts of numerous people. First, I would like to thank the many graduate students who assisted with the logistics of the conference. This student corps was ably led by Anna M. Malsch, and included Christina Aldrich, Michelle Bovin, Bettina Casad, Walter Chang, Bridgette Cheeks, Cindy Gilbert, Alana Olschwang, Michele Schlehofer-Sutton, Viviane Seyrayani, and LaRease Thomas. Simply put, the conference would never have happened without the dedication and work of these students.

The speakers and the contributors to this volume have been, without exception, a pleasure to work with and consummate professionals. I cannot imagine a more congenial group, and I thank them for their time and patience and for sharing their ideas in the chapters in this volume. I also thank Stuart Oskamp of the Claremont Graduate University, the "father" of the Claremont Symposium on Applied Social Psychology, and Mark Costanzo of Claremont McKenna College for their assistance in organizing the conference and hosting it on the day of the event.

In addition, I extend special and heartfelt thanks to Larry Rosen, President and CEO of the YMCA of Metropolitan Los Angeles, and Vera Mijojlic of the International Rescue Committee, Los Angeles. Although they do not have chapters in this volume, both participated in the Symposium by providing valuable commentary on the presentations from their respective perspectives as individuals working at the front lines of community change and social action. In short, they helped to place the theorizing and research into a "real world" context, and to put a human face on the abstract concepts and processes under discussion. The value, interest, and excitement that they expressed about the conference presentations and speakers, I believe, come through in the pages of this volume.

The institutions in the Claremont Colleges consortium also deserve special thanks. These prestigious institutions have consistently supported the Claremont Symposium on Applied Social Psychology, including with generous financial assistance. This important series would not have attained its outstanding reputation or been able to continue for so many years without the long-standing and continuing support of these institutions and their faculties. I also thank Lawrence Erlbaum Associates and its staff for making possible the publication of this volume and for their assistance at various stages of the production process.

Finally, Anna M. Malsch and Carli Straight deserve special thanks for all of their assistance in the preparation of this volume. It is a better product for their efforts, and their time, carefulness, and pleasant dispositions have been greatly appreciated in bringing this volume to fruition.

Ultimately, I hope that this volume not only advances research on processes of community change and social action, but also helps to make more efficient, successful, and complete the social change attempts that so many people throughout the world work for everyday. It is in this spirit that I trust that the reader will learn from and enjoy the chapters in this volume.

Allen M. Omoto
Claremont, California

UNDERSTANDING SOCIAL CHANGE: INTRODUCTION TO THE VOLUME

Allen M. Omoto
Claremont Graduate University

The Civil Rights movement. Environmental protection and conservation. AIDS education and care for people affected by HIV disease. Soup kitchens and homeless shelters. Women's rights. What do all of these have in common? They are a few examples of highly visible, and arguably very successful, attempts to change communities and society. Beginning with the grass roots efforts of a few committed individuals, these and many other social movements have developed and grown, and in some cases, evolved into industries and institutions that wield considerable influence in public opinion, in social policy decisions, and in initiatives that create social change. In short, it is indisputable that these and many other movements and collective efforts have helped to shape contemporary society, and to profoundly affect the ways that people live their lives. Such is the power of the processes of community change and social action.

Obstacles to Understanding

Although efforts to create and sustain change and social action occur everyday and around the globe, scientific and research-based knowledge of these processes appears somewhat fragmented and uneven. Why might this be? For one, efforts directed at creating change frequently proceed without theoretical or research guides. Citizens take action, movements are begun, and social programs are initiated to meet immediate needs and alleviate pressing problems. These efforts are not necessarily planned and tested by researchers and theorists, but instead represent the best attempts of people to collectively address common concerns or problems. Thus, as ubiquitous as social change attempts may be, there may not be involvement of researchers or even research tracks to follow in stalking scientific understanding of them. A related problem is that by the time researchers direct attention to an issue or movement, a good deal of its growth and development has already taken place. In this case, science lags behind "real world" attempts at change or is simply absent from the effort all together.

Perhaps obvious, social movements, social action, and civic involvement occur across a variety of domains and in response to a myriad of issues. Activists for and researchers who study the women's movement and rights, for example, may not necessarily deem investigations of environmental activism relevant to the understanding or change they are attempting to achieve. Or as another example, researchers who study service learning activities among youth may not look to work on older adults' political volunteerism for information and inspiration. A consequence of these myopic tendencies is that research fails to inform across different topic areas or different populations. To the extent that researchers and practitioners focus only on action in a particular domain, they may be unlikely to be exposed to potentially relevant findings or practices from another domain or on a different social issue. Therefore, while a good deal of information can accumulate on one topic, how translatable or generalizable this information is to other domains remains unexamined. And, it may lead to the perception of uneven development or knowledge across different domains of social action and attempts at community change.

Sometimes research and even sophisticated methodological and statistical techniques are utilized to analyze or evaluate change attempts and community programs. This research does not always receive widespread attention, however, especially because it may be disseminated in summary or technical reports or in presentations to boards of directors of even funding agencies. And, of course, much of this research is conducted only after a program has been implemented and for the purposes of evaluating its effectiveness or efficiency. The evaluated program may or may not have theoretical foundations, and thus its ability to speak to theoretical concerns may be limited. Furthermore, it is often impossible to collect information on the processes responsible for program outcomes after-the-fact. In summary, research on social movements and change that is restricted to evaluation work may possess limitations related to targets and means of dissemination, theoretical ties, and the nature of the information available for analysis.

Still another reason for the seemingly uneven literature on social action and change is that research on these topics occurs across a wide variety of social science (if not other) disciplines. Indeed, social scientists of many different stripes can and do legitimately claim interests in social issues and social change, often with good historical precedent and legacy. Thus, research and theorizing on processes of community change and social action have not one, but many "homes." Thus, to be master of the literature requires that an individual be part psychologist, part sociologist, part anthropologist, part political scientist, and so on, and also to read broadly across many different fields. Precisely because of its popularity and these multiple perspectives, then, research on community change and social action may actually suffer because its "core" is harder to situate than some other topics of theory and research.

And finally, research and theorizing on topics of community change and social action can serve several different purposes. One key distinction is the relatively applied or practical focus of the work versus its more theoretical or basic, knowledge-based end. The applied -- basic chasm has proved difficult to bridge across many disciplines and in numerous realms and is not unique to research in this area. However, it runs right through the heart of issues of social change and social movements. The desire to change conditions and improve human welfare has to be weighed against the desire for rigorous and systematic research on such attempts at change. From a practical standpoint, change may be needed sooner rather than later and by whatever reasonable means. From a basic research standpoint, however, studying change may be most informative if it is carefully planned, incrementally implemented, and perhaps even excludes some people from receiving potential benefits of change. In short, applied and basic goals can conflict and confuse social change practitioners and researchers. Complicating this picture, the outlets for reporting applied and basic work differ, so that the ability to discern a cumulative body of knowledge in this area can be further compromised.

The Causes and Consequences of Social Action

These are but a few of the most obvious challenges faced by social scientists and even practitioners interested in achieving a general understanding of processes of community change and social action. In spite of these obstacles, developing a clear understanding of the facets and forms of social change, as well as people's reactions to societal changes, is critical for both theoretical and applied reasons. Technological changes, increased travel and globalization, and the rise of urbanization all continue to shape the socio-political landscape of the modern world. Many of these changes are driven by social forces and factors. In addition, they impact personal well being and social functioning. Thus, a complete accounting of change can only be achieved by including analyses of the personal and social factors and influences. The knowledge that emerges is likely to inform theoretical understanding of political thought and behaviors, social movements, volunteerism and prosocial action, social capital, and the like. To be sure, it is also practically important, especially for people and issues "in the trenches," attempting to create social change.

This volume brings together the theorizing and research of a number of leading investigators from across several social science disciplines all of whom have devoted substantial time and energy to studying processes of community change and social action. Far from a fragmented literature, the volume chapters reveal a fascinating and ever-growing body of knowledge about different aspects of social action and change. The collective work of the scholars who have contributed to this volume is nothing short of first-rate; each of them has a well-established program of research devoted to understanding one or more aspects of civic participation and social action. Taken together, they have used methods that range from experimental work, even conducted in the laboratory, to analyses of large representative data sets. Traditional cross-sectional and longitudinal data collection methods have also been utilized. In addition, some of the work reported here derives from intervention projects -- intentional and informed attempts to foster community change, connections, and communication. Some of the work in the chapters focuses on members of hard-to-reach populations, on people actively engaged in social change initiatives, and on individuals in educational settings participating in service learning activities. There is also considerable variability in the ages of the research participants in the studies described in this volume, from adolescents to older adults. Furthermore, the research that is described draws from data collected from across the U.S. and also from countries the world over. Finally, in some cases, the data span long historical periods, either decades of people's lives or periods of time during which significant social change has occurred.

In analyzing and empirically investigating processes of community change and social action, a wide range of possible causal antecedents have been identified. Some of the chapters discuss "mandatory" efforts, such as required service learning programs, whereas others focus on the different kinds and magnitude of motivations that lead people to work for social change. Some of the chapters emphasize the dispositional and personality predictors of who gets involved in civic activities, whereas others focus on larger, systemic factors that compel people to involve themselves in organizations and the lives of their communities. And, still other contributors seek to explain volunteerism and other forms of civic participation in terms of the psychological experiences and manifestations of certain systemic and structural factors, or also, to document demographic differences in rates and types of participation. None of the authors claim to have isolated the most important or influential cause for stirring people to action. Rather, the chapters can be read as presenting the beginning of a complex and multi-layered explanation for these actions. Any one explanation alone may sufficiently explain some social action, but when considered together, the full power of the multiple perspectives represented in this volume becomes evident. Social action is likely multiply determined. Collectively, the chapters point an informed and useful finger at some of the most likely suspects responsible for creating and promoting social change and civic participation.

Just as there are differences in the preferred causal constructs and mechanisms invoked in explaining civic participation and social action, the different chapters focus on different outcomes or effects of these actions. What seems to be generally assumed that communities and society are somehow changed, and usually improved, by volunteerism, civic participation, and social movements. Rather than emphasize change at a societal level, the chapters focus relatively more thoroughly on some of the ancillary, but no less meaningful, changes in individuals and social networks that result from participation in community change activities and volunteerism. For example, some of the chapters outline attitudinal shifts that take place after participation in these or similar (e.g., service learning) activities. Some chapters illustrate psychological changes, including in self-esteem, trust, depressive symptomology, whereas some chapters examine commitment to and reports of civic participation, volunteerism, and collective action as important outcomes to be traced. There is not an exclusionary focus on only one type of outcome or consequence. Rather, the volume as a whole speaks the numerous effects of social change attempts and of participation in these processes.

Dialectical Tensions and Avenues for Future Research

Several what can be labeled "dialectical tensions" are evident in research on civic participation and social action, including in the work described in the chapters in this volume. How it is that individuals resolve these tensions, if indeed they do, may have important implications for their willingness to embark on or sustain civic involvements. Some of the tensions, meanwhile, are not intra-individual, but are between individuals, groups, or organizations. The existence and resolution of these tensions likely affect the relative success of attempts at social change.

Among the countervailing forces that can be seen in the literature on social movements and civic participation, including in the chapters in this volume, are that some individuals work in organizations because of the trust and support that they feel, whereas other individuals experience mistrust and ill-will working with and in organizations. The tension between self and society, legion across the sociological and psychological literatures, is also evident in this area of theorizing and research. As a concrete example, some individuals appear to appreciate and seek broad impact for their efforts, whereas others remain more narrowly focused on their own personal gains and effects. A related tension emerges between benefiting oneself, or being motivated by potential personal gain, and contributing to the well-being of another (recipient of service). Although not necessarily mutually exclusive, the distinction between benefiting the self and benefiting others has important implications for creating and sustaining social change efforts. It also likely has important implications for who attempts to help others or to create change and for how recipients of assistance or targets of change react to such efforts.

Furthermore, some social actions are aimed at working for a cause or instantiating a new culture, ethic, or set of beliefs, whereas others may be more appropriately labeled as working against an entity or status quo. In these cases, there is a tension between those who seek to create social change and those who wish to squelch it. Yet another dialectical tension, illustrated in more than one of the chapters, concerns the pull and push between the costs and the benefits of civic participation and social change attempts. It seems clear that both costs and benefits are important to consider in predicting, and also encouraging, civic participation and volunteerism. A potentially fruitful avenue for future research will be to investigate the relative emphasis on costs and benefits, and also to give attention to the different types of costs and benefits that participants deem relevant to creating and sustaining social change. Answers to some of these questions about costs and benefits are likely to have important implications for determining the success of social actions and change attempts, but they also may need to be refined so as to take into account who it is that is attempting to create change.

While it may not be wholly appropriate to describe these distinctions and relative emphases as tensions, it is a convenient heuristic for organizing some of the work that has been done and that remains to be conducted on community change and social action. It also serves as a good reminder that any explanation for social action must also be able to account for its contrary, namely inaction. For that matter, explanations must also account for successes and failures in attempts at social change. While the chapters in this volume present a wealth of information and insights on processes of community change and social action, they are the beginning and not the end. There is a good deal more to be learned about these important, fundamental processes. Thus, instead of merely listing themes to be found across the chapters in this volume, these tensions are presented as intriguing possibilities or challenges for future research. As suggested by the chapters in this volume, in fact, they are some of the more promising and provocative directions for new work, if only a partial set of possibilities.

Preview of Chapters

There are a number of possible organizational schemes and orderings for the chapters in this volume. Each chapter was written to stand alone, as a reasonably complete analysis or description of a core issue in understanding processes of community change and social action. Thus, they need not be read in any particular order, nor should they be expected to build on one another. However, many of the chapters are focused on fundamental issues related to volunteering and voluntary affiliations, including some of its determinants, consequences, and the processes at work among individuals who volunteer. These chapters have generally been grouped together at the beginning of the volume. Much of this work, furthermore, includes data at the level of the individual or with the individual as the unit of analysis. The latter chapters consider additional types of social action, including participation in community coalitions, civil society organizations, club and school groups, and service learning programs. In addition, some of the chapters go beyond individual-level data and examine group-level data. Thus, the general scheme that has been applied in organizing the chapters is to go from those with relatively specific foci on volunteerism and social involvement with individual-level data to chapters that include group-level data or which focus on other forms of social action and civic participation. A brief summary of the chapters in the order in which they appear follows.

In an extensive review chapter, John Wilson brings to light several critical issues regarding research and theorizing on volunteerism. He describes different units of analysis that have and can be used to study volunteerism, as well as differences in the picture of the phenomenon that emerge depending on the unit of analysis that is adopted in research. Embedded in Wilson's analysis is a critique of an over-reliance on survey methodology, especially when surveys are completed by individuals about their own attitudes and beliefs, to understand volunteerism. Wilson makes suggestions for future research on volunteerism, including paying attention to multiple and potentially interactive characteristics of individuals as predictors of volunteerism, contextual factors that influence prosocial and other helping behaviors, and the need for serious consideration of developmental issues (and methods) in research. As Wilson notes, much volunteer behavior is multiply determined and discontinuous in nature. Therefore, an exclusionary reliance on cross-sectional survey methodology, while providing important pieces to understanding the puzzle of volunteerism, is inadequate for future work in this area.

Next, Jane Allyn Piliavin's chapter reviews the psychological and sociological literature for evidence of health consequences of social participation, especially volunteerism. She describes several different theoretical models that would lead to predicting beneficial health effects for people who are involved in volunteer and service activities. Then, she reviews empirical work on adolescents, adults, and the elderly, all of which supports the volunteerism – health link, and poses important questions about the mediating mechanisms and possible moderators of these effects. To begin to answer some of these questions, Piliavin presents the results of her analyses of data from the Wisconsin Longitudinal Study, a multi-wave survey study conducted with a sample of over 10,000 women and men who graduated from Wisconsin high schools in 1957. Her analyses of data from over a nearly four-decade period suggest that volunteering leads to psychological well-being, and that more volunteering enhances health to a greater extent. The effects of volunteering also appear to be particularly powerful for those individuals who are least socially involved and integrated to start with.

Another chapter that explores some of the consequences of community involvement, and especially involvement in social change and support organizations, is provided by Jesus Ramirez-Valles and Rafael M. Diaz. Utilizing a probability sample of self-identified Latino gay men in New York City, Miami, and Los Angeles (no small feat), they explore the characteristics of who gets involved in gay, Latino, and Latino-gay organizations. They also go on to examine the social support and self-esteem correlates of community involvement. Even after statistically controlling for a variety of factors that are themselves related to social support and self-esteem (e.g., acculturation, poverty, and experienced homophobia), Ramirez-Valles and Diaz find significant contributions for community involvement. Some distinctive features of this chapter are that it brings together currents of research from several different areas and that it also includes presentation of data taken from a relatively understudied population. Social movements help to change the culture and social fabric in which they operate. As evidenced by this chapter, however, there are additional implications of community involvement and activism for the mental health of individual participants that are important to consider both for future research and in the design of intervention and empowerment programs.

Mark H. Davis's chapter presents the results of four studies, some with college students and some with actual community volunteers, which address issues of whether and how much personality factors matter in decisions to engage in and continue with volunteering. Specifically, Davis assesses dispositional empathic concern and personal distress among his participants and attempts to link these tendencies to decisions and feelings about volunteering, extensiveness of volunteer involvement, and actual volunteer persistence. He also explores the role of anticipated and experienced emotion as potential mediators between the personality characteristics and volunteer outcomes. Based on the results of his research, Davis concludes that certain personality characteristics do matter in initial decisions to volunteer and are also likely important in predicting the subjective experiences of volunteers over the course of their volunteer activities. Furthermore, he finds an intriguing pattern of difference between sympathy and distress in the strengths of their associations with satisfaction with volunteer work. Davis explores some of the implications of these findings and the chapter concludes with several practical recommendations for increasing volunteer satisfaction and involvement.

In the next chapter, Anna M. Malsch and I focus on the conceptual status of psychological sense of community and examine individual and group processes in the context of volunteering and volunteer organizations. Specifically, we make the case for recognizing and testing the differences between psychological sense of community, social support, and feelings of belonging and distinctiveness engendered by social identity processes. Our analyses are restricted to data taken from active volunteers about their individual-level experiences, but as is explained in the chapter, there are clear implications for group-level processes. Moreover, we find that sense of community is at least as good as, if not a better, predictor of future activism and volunteer-related activities than expected social support for volunteerism. Social identity considerations in our data were not related to future volunteer activities, although our measurement of social identity was less precise and reliable than might be preferred. We conclude by emphasizing the potential value and importance of continuing to explore psychological sense of community, especially for understanding communities that are developed and organized around interests, characteristics, and opinions, and for practical attempts to encourage volunteerism and related forms of civic participation.

Matthew Chinman, Abraham Wandersman, and Robert M. Goodman offer a cost-benefit analysis of participation in voluntary organizations. Their chapter reviews some of the research on volunteerism and volunteer participation, including organizing this work in terms of different categories of costs and benefits that have been explored. After presenting this framework, Chinman et al. go on to examine the implications of different costs and benefits for volunteer participation by drawing from data taken from participants in community-based coalitions at the frontlines of public health promotion campaigns. Specifically, they assess the costs and benefits of participation for individuals who take part in substance abuse prevention efforts either as representatives of organizations or as individuals (not explicitly organizational representatives). This distinction in participation role calls attention to different levels of analysis that may be important in research on civic participation, in this case, individual versus group (coalition or committee). In fact, Chinman et al. report analyses that reveal differences in perceived costs and benefits between individuals who represent only themselves and those who represent organizations, and also different patterns of correlation between participation and costs and benefits depending on whether these analyses were conducted at the individual- or group-level. The chapter concludes with practical recommendations and suggestions for future research that take account of costs and benefits and multiple levels of analysis.

Bert Klandermans, Marlene Roefs, and Johan Olivier also explore social involvement, but in this case, in civil society organizations broadly defined. Specifically, these researchers examine the extent to which South Africans were involved in organizations as diverse as trade unions, street block committees, youth organizations, environmental organizations, and churches for the unique historical period 1994-2000. This chapter draws from literature on social movements and attempts to link systematic factors (e.g., racial and economic groups), individual characteristics (e.g., employment status, education, location of residence), and psychological and attitudinal factors (e.g., trust in government, preparedness to participate in peaceful action) to participation in civil society organizations. The integration of these variables at different levels makes for an intriguing and inclusive chapter. By investigating a society in transition, this chapter also gives clues as to how the nature and types of involvement in voluntary organizations develop and change. In addition, it speaks to the ways in which individuals interact with broad and diffuse entities such as government though mediating civil society organizations.

In their chapter on social participation and social trust among adolescents, Constance Flanagan, Sukdeep Gill, and Leslie Gallay provide data from a multi-ethnic group sample of youth that trace some the effects of community service and involvement on the youth. As part of their investigation, Flanagan et al. also explore some of the potential mediators or processes that are hypothesized to produce changes in the adolescents. Based on questionnaire data collected from over 1000 youth, these investigators find that youth who participate in service activities and organizations have more positive views of others, including the study body at their schools and people in the communities in which they live. And, echoing the findings from some of the other chapters, the more that youth participate in both clubs and community service, the more positive are their views. In addition, the results indicate that youth who reported learning from their service experiences also had more positive views of their schools and communities. The implications of these findings for service learning programs, and the effects of these programs on creating greater social trust among adolescents are discussed.

In the final chapter, Robert G. Bringle explains some of the philosophy and assumptions behind service learning programs and then goes on to apply theory and principles from close relationships and social psychology to understand these programs and their potential effects on participants. Bringle also considers the various motivations that lead people to take part in service learning programs and the types of activities that students desire in these programs, including presenting illustrative data from surveys of university students. Then, he presents the results of three studies that explore the effects of service learning on participants. Across the studies, there is a tendency for students who engage in optional rather than required service learning to report greater civic responsibility at the conclusion of their experiences. Interestingly, the effects of service learning also seem to depend on students' prior inclination toward civic activities; required service resulted in less civic responsibility than optional service among students with little history of civic involvement. Bringle's conclusions focus on the role of service learning in higher education and the components that should be included in creating effective programs. In addition, he suggests some ways in which basic social psychological theory can be advanced by research conducted in the context of service learning programs.

Concluding Comments

Clearly, the topics covered in this volume and the rigorous scientific approaches taken by the chapter contributors vary considerably. It should be noted, though, that they also represent only the tip of the ice berg when it comes to viable approaches and issues that are ripe for study in this domain. They also represent the wedding of systematic research with social movements and civic participation across a number of different realms. To the extent that the volume as a whole effectively speaks to both researchers and practitioners of social change, it provides powerful illustration of the value and capacity of applied social science and applied social psychology.

The value, importance, and impact of research on community change and social action cannot be underestimated. Effective social action has the power to change the world, and understanding it may be critical for predicting and determining the quality of life of future generations. It would be a great contribution, indeed, if social scientists were able to explain when and why change occurs, as well as to fully articulate the causal mechanisms that give rise to such changes. And, in the service of putting research into action, such knowledge could serve as foundation for designing and implementing effective programs, social movements, and civic engagement efforts that improve the lives of individuals and the communities in which they live. Research like what is described in this volume benefits both science and humanity. This is at one and the same time its value and its promise.

ACKNOWLEDGMENT

The preparation of this chapter was supported by a grant from the National Institute of Mental Health to Allen M. Omoto.

1

SOME THINGS SOCIAL SURVEYS DON'T TELL US ABOUT VOLUNTEERING

John Wilson
Duke University

The volunteer has long been a subject of curiosity to the sociologist. In a world largely given over to the self-interested pursuit of material gain, how is this altruistic behavior to be accounted for? In this chapter, I describe and comment on the research on volunteering that has relied principally on the survey research method. I point to a number of missed opportunities and to ways in which survey methods, and the theoretical assumptions on which they typically rest, distort our view of volunteering. I suggest improvements in the use of survey methods to study volunteering, illustrating some of these with analyses of data from the National Longitudinal Survey of Labor Market Experience as well as citations to previous findings of my own and those of other scholars working in this field. The purpose of the chapter is less to summarize existing sociological knowledge than it is to provide an agenda for further sociological research on volunteering. Data are presented not for the purpose of testing specific hypotheses but to illustrate the potential for a program of research using survey methods.

The Unit of Analysis Problem

In the vast majority of social surveys, the individual is both the unit of observation and the unit of analysis. As a result, the impact of social relations and social structures on the range of choices open to actors is largely obscured. The research on volunteering using social survey data is typical in this regard. The result is a somewhat myopic view of volunteer behavior. In this section I will describe some of the problems created by focusing too much on the individual.

The Household

Although the people who complete social survey questionnaires are typically members of a household, this is rarely acknowledged in studies of volunteer behavior. This is in contrast to studies of philanthropy, where it is simply assumed that decisions about how much money to give to charity are made as part of the household budget management. In just over one third of all American households, two members of the family volunteer together, rising to nearly one half in middle-class families (Points of Light Foundation, 1994). Spouses encourage each other to volunteer and often volunteer together (Freeman, 1997). Parents take their children with them to share the experience of volunteering. In order to fully understand the practice of volunteering, we must take into account the inner dynamics of the household.

Volunteering often costs money, but *personal* wage or salary income makes surprisingly little difference to how much people volunteer (Carlin, 2001; Freeman, 1997). The solution to this riddle is that, in most cases, income is a household phenomenon—jointly produced and jointly consumed. How it is spent depends to a great degree on whether one or two people produce it and who contributes the larger share. For example, one study showed that family income had a positive effect on volunteering, but only for women. This is easily explained once we recall that women typically earn less than men, which means they enjoy the benefits of higher family income without paying the high opportunity costs (of volunteering rather than working for pay) that men face. They can switch from paid work to volunteering at less cost to themselves than can the men to whom they are married (Wilson & Musick, 1997a).

Surveys encourage us to believe that people's paid employment makes a difference regarding how much they volunteer. But this is to ignore entirely the labor inputs of other members of the household. In the typical American household, the hours spouses work are jointly determined. For example, spouses in two-earner families have less time for nonwork activities than those in single breadwinner families. Kingston and Nock (1992) examine rates of "active work" for voluntary associations in a sample of married respondents. They find that wives' active participation is affected by how their labor force participation combines with their husbands'. "If any group of women can be defined as the 'joiners' it is those with part-time employment who are married either to full or part-time employed husbands" (Kingston & Nock, 1992, p. 842). They enjoy the benefits of the social contacts their job provides while at the same time having the leisure granted by the part-time nature of their work. Wives with unemployed husbands have low activity rates, regardless of their own work arrangements. However, the opposite is not true. Husbands' activity rates are unaffected by how the spouses' work arrangements are combined.

Focusing on the household rather than the individual makes us more aware of the impact of other kinds of unpaid work on volunteering because we think about the work of running a household as a whole. Caring for kin is usually regarded as a higher priority than volunteering. This would suggest that the more time people spend caring for kin, the less time they have for volunteering. In fact, the data on this topic indicate precisely the opposite (Farkas & Himes, 1997). Also, the more time spouses invest in housework, the more time they contribute to volunteer work, especially wives. Rossi (2001) speculates that "time invested in domestic maintenance may function as an index of commitment to the personal care and pleasures of others at home, which is then generalized to include concern for the welfare of more distant members of the community" (p. 454).

Social Networks

The individual persons who supply the data for social surveys are actually embedded in complex networks of social relations that exert considerable influence over how they behave. Social networks are comprised of friends, extended kin, workmates, fellow church or club members, and so on. These networks connect us to volunteer opportunities and increase the chance of being invited to help. Unfortunately, social surveys typically use inadequate network measures, if they use them at all. Typically, information is drawn from the respondent. The social networks are therefore ego-centered. Because little is known about the linkages between other members of the respondent's circle of acquaintances, it is a misnomer to call them social networks at all. We know how often the respondent has contact with friends but not how often those friends contact each other. We know if the respondent draws friends from all walks of life but we know nothing of the heterogeneity of the social networks of which he or she is a member. We can therefore examine the impact of the number of friends on volunteering but we cannot examine the impact of different kinds of friendship networks on volunteering.

Neighborhoods and Communities

Focusing on the individual, social surveys leave ecological phenomena such as neighborhoods or communities very much in the background. But neighborhoods shape our lives in many ways, including the kinds of jobs we have, the kinds of houses we live in, whether there are parks nearby, and how safe we feel going to them. A recent study of voluntary association memberships (not volunteering) suggests that context has a powerful effect on volunteering. The study notes that racial differences in memberships are usually attributed to differences in human capital. However, residence also plays a role. Poorer neighborhoods are less likely to have branches of voluntary associations located in them, and they lack the highly educated people who are most likely to act as recruiters. Stoll (2001) found that, in poorer neighborhoods, fewer people belong to voluntary associations. The entire difference between the level of Black and White memberships is attributable to the poor neighborhoods in which Blacks live.

Neighborhoods rich in voluntary associations have high rates of volunteerism for another reason. They help foster "collective volunteering," in which people volunteer as members of a team. The "team" might be a religious congregation, a youth organization, or the local branch of the American Legion. A team agrees to supply volunteers to the community for a specific purpose, such as mounting a Christmas-gift-to-the needy drive. Many individual members of such groups are drawn into volunteer work in this way. However, this kind of volunteering is not merely the aggregation of individual decisions to volunteer because community characteristics have made the collective mobilization possible. Research methods that focus on the individual, rather than the community, are "inappropriate for fully capturing communal roots of volunteerism" (Eckstein, 2001, p. 847).

It makes sense that more people will volunteer if they live in a neighborhood with strong norms of community building or one that is institutionally well endowed with voluntary organizations. And, since we know that the quality of schools, the availability of parks and clubs, and the outreach programs of religious congregations vary across neighborhoods, we can expect the volunteer rate to vary also. The intriguing point is that an increase in volunteering could be brought about by improving neighborhoods as well as "improving" individuals. Conversely, failure to maintain a given rate of volunteering or community involvement might be attributable to the disintegration of a neighborhood rather than to a decline in altruism.

Political Units

Paradoxically, the most individualistically competitive of all modern nations, the United States, is also the nation with the highest volunteer rate. How could all of these self-interested and materialistic people produce so much altruism? The paradox melts away once demand factors are recognized. Larger structural forces in the United States have combined a free enterprise economy with a relatively small and nonintrusive government, creating a much stronger demand for volunteer labor than is found in most other countries. The nonprofit sector is also more clearly defined in the United States (Salamon, 1997). The result is a high rate of "job-creation" in the nonprofit sector. Recent analysis of data on voluntary association memberships [not volunteering] across 32 countries shows that differences can be explained by pointing to the opportunity structure in each country. "Statism" (the degree to which political power is centralized) and "corporateness" (the degree to which society is organized along corporate, or group, lines) both affect the variation in rate of membership across countries. Statism deters membership whereas corporateness encourages it. These country-level effects "operate strongly over and above individual-level variables such as individual education, employment and marital status, and so on" (Schofer & Fourcade-Gourinchas, 2001, p. 813).

Another theory of cross-national differences in volunteerism focuses on the role of the welfare state. The expansion of the welfare state in many capitalist countries after World War II threatened to crowd out volunteering in many areas. Do national differences in volunteering reflect differences in demand as governments step in and provide services formerly provided on a charitable basis? Or do governments actually serve to stimulate the demand for volunteer workers by funding nonprofit agencies? Intriguing data come from Canadian surveys of volunteering that show a positive correlation between government expenditures in a province and the rate of volunteering. When provincial governments lower welfare expenditures, fewer people volunteer. More detailed examination of the Canadian data reveals that some provincial expenditures increase volunteering (e.g., on recreation and culture), whereas others decrease it (e.g., social services; Day & Devlin, 1996). However, this line of research has yet to be extended to cross-national comparisons.

Cultural Frames

Survey research has been used to examine the impact of attitudes on volunteering in the belief that culture plays a role in shaping volunteer behavior. There is nothing wrong with gathering data on attitudes and beliefs and attempting to link them to behavior. But it is wrong to extrapolate from these data about the culture of the nonprofit sector at the macro level, and it is wrong to anticipate that by changing these attitudes and beliefs changes can be effected at the macro level. I discuss each of these criticisms in turn.

Political scientists do not assume that, having polled Americans concerning their beliefs about democracy, they have determined that America is a democracy. Public culture is not the sum of many private cultures. Deciding whether or not a society has a culture that encourages and warrants volunteering requires institutional analysis and cannot be based on data from individuals. The "health" of the nonprofit sector cannot be determined by conducting opinion polls. Rather, there are pre-existing "cultural frames" that shape the way we think about volunteering. These frames cannot be reduced to the internalized value systems of individuals. "Rather, they are cognitive scripts, embedded in long institutional traditions and organizational frameworks that shape the social behaviors and practices that are deemed legitimate, even 'thinkable'" (Schofer & Fourcade-Gourinchas, 2001, p. 810).

The second reason that surveys of attitudes and beliefs are misleading is that they imply we can get more people to volunteer by changing the way people think about it. This false belief overlooks the social organization of volunteering. Opinion polls might be useful for predicting the mass actions of individuals (e.g., purchasing toothpaste) but they are ill suited to predicting behavior that is socially organized in any way (Blumer, 1969). They deny the role of social forces, such as social networks or inequalities of power and resources, in forming opinion and mediating the connection between opinion and action. Leaping directly from changing individual opinion to changing behavior overlooks all the (unmeasured) mediating steps. It is easy to understand why survey methods are used to measure the culture of volunteering. "This idea is harmonious with individualistic American common sense, which tells us that what is inside is what counts: 'they care because they believe in helping people,' or 'they don't care because they don't have good values'..." (Eliasoph, 1998, p. 19). But, in reality, the rate of volunteering is more responsive to changing social and economic conditions and organizational opportunities than it is to changes in individual thinking about the topic. Forms of participation are not so easily engineered (Schofer & Fourcade-Gourinchas, 2001).

The Analysis of Data: Modeling Volunteering

Knowledge derived from social surveys is based largely on thinking about volunteers as bundles of personal characteristics, such as age, education, income, religiosity, and family status. The goal is to ascertain the partial effects of each characteristic using multivariate methods of statistical analysis. All too often, however, these characteristics are treated as if they existed independently of each other, as if each adds something to the variance explained. For a number of reasons, this assumption of independence runs counter to both common sense and sociological theory.

Resources in Combination

One prominent sociological approach to the study of volunteering relies heavily on "resource theory." Volunteering is compared to paid work, because both are forms of productive labor that consume resources. Individuals with more resources are better able to volunteer; they volunteer more often, volunteer for a wider range of activities, and volunteer longer (Wilson & Musick, 1997a, 1999). Chief among the resources are education, free time, occupation, and income, but social ties or connections are also important. It is customary to estimate models where these and other factors are treated as independent variables. These resources are seldom considered to operate in combination with each other, but many instances suggest that this might be the case. For example, the positive effect of education on volunteering is moderated by social ties: Educated people not only have more social ties but those ties "work" better for them when it comes to volunteering (Wilson & Musick, 1998). Another example demonstrates how race moderates the effect of education on volunteering. Whereas education results in more volunteering for Whites, it has no effect on African Americans. Conversely, African American volunteering is more strongly affected by church attendance than is White volunteering (Musick, Wilson, & Bynum, 2000).

The effects of many other combinations of factors on volunteering remain unexplored. Major social parameters, such as age, cohort, and gender, are viewed as if they do not intersect with factors such as education, occupation, and income. If professionals are more likely to volunteer, might this effect be stronger for women professionals than male professionals because women need to work harder to drum up business and make contacts? If volunteering is contingent on paid employment, does this effect diminish as one ages? Is it not likely that the effect of children is moderated by the work role? We know that having infant children has a negative effect on volunteering whereas having school-age children has a positive result. The negative effect having infant children has on volunteering would surely become stronger as the working day of the parent became longer. On the other hand, the positive effect of having school-age children would grow weaker, the longer the working day of the parent. Occupational prestige has a positive effect on volunteering (Wilson & Musick, 1997b), but high prestige jobs tend to demand long hours, which could inhibit volunteering. The positive effect of prestige might therefore be stronger for those holding part-time jobs or jobs that have not only high prestige but also flexible work schedules.

Role-Sets

The units of analysis in most sociological surveys are concrete persons. However, many believe that "persons-in-roles" are the fundamental unit of analysis in sociology. Regrettably, the idea that volunteering is a role embedded in a larger set of roles is almost entirely lost in the social survey research on volunteering. Instead, being a volunteer is reduced to a "state" of the individual, like being in the labor force. Attributes are taken as proxies for interaction and role incumbencies. Thus liberated from the network of roles in which it is embedded, volunteering is free to be causally connected to other individual "states," such as work hours or number of children.

In reality, work, family, and volunteering constitute a *set of roles*. Although survey researchers frequently gather information on these roles, they rarely consider the way they combine to affect choices. For example, it is typically assumed that people allocate their time in a sequence of decisions. First they choose how many hours to work for pay. Only then do they decide how many hours to volunteer. But it is intuitively more plausible that people choose how many hours to work for pay and how many hours to volunteer simultaneously. They decide how to allocate their time across paid and unpaid work at the same time, trading them off against each other (Tiehen, 2000). We cannot simply assume that people select their volunteer activities based on pre-existing work and family contingencies, each of which makes its independent contribution to the decision. Work and family roles combine to determine the decision to volunteer. We choose to volunteer under those conditions where our work and family roles can be combined in a satisfactory way. For example, some surveys show that married people are more likely to volunteer than single people. They also show that part-time workers volunteer more often than full-time workers. Must we assume that the effect of work is "added to" the effect of marriage? Is it not more likely that a certain marital arrangement (i.e., being married) has made possible a particular combination of work and volunteer roles? Married women find it easier to choose a combination of paid and unpaid work than single women.

We get a clearer picture of how volunteer work is gendered once we adopt the view that the volunteer role as embedded in a network of other roles. Three examples should help illustrate this point. First, the positive effect of marital status on volunteering is moderated by gender. Single women volunteer more than married women but single men volunteer less than married men (Vaillancourt, 1994). Marriage leads men to volunteer, but single women use volunteering as a form of social integration. Second, women who have paid jobs do more of the household chores than men who have paid jobs. Given this time squeeze, an extra hour of paid work costs women more than men in the currency of free time. An hour free from paid employment for a woman might be worth half the free time it is for a man and therefore has a weaker positive effect on volunteering. We also know that women's paid work roles are more taxing than men's work roles. An extra hour of women's paid work is more debilitating than an extra hour of men's paid work. Third, we know that women assume more responsibility for child care than men. If the presence of infants in the household is a disincentive to volunteering, its effect on women should be stronger than on men.

Explaining Volunteering: The Search for Social Mechanisms

Much of what passes for theory in sociology is little more than empirical generalizations that describe regularities in the data that have been elevated to the status of "laws." Such generalizations remain descriptions rather than explanations as long as they fail to specify the operative mechanisms that account for them. The use of statistical methods to tease out associations in survey data encourages the false idea that a correlation is an explanation. There are a number of empirical generalizations in the scholarship on volunteering that could be used to illustrate this argument, but two of the best known are the link between education and volunteering and that between occupation and volunteering.

Education

Education is a reliable predictor of volunteering. But why should education promote volunteering? There are many possible answers to this question. Education helps shape attitudes and dispositions that encourage volunteering. Better educated people have more self-esteem, self-efficacy, and ability to empathize, and they are more trusting. Education provides the skills needed to perform volunteer work and improves knowledge of social problems and an analytical understanding of their possible solutions. Education is a form of "ability signaling": It makes sense to recruit more highly educated people because if they are good at one thing they will be good at another. Educated people are more mobile and thus have weaker primary ties with kin and neighbors. They are more likely to use secondary associations and volunteer work as substitutes for these ties. Schools and colleges are similar to religious congregations, where volunteering is encouraged and the resources to perform it are provided. Prolonged exposure to these opportunities increases the odds of volunteering. Educated people know more people and know more different kinds of people. This increases their chances of coming into contact with opportunities to volunteer.

Occupation

Occupation is another predictor of volunteering but, again, we are not sure how it works. Perhaps the link is social-psychological. The kinds of jobs professionals and managers have increase self-confidence, which in turn makes it easier to volunteer. Blue-collar workers are simply too tired, too alienated from the "do-goodism" of middle-class volunteering, to feel much connection to it. A competing theory argues that people volunteer to compensate for what they lack in their jobs (Rossi, 2001). Professional and managerial occupations require, and enhance, "civic skills," such as the ability to organize and preside over a meeting, to write memoranda, letters, and newsletters, to be comfortable in the presence of strangers, to be assured in confrontations and dealings with opponents, and so on (Brady, Verba, & Lehman Schlozman, 1995). Job credentials can be a form of ability signaling. Professional and managerial workers enjoy a "halo effect" of their exalted work status. Those with higher status are believed to be somehow more able and are therefore more likely to be asked to volunteer (Herzog & Morgan, 1993). Professional and managerial workers are often encouraged, even required, to undertake volunteer work as part of their employer's campaign of corporate responsibility. This obligation is not pressed upon lower ranking workers. Self-employed businessmen and professionals volunteer in order to establish contacts, or give for nothing what they will eventually provide for pay.

The Only Constant Is Change: Cross-Sectional Versus Longitudinal Data

Social surveys can be likened to snapshots of the sampled population. They arrest motion, reinforce a static view of social life, and tell us about current rates of volunteering. If a population is surveyed at regular intervals we get useful trend data, but we learn nothing of the *individual* dynamics of volunteering from such studies. Two surveys conducted 5 years apart might indicate that one third of the population is volunteering on each occasion, but this could be the result of the same people volunteering on both occasions or of one group of volunteers replacing another. Cross-sectional data obscure altogether the patterns of volunteer activity over the course of people's lives. Some people volunteer only sporadically, whereas others make a career of it. Whether or not we are volunteering currently has a lot to do with whether we have volunteered in the past. At any given moment, "those who have a previous spell of volunteering have a higher rate of becoming volunteers and a lower rate of leaving volunteer roles" (Moen, 1997, p. 149). Cross-sectional data hide the long-term effects of life experiences. For example, what we learn from our parents about volunteering might not affect our volunteering until we become parents ourselves. Going to church frequently might affect our volunteering only when we reach old age. Spouses might affect each other's volunteer efforts but only once they reach retirement.

Volunteering Over the Life-Course

Sociologists with an interest in the individual dynamics of volunteering are inevitably drawn to the life-course approach to sociological analysis. This approach has two key ideas. The first is that the response of individuals to the social and economic conditions they face at any point in their lives is contingent on the pathways by which they reached those conditions. The second is that individual life transitions tend to be synchronized. The decision to volunteer, or to stop volunteering, is a "transition" that is tied to other transitions, such as getting married, having children, being promoted, and retiring.

By using longitudinal data we can analyze the "volunteer work history" of people in the same way we would analyze their employment history. One of the cohorts of women being followed by The National Longitudinal Survey of Labor Market Experience (NLS) was first interviewed in 1967 when they ranged in age from 30-44. They were first asked about their volunteer activities in 1974, when their mean age was 47. They were asked about their volunteer activities again in 1976, 1979, 1981, and 1984. These longitudinal data provide a glimpse of how middle-aged American women move in and out of the volunteer labor force over the span of a decade. Between 1974 and 1984 the women had five opportunities to indicate they had volunteered in the past 12 months. For 10 years, the proportion of women remained stable at about 28%. But this does not mean that the volunteer activity of particular women was stable. In fact, only 8% volunteered throughout the decade, while another 8% volunteered on four of the five occasions. The aggregate rate, therefore, overstates the level of involvement of women in volunteering measured over time. On the other hand, the aggregate rate understates the likelihood that a woman would volunteer at all. In fact, just over one half of the women (56%) volunteered at least once between 1974 and 1984.

The NLS data not only provide us with a picture of the overall pattern of individual involvement in volunteering across a decade, but they also allow us to see how much current states of volunteering are dependent on prior states. The positive correlation between volunteering in different panels of the NLS is strong, especially when measurements of volunteering are taken soon after one another. The correlation between volunteering in 1979 and 1981 is 0.53 ($p <$ .0001). Even across longer stretches of time there is a strong correlation. The correlation between 1974 and 1984 volunteering is 0.36 ($p < .0001$).

Nearly one half of the women in the NLS never volunteered at all. Just as there is a sizeable minority of the population who never vote, despite the issues, so there is a sizeable minority who never volunteer. Moen (1997) describes this pattern in her *Women's Roles and Well-Being Project*: "some women do in fact adopt a life pattern of continuity in their social role involvements, while others adopt a pattern of few such involvements" (p. 147). On the opposite end of the spectrum from the "abstainers" are the "career" volunteers. For career volunteers, being active in the community and helping others is an important part of how they think of themselves. They are not so much motivated by particular needs and causes as they are always predisposed to be active in some way. Vela-McConnell's (1999) interviews uncovered a group of people he calls "participatory activists" (p. 152). They were committed to involvement in general without being committed to any particular issue. Volunteering is what they did. They were passionate not about particular issues but about being involved.

Clearly, some people are more strongly attached to volunteer work than others. This shows up when we track individuals over time using longitudinal data. A study of two panels of the Americans' Changing Lives survey found that 28.3% of those volunteering in 1986 were no longer volunteering in 1989. Those who had dropped out worked longer hours at their regular jobs, had less education, had fewer children in the household, and attended religious services less frequently. And, since they also volunteered fewer hours in 1986 we can assume they were not very strongly committed to the volunteer role originally (Wilson & Musick, 1999).

It is possible to use the NLS data to see if sociodemographic differences exist between "participatory activists" and the more casually committed women. In this case, the time span is not 3 but 10 years. We can do this by constructing a variable to count the number of occasions on which a woman reported doing some volunteer work during the previous year and predicting variation in the amount by demographic variables measured at the onset of the period. Table 1.1 reports the results of regressing years volunteered on a number of sociodemographic variables that have been shown to predict volunteering in cross-sectional studies. The independent variables are measured in 1974. The number of times volunteered ranges from zero to five. It is worth noting that this coding says nothing about the precise year in which the volunteer work was reported. It is not a measure of the "longevity" of volunteering. For example, a score of "2" on this variable could indicate that a woman volunteered in 1974 and 1976, but it could also indicate she volunteered in 1974 and 1984 but at no time in between. However, it does give us a measure of how much volunteer work "occupied" a woman across this decade of middle life.

Both education and income have a powerful positive effect on how many times the women volunteered. The net effect of occupational prestige, however, is small. The effect of work hours reported is curvilinear. Women working the standard 40-hour week were the least likely to have volunteered often. Perhaps the most striking finding in the table is that *the "never employed" group of women are much more likely to volunteer over the five waves than any of the other group of women,* even more than the self-employed or government workers. This suggests that whereas being out of the labor force might have a negative effect on volunteering *concurrently,* a woman who reaches middle age and has never worked is more committed to volunteering regardless of current employment status. This indicates that work histories are as important as current employment status. Some of the women in the NLS study chose to be homemakers. They did not get a job but stayed at home and looked after their spouse and children. As part of this life-style choice, they also volunteered.

The career volunteer is probably distinctive in being more psychologically attached to the role. It makes sense to believe that people continue to volunteer if performance of the role is satisfying and rewarding to them. Intriguingly, however, it appears that this cost-benefit approach to career volunteers is not all that helpful. A survey conducted in 1982 "found that very few of the respondents who had resigned from a volunteer assignment during the previous three years said they did so for reasons indicating dissatisfaction with the experience" (Miller, Powell, & Seltzer, 1990, p. 904). Another study found that people who expressed dissatisfaction with their volunteer work were *more* likely to be volunteering 3 years later than those who were satisfied (Wilson & Musick, 1999). This seems to run counter to common sense. Workers normally leave unsatisfying jobs if they can. Some of this might have to do with the fact that survey researchers tend to think in terms of *absolute* satisfaction when predicting future volunteering. We need to know whether volunteer work is more or less satisfying than other roles being performed. A survey of teenagers found that 83% got a "great deal" or a "fair amount" of satisfaction from "doing things for others." Is this high or low? It is high in relation to satisfaction with schoolwork (70%) but low in relation to satisfaction with family (94%; Wuthnow, 1995).

Table 1.1
Estimated Net Effects of 1974 Factors on Number of Waves Volunteered
(Ordinary Least Squares Estimates)

	Five-Wave Volunteering	
Sociodemographics		
Nonwhite	-.064	
Age	-.002	
Socioeconomic status		
Education	.555	***
Income		
$11,000 - $16,000	.157	*
$17,000 +	.241	**
Missing income	-.168	*
Work factors		
Occupational prestige	.009	***
Work hours per week		
1 – 19 hours	.225	*
20 – 39 hours	-.291	***
40 hours	-.425	***
41+ hours	-.204	*
Employment sector		
Never employed	.597	***
Government	.289	***
Self-employed	.482	***
Family status		
Married	.202	**
Preschool children	-.031	
School-age children	.084	***
Adjusted R^2	.192	**

Key: $*p < .05$; $**p < .01$; $***p < .001$.

More importantly, we need to know whether volunteer work is more or less satisfying in relation to expectations, and this takes us into the area of people's reasons for volunteering in the first place. The volunteer might be thinking: "Does the activity satisfactorily express who I am?" The soup kitchen volunteer is there because she wants to learn more about herself or to affirm an identity as a caring person. Ridding the world of hunger is not necessary to reach these goals. By the same logic, the opposite set of circumstances can be imagined. A woman might sign up to prevent rezoning of nearby land in order to protect the quality of the neighborhood in which she lives. But she learns little more about herself as a result of her participation and her expressive satisfaction is low although the rezoning is prevented. In both cases, value is endogenous to participation because the volunteer herself instills it through her participation.

Theories of motivation have been developed to help explain why people volunteer in the first place, but they can also be used to explain why people continue volunteering. Although the designers of the NLS did not have motivational theory in mind, they did occasionally ask women why they had volunteered. The women were given the option of listing three reasons. The answers were open-ended but subsequently coded by survey staff into seven categories: "perceived need or sense of obligation," "personal enjoyment or interest in people," "personal enjoyment or interest in the activity," "family member involved," "was asked to do it or volunteered by someone else," "have the time or something to do," "sense of self-fulfillment or personal satisfaction," "other." This question was asked of middle-aged women in 1974 and 1976. The NLS also gathered data on the volunteer activities of these women in 1979, 1981, and 1984. It is therefore possible to see if respondents who gave a particular reason were more or less likely to continue volunteering at a subsequent date.

The reason "perceived need or sense of obligation" was by far the most likely to be listed number one. To examine the possibility that career volunteers have different reasons for volunteering than those who participate more sporadically, a continuous variable was constructed from the data on reasons for volunteering. Each reason was given a weighted score: three points when mentioned first, two points when mentioned second, one point when mentioned third, and zero points if not mentioned at all. Each volunteer could then get a score for that variable ranging from zero to three. Of the reasons listed in 1974, "need or duty" predicted volunteering in 1976 ($r = 0.09$, $p < 0.05$) and 1981 ($r = 0.08$, $p < 0.05$). "Personal fulfillment" predicted volunteering in 1979 ($r = 0.09$, $p < 0.05$) and 1981 ($r = 0.08$, $p < 0.05$). On the other hand, women who, in 1974, indicated that they were asked by another person to volunteer were less likely to be volunteering in 1981 ($r = -0.08$, $p < 0.05$) and 1984 ($r = -0.08$, $p < 0.05$). This suggests that being "coerced" into volunteering results in weaker commitment to the role.

We should not overlook the institutional contexts that favor career volunteering. Some people find themselves (or choose to be) in institutions where the volunteer role is clearly legitimated and strongly supported (e.g., colleges). Two examples can be provided. As shown in Table 1.1, government workers volunteer more often than private sector workers. This could be a result of self-selection: "Do-gooders" choose government work to avoid the selfish and competitive world of business. But it could also be that public sector work provides a more congenial and supportive environment for pursuing volunteer opportunities (Wilson & Musick, 1997b). Volunteering in connection with a church also encourages volunteering over the long haul (Wilson & Musick, 1999). One study of hospital volunteers suggests that this is a reflection of religious teachings and beliefs. Those volunteers who rated religion as being very important in their lives were rated as more dependable by their supervisors (Zweigenhaft, Armstrong, Quintis, & Riddick, 1996). However, another explanation is that the support religion gives to volunteering is structural. Religious congregations provide more solid infrastructural support for the volunteer role than other voluntary associations and therefore make it possible to contribute help over several years.

Other than these studies, very little is known about the structures that foster attachment to volunteering over the life course. Of course, we must be careful to distinguish the study of attachment to a job or an agency from attachment to volunteering. Nothing has been said here about attachment to particular volunteer jobs. This is an entirely different area of investigation to which social survey research based on randomly drawn samples of the population can make little contribution. We have already mentioned public sector work and religious institutions as supportive environments for volunteer work. Do communities perform the same function and, if so, what are the characteristics of communities that enable them to do so? The density of nonprofit agencies varies significantly from one county to another (Gronberg & Paarlberg, 2001). Does this make a difference to how much people volunteer? Do ethnic groups provide a context for volunteering? We know that minority groups in the American population structure the provision of help to nonkin in ways that are different from those of the majority group. Does this make it more difficult for people to remain committed to contributing their time to strangers?

Conclusion

Sociologists are attracted to social surveys because they can use quasi-experimental design in their studies. Where the use of experimental and control groups is impractical or unethical, an approximation is to draw a random sample of the population. The data gathered can be examined for relationships among the properties and dispositions of the "units" surveyed. Typically these units are individual respondents. Over the past two decades, the analysis of social survey data has allowed sociologists to construct a fairly detailed profile of the volunteer, to identify the reasons why people volunteer and what they are most likely to volunteer for at any stage of their life. The extent to which social institutions, such as work, family, church, and school, combine to shape volunteer activities is more clearly understood today than it was 20 years ago. Some progress has been made toward a better understanding of how the social interactions in which people are involved and the communities in which they live influence their volunteer work.

As a result of this accumulating research, sociologists have begun to change the way they think about volunteering. No longer is it dismissed as a charitable pursuit of middle-aged and middle-class housewives with time on their hands, or subsumed under the study of voluntary associations and consigned to leisure time. Nor is it considered an altruistic anomaly in a society largely given over to the pursuit of self-interest. The study of volunteering has moved closer to center stage in the social sciences partly because prominent politicians are looking to the nonprofit sector to substitute for declining state spending, but also because we now think of volunteering as a vital contribution to the public household, the value of which can be estimated in billions of dollars. Consequently, if social surveys find blue-collar workers volunteering less than white-collar workers, or Hispanics volunteering less than Anglos, or evangelical Christians focusing all their volunteer work on their own churches, these are highly significant findings because it means the nation is not realizing its potential when it comes to drawing on the charitable impulses of its people.

In this chapter, I have described in detail some of the ways in which survey analysis has improved our understanding of volunteer behavior. I have not attempted an exhaustive survey of the sociological literature on this topic. Instead, I have used examples of the analysis of volunteering using survey data to: (a) suggest ways in which we could build on what we already know to improve our theoretical knowledge of the topic, and (b) indicate some of the limitations of the survey method when applied to testing theories of volunteering. On the first topic, I argue that the study of volunteering is poorly theorized. As a result, much of the analysis of volunteer behavior using survey data is descriptive or, at best, provides only empirical generalizations. We know that certain properties of individuals tend to be correlated but we do not know why. One promising line of investigation is to integrate the study of motives with the study of sociodemographic variables. In short, there are several ways, within the confines of the survey method, of improving our understanding of volunteer behavior. On the second topic, I have argued that social surveys share a number of limitations. Typically, they view the individual as the unit of observation and analysis. The result is a tendency to ignore, or measure incorrectly, relational phenomena, such as households, networks, and communities. This problem is compounded by the analytical tendency to estimate the effects of predictor variables as if they existed independently of each other. In short, social surveys encourage an atomistic view of the world, which runs counter to the structural or holistic approach that many sociologists believe identifies the discipline. Social surveys also are limited in being snapshots of motion. Longitudinal surveys allow us to track an individual's volunteer activities across a span of time. They allow us to measure "spells" of volunteering and "spells" of inactivity. But even the best of these studies fails to capture the processual nature of social interaction. They can measure identities by asking people with whom they identify. They can measure changes in identity by repeating this question 1 year later. But they cannot reveal the process of identification. At this point, it seems, we reach the boundary of what the social survey method can achieve.

References

Blumer, H. (1969). *Symbolic interactionism*. Englewood Cliffs, NJ: Prentice Hall.

Brady, H. E., Verba, S., & Lehman Schlozman, K. (1995). Beyond SES: A resource model of political participation. *American Political Science Review, 89*, 271-294.

Carlin, P. (2001). Evidence on the volunteer labor supply of married women. *Southern Economic Journal, 67*, 801-824.

Day, K. M. & Devlin, R. A. (1996). Volunteerism and crowding out: Canadian econometric evidence. *Canadian Journal of Economics, 29*, 37-53.

Eckstein, S. (2001). Community gift-giving: Collective roots of volunteerism. *American Sociological Review, 66*, 829-851.

Eliasoph, N. (1998). *Avoiding politics: How Americans produce apathy in everyday life*. Cambridge, England: Cambridge University Press.

Farkas, J., & Himes, C. (1997). The influence of caregiving and employment on the voluntary activities of midlife and older women. *Journal of Gerontology, 52B*, S180-S189.

Freeman, R. (1997). Working for nothing: The supply of volunteer labor. *Journal of Labor Economics, 15*, 140-167.

Gronberg, K., & Paarlberg, L. (2001). Community variation in the size and scope of the nonprofit sector: Theory and preliminary findings. *Nonprofit and Voluntary Sector Quarterly, 30*, 684-706.

Herzog A., & Morgan, J. (1993). Formal volunteer work among older Americans. In S. Bass, F. Caro, & Y. Chen (Eds.), *Achieving a productive aging society* (pp. 119-142). Westport, CT: Auburn House.

Kingston, P., & Nock, S. (1992). Couples' joint work status and community and social attachments. *Social Science Quarterly, 73*, 862-875.

Miller, L., Powell, G., & Seltzer, J. (1990). Determinants of turnover among volunteers. *Human Relations, 43*, 901-917.

Moen, P. (1997). Women's roles and resilience: Trajectories of advantage or turning points? In I. Gottleib & B. Wheaton (Eds.), *Stress and adversity over the life course* (pp. 133-145). Cambridge, England: Cambridge University Press.

Musick, M. A., Wilson, J., & Bynum, W. B., Jr., (2000). Race and formal volunteering: The differential effects of class and religion. *Social Forces, 78*, 1539-1571.

Points of Light Foundation. (1994). *Family volunteering: A report on a survey*. Washington, DC: Author.

Rossi, A. (2001). The interplay between work and family and its impact on community service. In A. Rossi (Ed.), *Caring and doing for others* (pp. 427-462). Chicago: University of Chicago Press.

Salamon, L. (1997). United States. In L. M. Salamon & H. Anheier (Eds.), *Defining the nonprofit sector: A cross-national analysis* (pp. 280-320). Manchester, England: Manchester University Press.

Schofer, E., & Fourcade-Gourinchas, M. (2001). The structural contexts of civic engagement: Voluntary association membership in comparative perspective. *American Sociological Review, 66,* 806-828.

Stoll, M. (2001). Race, neighborhood poverty, and participation in voluntary associations. *Sociological Forum, 16,* 529-557.

Tiehen, L. (2000). Has working more caused married women to volunteer less? Evidence from time diary data, 1965 to 1993. *Nonprofit and Voluntary Sector Quarterly, 29,* 505-529.

Vaillancourt, F. (1994) To volunteer or not: Canada, 1987. *Canadian Journal of Economics, 27,* 813-826.

Vela-McConnell, J. A. (1999). *Who is my neighbor? Social affinity in a modern world.* Albany: State University of New York Press.

Wilson, J., & Musick, M.A. (1997a). Who cares? Toward an integrated theory of volunteer work. *American Sociological Review, 62,* 694-713.

Wilson, J., & Musick, M.A. (1997b). Work and volunteering: The long arm of the job. *Social Forces, 76,* 251-272.

Wilson, J., & Musick, M.A. (1998). Social resources and volunteering. *Social Science Quarterly, 79,* 799-814.

Wilson, J., & Musick, M.A. (1999). Attachment to volunteering. *Sociological Forum, 14,* 243-272.

Wuthnow, R. (1995). *Learning to care.* New York: Oxford University Press.

Zweigenhaft, R., Armstrong, J., Quintis, F., & Riddick, A. (1996). The motivation and effectiveness of hospital volunteers. *Journal of Social Psychology, 136,* 25-34.

2

FEELING GOOD BY DOING GOOD: HEALTH CONSEQUENCES OF SOCIAL SERVICE

Jane Allyn Piliavin
University of Wisconsin - Madison

The question raised in this chapter regards the personal health benefits of volunteering and other social participation. Stated crassly, does one do well by doing good? This is not the first investigation of this question, and other research—which will be briefly reviewed—has found affirmative answers to it. But first I want to address more theoretical concerns. Why would one even suggest that social participation would be good for you?

Theories from both sociology and psychology have relevance for the relationship between social participation and well-being. First, sociologists have proposed for many years that there are benefits of social participation. In the 19th century, Durkheim (1898/1951) argued convincingly for the importance of group ties, norms, and social expectations in protecting individuals from suicide. Van Willigen (2000) states, "Beginning with Durkheim (1951) . . . sociologists have argued that some positions in society foster a subjective sense of alienation . . . while others promote a sense of attachment or integration" (Mirowsky & Ross, 1989; Seeman, 1959). Referring to Seeman's five types of alienation, she goes on to suggest that "the extent to which individuals feel they control the outcomes of their lives, believe they are part of a supportive community, find their daily work rewarding, have a sense of purpose to their lives, and expect that rewards can be achieved through socially normative means affects their psychological well-being" (p. S2). Volunteering, she suggests, can facilitate the development of these "psychosocial resources" and thus lead to positive effects on well-being.

Second, there is role theory. If one is involved in society, one takes on many roles vis-a-vis others, including family roles, work roles, and roles as group member. In early discussions of the optimal number of roles, two opposing positions were staked out. The *scarcity* approach posited that the demands of different roles will conflict, and predicts that as the number of roles an individual holds increases, so does the likelihood of role strain (Goode, 1960). In contrast, the *role accumulation* approach (Sieber, 1974) assumes that social roles provide status, role-related privileges, and ego-gratification, as well as identities that provide meaning and purpose. Thus adding roles should enhance psychological well-being. In general, the literature provides far more support for the role accumulation approach than for the scarcity approach.

This conclusion is qualified, however, by reference to the kind of role. Thoits (1992, 1995) suggests that voluntary roles, such as friend or group member, may be more responsible for the positive effects of multiple roles than are obligatory roles such as parent or spouse. Keyes (1995) found that, indeed, the number of voluntary social roles predicted higher levels of social and psychological well-being whereas the number of obligatory roles did not. The relevance of these results for our concerns here is that half of the voluntary roles he asked about are clearly helping roles: community activist, blood donor, volunteer, and caregiver.

Finally, consistent with this emphasis on integration into society and the performance of multiple roles, activity theorists suggest that the *elderly in particular* will benefit from remaining engaged with society, active, productive, and involved in their social networks. The argument is based on the fact that many roles central to identity are lost or heavily decreased as we age. Thus adding new volunteer or activist roles in old age should have positive effects on mental and physical health. These benefits would not necessarily be specific to community service per se. However, given the public esteem in which such activities are held, engaging in such activities should provide a particularly strong psychological boost.

I also discuss three theoretical approaches from psychology. First, Cialdini (Cialdini, Kenrick, & Baumann, 1982) believes that helping others serves as a reward, although children have to learn that helping others can make a person feel good. They learn this because parents reward such behavior, and it therefore becomes "a socialized, secondary reinforcer" (p. 343). He presents a convincing series of studies to show that as children move into adolescence, they change from helping more when in a neutral mood to helping more when they feel sad or guilty (e.g., also see Cialdini & Fultz, 1990). Individuals who have been socialized to take pleasure from helping others should thus feel better when they help. This could lift the spirits of those who are depressed, and could—if the psycho-neuro-immunologists are correct—strengthen the immune system and lead to reduced morbidity and mortality.

Second, research by Langer and Rodin (1976; Rodin & Langer, 1977) has indicated that being the cause of action, being in control, provides protection against morbidity and mortality. They randomly assigned 91 nursing home residents aged 65 to 90 to either a "personal responsibility and choice" condition or to a "comparison information only" condition. They found short-term effects both on self-reported happiness and activity, and on ratings of alertness, general improvement, and socialization with patients, staff, and others favoring the experimental condition. More striking, they report significant differential mortality (15% vs. 30%) favoring the group encouraged to take control. In a more recent review of the literature on control and efficacy, Haidt and Rodin (1999) provide a possible, provocative link between these psychological effects and the sociological theories presented earlier. They state, "Reading Durkheim while thinking about control and efficacy leads to the following speculation: Normlessness and chaos breed misery and suicide in part because they are structural impediments to the satisfaction of effectance motivation" (p. 323).

Finally, Snyder, Clary, and Stukas (2000) and their colleagues have been carrying out a systematic program of research focused on understanding volunteer motivation. They have identified six functions that volunteering serves: value-expressive, social, knowledge, defensive, enhancement, and career. They have consistently found greater satisfaction on the part of volunteers based on meeting their motivational needs. For example, if a volunteer is mainly motivated by social needs, and those needs are met, that volunteer is happier and more satisfied than he or she would have been if value-expressive or career rewards were provided (Clary et al., 1998). Snyder and Omoto (1992) in fact found, paradoxically, that volunteers who were motivated by esteem enhancement or personal development (relatively selfish motives) were more likely than those who were more altruistically motivated to remain as active volunteers for an AIDS organization.

Thus, both sociological and psychological theories predict that performing community service will have benefits for the helper. Mechanisms are suggested from the very macro, based on integration into society, to the very micro—psycho-neuro-immunologic. From both sets of theories we are led to believe that the impact will vary depending on a "fit" between the helper's needs and the nature of the actions performed. In addition, both sets of theories suggest that having a feeling of volition and control will enhance the positive effects.

Literature Review

Does Helping Others Lead to Positive Emotions?

Although there is little direct evidence that helping others makes you "feel good," there is indirect evidence. Harris (1977) presents survey data indicating that college students believe that altruistic actions have a mood-enhancing component. Newman, Vasudev, and Onawola (1985) interviewed 180 older adults (ages 55 to 85) volunteering in three school programs in New York, Los Angeles, and Pittsburgh. Sixty-five percent reported improved life satisfaction, 76% better feelings about themselves, and 32% improved mental health. In response to the question, "How has the volunteer experience affected you?" the authors received many answers such as, "It is an experience that I will keep with me as long as I live. . .it has enriched my life. I think that associating with children is rejuvenating; it is energizing. . ." (p. 125). Blood donors also talk about how good it makes them feel to give blood (Piliavin & Callero, 1991).

Are There Long-Term Positive Behavioral, Psychological, and Physical Health Effects of Community Service?

I have reviewed elsewhere the existing literature on this question (Piliavin, in press), and will discuss only a few central findings here. Research on the effects of volunteering at different points in the life span has focused on different outcomes; I will give a few examples of each.

Adolescents.   In adolescence, the focus has largely been on whether volunteering can teach values and prevent self-destructive behaviors.   For example, results from an 8-year longitudinal evaluation of a very large volunteering program (over 8,000 participants and controls) showed that "Teen Outreach" students had "a 5% lower rate of course failure in school, an 8% lower rate of school suspension, a 33% lower rate of pregnancy, and a 50% lower rate of school dropout" (Moore & Allen, 1996, p. 235). [1]   Uggen and Janikula (1999) studied a panel of 1,139 teenagers in St. Paul, Minnesota, and found that measures of volunteer activity in their junior and senior years were related to self-reported first arrest data for ages 17-21, obtained when they were 21. The authors concluded, "Only 3% of the volunteers were arrested in the four years following high school compared to 11% of the nonvolunteers" (p. 344). Finally, Stukas, Clary, and Snyder (1999) concluded that service learning can positively affect personal efficacy, self-esteem, and confidence.

Adults.   Among adults, the focus of research has mainly been on mental health. Voluntary association membership has been found to be related to self-esteem, personal happiness, life satisfaction, improved well-being, and decreased depression.   Keyes (1998) found that recent volunteers reported higher levels of social well-being than did those who had volunteered over 1 year previously or had never volunteered.   Van Willigen (1998) found effects both of attending voluntary association meetings and of hours of volunteer work on life satisfaction (positive) and depression (negative).

Thoits and Hewitt (2001), using the Americans' Changing Lives data set (House, 1995), found effects of volunteer hours at Time 1 (1986) and the change in volunteer hours T1 - T2 (1989) on six measures of well-being: happiness, life satisfaction, self-esteem, mastery, depression, and physical health at Time 2. The most highly significant are on life satisfaction and feelings of mastery. [2] The authors note that one important remaining question is "how are the beneficial effects of volunteer work on well-being generated?"

---

[1]These effects were statistically significant, controlling for a number of demographics and for preprogram problem behavior.   (See also Allen, Philliber, Herrling, & Kuperminc, 1997; Allen, Philliber, & Hoggson, 1990.)

[2]Controls for demographic factors as well as for other forms of community participation (and change in participation), such as church attendance and participation in other

The Elderly. In a recent meta-analysis, Wheeler, Gorey, and Greenblatt (1998) found that over 37 studies of the impact of volunteer activities, the average correlation between helping (or membership) and some measure of well-being, most commonly life satisfaction, was .252 (p < .001), with a range from zero to .582. Those who engaged in direct helping (12 studies) "seemed to derive greater rewards from volunteering . . . than other elders engaged in more indirect or less formally 'helping' roles" (p. 75).

Researchers have also looked at the impact of volunteering on health and mortality among the elderly. Young and Glasgow (1998) found that self-reported health increased as instrumental social participation increased for both men and women in a sample of 629 nonmetropolitan elderly. Moen, Dempster-McClain, and Williams (1989) found, in a sample of women who had been ages 25 to 50 in 1956, that those who had participated in clubs and volunteer activities were less likely to have died by 1986.[3] Interviews done in 1986 with the 313 surviving women show significant, or nearly significant, effects of organizational participation in 1956 on three health measures: self-appraised health, time to serious illness, and functional ability (Moen, Dempster-McClain, & Williams, 1992). Oman, Thoresen & McMahon (1999) found, among 2,025 community-dwelling elderly aged 55 and older, that high volunteers (2 or more organizations) had 44% lower mortality than nonvolunteers.[4] The impact of volunteering on mortality increased with increasing age; that is, those most at risk were helped the most.

Dose-Response Curve. How much volunteering is best? Musick, Herzog, and House (1999) found that moderate volunteering (< 40 hours per year or for only one organization) in the year preceding the Americans' Changing Lives survey (1986) had a protective function on mortality over the following 8 years among those 65 and older. Volunteering more than that was no more beneficial than not volunteering at all.[5] More recently, using all three currently available waves, Musick and Wilson (2003) found a strong effect of volunteering on depression,

---

organizations do not eliminate the impact of volunteer participation on the well-being measures at Time 2.

[3]The analysis controlled for many other relevant factors, including the number of other roles and health in 1956, and the article makes clear that the activities were indeed largely community-oriented (PTA, scouting, book drives, etc.)

[4]Their measure of volunteering was developed from two questions, whether respondents did "any volunteer work at the present time" and then "how many voluntary organizations are you involved with?" Analysis controls for health habits, physical functioning, religious attendance, social support, and many other factors.

[5]Analysis controls for health, race, age, income, physical activity, and initial health and impairment.

but only among those over 65. There is a dose-response curve: Volunteering in all three waves has a highly significant effect, whereas volunteering in only one wave is unrelated to depression at Time 3.

Moderating and Mediating Factors. Of perhaps greater interest, the protective effect on mortality in the Musick and Wilson (2003) study was found only among those low in informal social interaction,[6] conceptualized as a measure of social integration. Van Willigen (2000), using the same data, found that the positive relationships between volunteering and both life satisfaction and better perceived health are significantly stronger in the elderly sample, regardless of what measure of volunteering is used.

The inescapable conclusion regarding volunteering by the elderly is that it is highly beneficial. There appears to be a strong and consistent effect, such that the more an elderly person volunteers, the higher is his or her life satisfaction. The impact is greater on those who need it most. Similarly, some volunteering enhances physical health and even can stave off death. Volunteering in moderation that does not physically tax the elderly individual appears to be best—as with exercise, food, and wine, moderation in all things.

The Present Study

Most of the research on the volunteering - health relationship to date has used the Americans' Changing Lives data set. This analysis tests whether these same relationships are found in the Wisconsin Longitudinal Study (WLS). Because the most recent wave of data was collected when respondents were in their early 50s, we cannot expect to find the larger effects demonstrated among the elderly.

Sample and Data

The WLS began with a one third random sample (N = 10,317) of women and men who graduated from Wisconsin high schools in 1957. The next two waves of survey data were collected from the graduates or their parents in 1964 and 1975. Critical to this study, measures of social participation were included at that time. In 1992, telephone and mail surveys of 8,500 of the WLS graduates were done.[7]

---

[6]This is measured by how often they talk on the telephone with friends, neighbors, or relatives in the typical week and how often they get together with them.

[7]In 1992, there were 6,900 responses to both the telephone and mail surveys of graduates.

These surveys expanded the content of earlier follow-ups to include key inventories of personality (John, 1990, 1991), psychological well-being (Ryff, 1989; Ryff & Keyes, 1995), mental health (depression and alcohol use), physical health and health practices, and many others. The measures of social participation are repeated.[8]

Measures

This report uses the core WLS sample for whom complete data from the 1957, 1975, and 1992 waves are available.

Volunteering. The key independent variable of volunteering is taken from the measures of social participation asked in both 1975 and 1992. Respondents were asked how much involvement they had had in each of a list of possible kinds of groups, for example, labor unions, youth groups, sport teams, and charity or welfare groups. The 1975 wave measured involvement as *none, some,* and *very much*; the 1992 wave used a 5-point scale, ranging from *not involved* to *involved a great deal*. A number of measures are used in the present analysis, but they are all based on the sum of respondent's answers regarding the PTA, youth groups, neighborhood organizations, community centers, and charitable or welfare groups. In 1975, this can range from 0 to 10, in 1992, from 0-20. Means and standard deviations of all variables are given in Table 2.1.

Psychological Well-Being and Mental Health

1. Psychological well-being (Ryff, 1989) and four of its subscales: environmental mastery, personal growth, positive relations with others, purpose in life
2. Depressive symptoms (as measured by the CES-D; Radloff,1977)

Analyses were also done using measures of self-reported health, symptoms, and diseases, but none of these showed any effects. Thus description of the variables is omitted here.

---

[8]The strengths of the WLS as a resource for studies of midlife and aging lie in its longitudinal scope, its exceptional sample retention, the content and quality of survey and administrative data, and its relational design. It has followed a large and diverse sample from high school graduation to the cusp of retirement, and it has followed a number of social and economic relationships between the graduates and their significant others.

Table 2.1
Descriptive Statistics on All Variables in the Analyses

Variable	Percentage/Mean	Minimum/ Maximum	Standard Deviation
A. Indepdendent Variables			
Sex: Female	53.6		
Married, 75: Yes	89.3		
Married, 92: Yes	83.1		
Working, 75: Yes	76.2		
Working, 92: Yes	85.0		
Some involvement in church-connected groups	32.7		
Church attendance:			
Once a week or more	51.6		
Seldom or never	10.6		
IQ in 1957	102.09	61 /145	14.62
Years of education	13.68	12 / 21	2.30
# children 6 - 12 in 1975	1.257	0 / 6	1.08
Service, 1975	1.28	0 / 10	1.60
Expressive participation, 1975	.858	0 / 8	1.19
Visits with friends, 1975	5.32	0 / 69	4.87
Integration	7.27	2 / 10	1.28
B. Dependent Variables			
Psychological well-being	69.18	0 / 84	9.30
Positive relations to others	33.81	4 / 42	5.94
Purpose in life	33.69	1 / 42	6.14
Environmental mastery	33.59	2 / 42	5.49
Personal growth	32.94	2 / 42	5.92

Control variables

Controls for activity, social integration, social contact:

3.   Visits with friends in last 4 weeks

4.   Social participation index parallel to volunteering index: Sum of participation in five self-oriented social activities (sports teams, country clubs, fraternal organizations, veterans' organizations, groups of people of the same nationality) in 1975

5.   Integration index: Sum of marital status (0, 1), work status (0, 1),

perceived social support (0, 1, 2), rural-urban residence (0, 1, 2), and visits with friends (0, 1, 2) in 1992

Controls for selection into volunteering: sex, IQ, Duncan SEI of head of household in 1957, education, marital status, work status, number of children age 6-12, and church attendance in 1975.

Research questions

6.   What is the impact of past and continuing volunteering on the psychological well-being, and self-reported health of adults at midlife? How much volunteering is the right amount? Do respondents who volunteer a moderate amount in only one or two contexts benefit the most? Is continuous volunteering over the life course more beneficial than intermittent volunteering?

7.   What are the moderating variables that may qualify this relationship? Is volunteering most beneficial among those who lack social support and other social activities, who are unemployed, widowed, or divorced? Is there a gender difference?

Other questions, about mediating factors, can be asked but not answered until the next wave of the WLS, to be collected in 2002-2003, is available. This is because the potential mediators—psychological well-being, proxies for immune function—are measured at the same time as the well-being and self-reported health measures.

Analysis and Results

Volunteering

The typical respondent in the WLS claimed to be involved "some" with one of the five service organizations both in 1975 and in 1992. Slightly over 25% of respondents did not volunteer in either wave; 32.4% volunteered in both waves; 42% volunteered in one wave but not the other. Before we can examine the consequences of volunteering for well-being, we need to build a model that predicts who is and who is not involved in volunteering in 1975.

Table 2.2 shows the best model predicting our continuous measure of volunteering in 1975, which has been logged because of its extreme skewness. Adjusted R^2 is .149. The most important predictors are sex, level of education, the number of school age children in the household, church membership, visiting with friends, and marital status. These findings are quite consistent with the literature on the determinants of volunteer participation (see Hauser, 2000).

To control for selection, these variables are used in the regressions about to be presented.

Table 2.2
Regression of Service in 1975[a] on Predictor Variables

Independent Variables	B	Std. error	Beta
Female	.339 ***	(.031)	.146
Duncan SEI, head of household in 1957	.00026***	(.000)	.054
Education in years	.0636 ***	(.007)	.126
Number of children age 6-12 in 1975	.244 ***	(.013)	.226
Married in 1975	.338 ***	(.045)	.091
IQ	.0033 ***	(.001)	.041
Working in 1975	-.0280	(.036)	-.010
Church attendance, 1975	.105 ***	(.009)	.146
R^2; df	.149	8/6360	

Note. Indicators of significance: *** $p < .001$.
[a]The dependent measure is the log (base 10) of Service, 1975.

First-Order Relationships With Health Measures

The next question is whether volunteering is related to psychological or physical health in the WLS sample. There is no relationship between perceived health and volunteering.[9] Thus, analyses of physical health will not be presented in this chapter. Table 2.3 presents the means for six measures of psychological well-being as a function of two measures of volunteering: a trichotomized measure of service in 1975 (no volunteering, volunteering for one organization, volunteering for more than one) and a trichotomy of longitudinal participation (never volunteered, volunteered in one wave, volunteered in both waves). Volunteering is significantly related to all six measures, although the relationship with depression is very small.

Regressions of Well-Being on Volunteering

Table 2.4 shows the relationship of the six measures of psychological well-being with four different ways of measuring volunteering. First, our basic

---

[9]It is a valid measure: ratings are related to mortality since 1992, to smoking, body mass, diseases, and symptoms. There is also a strong relationship with all of the psychological well-being measures. However, only 11% of the sample reports feeling less than good to excellent.

measure of volunteering—Service, 1975—remains significantly related to five of the six measures of well-being at $p < .001$, after controls for selection (the variables that predicted volunteering in 1975) as well as controls for other forms of social participation that is not "altruistic:" visits with friends, involvement with church-connected groups, and "expressive" social participation. It is not related to depression after these controls, and the effect on environmental mastery is quite small. Similar findings result in the regressions using our three-valued measure of longitudinal participation. Here, however, a small significant effect on depression remains.

Table 2.3
Means of Six Psychological Well-Being Factors as a Function of Two Trichotomized Measures of Volunteering

	Measure of Psychological Well-Being					
	Positive Relations	Personal Growth	Purpose in Life	Environmental Mastery	Depression	Psychological Well-Being
1975 Service[a]						
None	33.0	32.3	33.1	33.2	17.0	68.2
1 Organization	34.1	33.0	33.9	33.8	16.5	69.7
2+ Organizations	35.1	34.2	34.6	34.1	15.7	70.8
Over time[b]						
None	32.4	31.5	32.6	33.0	17.7	67.2
1 Wave	33.7	32.9	33.6	33.5	16.8	69.2
2 Waves	35.0	34.2	34.8	34.3	15.3	70.8

Note. [a]All comparisons are significant at $p < .001$, by ANOVA.
[b]All comparisons are significant at $p < .001$ except depression, at $p < .05$, by ANOVA.

The Dose-Response Curve. Previous research has found that the effect of doing service in some cases follows a dose response curve. Usually, more is better. To test this, two sets of dummy variables have been constructed from the measures of volunteering. For the 1975 measure, the first dummy indicates that the respondent reports participation in just one of the service organizations; the second indicates participation in two or more. The omitted category is nonparticipation. For the measure over time, the first dummy indicates participation in one wave; the second indicates participation, both in 1975 and in 1992. In the first case, the unstandardized coefficient for the two dummy variables are about equal, indicating that about the same amount of "boost" to

Table 2.4
Coefficients for Volunteering Predicting Mental Health: WLS Core Sample

Volunteering Measure	Measures of Psychological Well-Being					
	Positive Relations	Personal Growth	Purpose in Life	Environmental Mastery	Depression	Psychological Well-Being
Service, 1975	.305 *** (.050) .083	.298 *** (.050) .081	.247 *** (.052) .066	.120 * (.047) .035	~	.438 *** (.087) .062
Service over time	.908*** (.105) .117	.979 *** (.104) .128	.728 *** (.109) .093	.377 *** (.100) .053	-.805* (.282) -.039	1.02 *** (.188) .084
1975 dummies: 1 Organization	.504** (.173) .040	.373* (.172) .033	.407* (.180) .032	.298@ (.164) .026	~	.694* (.304) .036
2+ Organizations	.578 *** (.105) .080	.549*** (.102) .085	.427*** (.109) .058	.206* (.100) .031	~	.587*** (.190) .053

Table 2. 4 Continued

Over time dummies:																	
One wave	.949***	(.188)	.080	1.117***	(.186)	.095	.752***	(.195)	.062	.385*	(.178)	.035	-.649 ~	(.515)	-.021	1.329***	(.336)	.072
Two waves	1.817***	(.210)	.145	1.97***	(.208)	.159	1.459***	(.217)	.114	.883***	(.196)	.077	-1.334*	(.579)	-.040	2.052***	(.377)	.105

Note: Cells: Unstandardized coefficients (standard error) standardized coefficients

Note. [a]Controlling for: female, IQ, 1975 church attendance, education, Duncan SEI of head of household, 1957; married in 1975, # children age 6-12 in 1975, visits from friends, 1975; measure of "expressive" participation, working 1975; involvement with church-connected groups.

Note. Indicators of significance are as follows: ~ = n.s.   @ = $p < .10$ * = $p < .05$ ** = $p < .01$ *** = $p < .001$

psychological well-being is obtained for participating in one or in two or more organizations. The variance for participation in only one, however, is higher for all of the variables, leading some of the effects to be of borderline significance. On the other hand, volunteering over two waves explains nearly twice the variance of volunteering in only one wave for all six of the measures of well-being. Results are thus clear: For this sample of 50ish Wisconsinites, doing well leads to feeling good. Doing more in early mid-life does not seem to contribute to more well-being in late mid-life than just doing some. However, consistent volunteering over the life-span leads to stronger effects on well-being than does intermittent volunteering.

Moderators. Some research has found that effects are stronger among the elderly. With essentially no variation in age in this sample, an age effect cannot be tested. It has been suggested that the effect should be greatest among those who are the least integrated into society. Thus several multivariate analyses of variance were carried out, focused on positive relations with others, purpose in life, and personal growth as the three dependent variables, and controlling for all the same variables as in the previously reported regressions. What was added were interaction terms involving service and social integration indicators in 1992: marital status, employment status, more or less social support, rural and urban residence, and extent of social visiting with friends. The few significant interaction effects found were three way interactions of sex and service with marital status and employment status. One of these is shown in Figure 2.1, which shows that the impact of volunteering for men on personal growth is almost entirely among the unmarried, whereas married women show a slightly, but probably not significantly, larger impact than do unmarried women.[10] This is consistent with what we know about the functions of marriage for men, namely, that unmarried men are at risk of social isolation and consequent poor mental and physical health.

The final analysis to be presented further tests the hypothesis concerning the moderating effect of social integration. This analysis consists of regressions employing an index made up of marital status, work status, perceived social support, rural-urban residence, and social visiting with friends, which ranges from 2 to 10, with an average score of 7. Also included is an interaction term formed by multiplying this index by the measure of volunteering over time. Table 2.5 presents the regressions on overall psychological well-being and on personal growth. Standardized regression coefficients are shown for all variables; unstandardized coefficients are also shown for the service, integration, and interaction terms.

---

[10]Similar effects are found on the variable purpose in life.

Figure. 2.1.
Interaction of sex, marital status in 1992, and service over time on personal growth scores. [a]

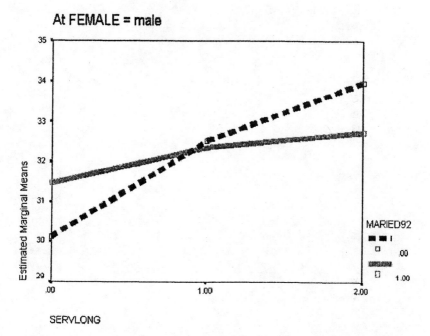

Estimated Marginal Means of raw personal growth score

At FEMALE = male

[a] Derived from a MANOVA in which the following were controlled: IQ, 1975 church attendance, education, Duncan SEI of head of household in 1957; married in 1975, # children age 6-12 in 1975, visits from friends in 1975; measure of "expressive" participation, working 1975, involvement with church-connected groups.

Figure 2.1 Continued.

Estimated Marginal Means of raw personal growth score

At FEMALE = female

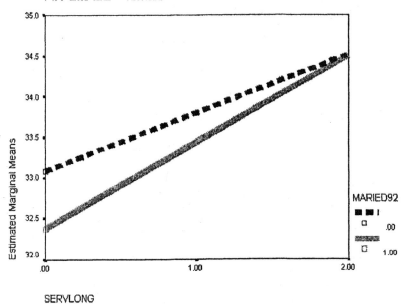

SERVLONG

The hypothesis that the degree of integration moderates the impact of volunteering on psychological well-being is supported in these analyses. The index of integration itself is strongly positively related to psychological well-being, as is service; the relationship of the interaction term to well-being is negative. As predicted, continued volunteer activities appear to have the *most* impact for those members of the WLS who are *least* integrated into society when in their early 50s. The only difference between the analyses of the two dependent variables is a curious reversal of the positive impact of church attendance when the dependent variable is personal growth.

Alternative Explanations. The question can be raised, concerning all of these analyses, about whether there is anything special about volunteering, that is, about activities that focus on helping others. Perhaps more activity is just better than less activity, and the kind does not matter. The data, however, seem to indicate that the kind of activity does indeed matter. The measure of "expressive" social activity, made up of participation in sports teams, fraternal organizations, and so on, does not contribute to improved mental health in these analyses.

A more serious issue that can be raised is that psychological well-being may well cause volunteering, rather than the reverse, or that there is a reciprocal relationship between well-being and volunteering. Previous research has found such reciprocal relationships, but it cannot be tested in this data set, since there are no measures of psychological well-being in 1975. We must wait until the next wave—to be collected in 2003—to be able to do such analyses. One argument against such reverse causality is that one might think that depression would be the most likely characteristic predicting volunteering (negatively) and it is barely related in these data.

Conclusion

In terms of replication of previous research, this analysis confirms that, at least up to a point, more volunteer participation is better for psychological well-being. More participation at a given time is certainly no worse than less participation, with any volunteering being better than none. Continuous (as compared to intermittent) participation across the life-span clearly contributes to better

Table 2.5

Regression of Psychological Well-Being and Personal Growth on Volunteering Over Time, Integration, Their Interaction, and Control Variables

Variables	Dependent Variable: Psych. Well-being			Dependent Variable: Personal Growth		
	Step 1	Step 2	Step 3	Step 1	Step 2	Step 3
Service	1.720*** (.180) .143	.996*** (.194) .083	3.111*** (.993) .258	1.367*** (.100) .179	.962*** (.107) .126	2.405*** (.555) .315
Controls:[b]						
Female		*** .053	@ .033		***	*** .103
Education		*** .081	*** .067		***	*** .135
Married 75		*** .093	*** .075		***	* .029
IQ		*** .085	** .085		***	*** .083
Church Attendance		** .050	** .042		@ -.025	* -.031
Visits w. frnd		*** .078	*** .050		*** .070	*** .046
Working 75		– –	– –		*** .048	** .040
Integration			1.784*** (.172) .248			.952*** (.096) .210
Integration X Service			-.339** (.134) -.222			-.226** (.075) -.233
R^2 change; df	.02 1/4415	.033 1/4404	.038 1/4402	.032 1/5596	.052 1/5585	.025 1/5583

Note. Cell entries are unstandardized coefficients (standardized errors) and standardized coefficients
Note. [a] Indicators of significance: *** $p < .001$; ** $p < .01$; * $p < .05$; @ $p < .10$. Dashes mean that coefficient was not significant.
[b] Controls shown were significant when added at $p < .01$ in either analysis; other controls included were Duncan SEI of head of household, 1975 number of kids 6-12, involvement in church-connected groups, and the index of expressive involvement.

mental health; dummy variable comparisons suggest that doing twice as much is roughly twice as valuable.

In terms of the theoretical approaches set forth in the introduction of this chapter, support has been provided for the social integration interpretation (à la Durkheim) of the role of volunteering in improving psychological well-being. People who are better integrated display higher well-being, controlling for many other factors, but, more critically, there is an interaction of the degree of integration with volunteer participation. The effect is that those who are least integrated appear to benefit the most from such participation. Little support was provided for the psychological approach of Langer and Rodin, in that environmental mastery, of all the facets of psychological well-being, was least related to volunteer participation. Activity theory was demonstrated to provide an incomplete explanation for the positive effects of volunteering on psychological well-being, because just any activity was not sufficient.

What are some implications of this research for community change and social action? First, these findings provide a good argument for volunteer organizations to use for getting people involved in other-oriented social action: "Not only is it good for the community, it is good for you." This is, in fact, an argument that volunteers, blood donors, and activists have been using for years, namely, that such actions are empowering and invigorating, and keep you involved in and tied to the community. Second, these findings, and those of other researchers who have had similar results, may be useful to senior citizen organizations in their planning of activities. It seems clear from these data that socially useful activities improve psychological well-being, whereas simply social activities do not, when controlling for other factors. Others find the effects to be stronger among older individuals. Thus it would seem sensible for seniors to do as much volunteering and active social service as they feel comfortable doing, and for organizations for seniors to encourage them in this.

References

Allen, J. P., Philliber, S., Herrling, S., & Kuperminc, G. P. (1997). Preventing teen pregnancy and academic failure: Experimental evaluation of a developmentally based approach. *Child Development, 64*, 729-742.

Allen, J. P., Philliber, S., & Hoggson, N. (1990). School-based prevention of teenage pregnancy and school dropout: Process evaluation of the national replication of the Teen Outreach Program. *American Journal of Community Psychology, 18*, 505-524.

Cialdini, R. B., & Fultz, J. (1990). Interpreting the negative mood/helping literature via meta-analysis. *Psychological Bulletin, 107*, 210-214.

Cialdini, R. B., Kenrick, D. T., & Baumann, D. J. (1982). Effects of mood on prosocial behavior in children and adults. In N. Eisenberg (Ed.), *The development of prosocial behavior* (pp. 339-359). New York: Academic.

Clary, E. G., Snyder, M., Ridge, R. D., Copeland, J., Stukas, A. A., Haugen, J., & Miene, P. (1998). Understanding and assessing the motivations of volunteers: A functional approach. *Journal of Personality and Social Psychology, 74,* 1516-1530.

Durkheim, E. (1951, Trans.). *Suicide* (J. Spalding & G. Simpson). New York: Free Press. (Original work published 1898)

Goode, W. J. (1960). A theory of role strain. *American Sociological Review, 25,* 483-496.

Haidt, J., & Rodin, J. (1999). Control and efficacy as interdisciplinary bridges. *Review of General Psychology, 3,* 317-337.

Harris, M. B. (1977). Effects of altruism on mood. *Journal of Social Psychology, 91,* 37-41.

Hauser, S. M. (2000). Education, ability, and civic engagement in the contemporary United States. *Social Science Research, 29,* 556-582.

House, J. S. (1995). *Americans' changing lives: Waves I and II, 1986 and 1989.* Ann Arbor, MI: Interuniversity Consortium for Political and Social Research.

John, O. (1990). The Big Five factor taxonomy: Dimensions of personality in the natural language and questionnaires. In L. A. Pervin (Ed.), *Handbook of personality theory and research* (pp. 66-100). New York: Guilford.

John, O. (1991). Big Five inventory (BFI-54). University of California, Berkeley. Institute of Personality Assessment and Research.

Keyes, C. L. M. (1995). *Social functioning and social well-being: Studies of the social nature of personal wellness.* Unpublished doctoral dissertation, University of Wisconsin-Madison.

Keyes, C. L. M. (1998). Social well-being. *Social Psychology Quarterly, 61,* 121-140.

Langer, E. J., & Rodin, J. (1976). The effects of choice and enhanced personal responsibility for the aged: A field experiment in an institutional setting. *Journal of Personality and Social Psychology, 34,* 191-198.

Mirowsky, J., & Ross, C. E. (1989). *Social causes of psychological distress.* New York: Aldine de Gruyter.

Moen, P., Dempster-McClain, D., & Williams, R. M., Jr. (1989). Social integration and longevity. *American Sociological Review, 54,* 635-647.

Moen, P., Dempster-McClain, D., & Williams, R. M., Jr. (1992). Successful aging: A life-course perspective on women's multiple roles and health. *American Journal of Sociology, 97,* 1612-1638.

Moore, C. W., & Allen, J. P. (1996). The effects of volunteering on the young volunteer. *The Journal of Primary Prevention, 17,* 231-258.

Musick, M.A., Herzog, A.R., & House, J.S. (1999). Volunteering and mortality among older adults: Findings from a national sample. *The Journals of Gerontology: Psychological sciences and social sciences, 54B,* S173-S180.

Musick, M. A., & Wilson, J. (2003). Volunteering and depression: The role of psychological and social resources in different age groups. *Social Science and Medicine, 56,* 259-269.

Newman, S., Vasudev, J., & Onawola, R. (1985). Older volunteers' perceptions of impacts of volunteering on their psychological well-being. *Journal of Applied Gerontology, 4,* 123-127.

Oman, D., Thoresen, E., & McMahon, K. (1999). Volunteerism and mortality among the community-dwelling elderly. *Journal of Health Psychology, 4,* 301-316.

Piliavin, J. A. (in press). Doing well by doing good: Benefits for the benefactor. In C. L. M. Keyes & J. Haidt (Eds.), *Flourishing: Positive psychology and the life well-lived* . Washington, DC : American Psychological Association.

Piliavin, J. A., & Callero, P. L. (1991). *Giving blood: The development of an altruistic identity.* Baltimore: Johns Hopkins University Press.

Radloff, L. (1977). The CES-D scale: A self-report depression scale for research in the general population. *Applied Psychological Measurement, 1,* 385-401.

Rodin, J., & Langer, E.J. (1977). Long-term effects of a control-relevant intervention with the institutionalized aged. *Journal of Personality and Social Psychology, 35,* 897-902.

Ryff, C. D. (1989). *The parental experience in midlife.* Chicago: University of Chicago Press.

Ryff, C. D., & Keyes, C. L. M. (1995). The structure of psychological well-being revisited. *Journal of Personality and Social Psychology, 69,* 719-727.

Seeman, M. (1959). On the meaning of alienation. *American Sociological Review, 24,* 783-791.

Sieber, S. D. (1974). Toward a theory of role accumulation. *American Sociological Review, 39,* 567-578.

Snyder, M., Clary, E. G., & Stukas, A. A. (2000). The functional approach to volunteerism. In G. R. Maio & J. M.Olson (Eds.), *Why we evaluate: Functions of attitudes* (pp. 365-393). Mahwah, NJ: Lawrence Erlbaum Associates.

Snyder, M., & Omoto, A. M. (1992). Who helps and why? The psychology of AIDS volunteerism. In S. Spacapan & S. Oskamp (Eds.), *Helping and being helped: Naturalistic studies* (pp. 213-239). Newbury Park, CA: Sage.

Stukas, A. A., Clary, E. G., & Snyder, M. (1999). Service learning: Who benefits and why. *Social Policy Report: Society for Research in Child Development, 8,* 1-19.

Thoits, P. A. (1992). Multiple identities: Examining gender and marital status differences in distress. *Social Psychology Quarterly, 55*, 236-256.

Thoits, P. A. (1995). Identity-relevant events and psychological symptoms: A cautionary tale. *Journal of Health and Social Behavior, 36*, 72-82.

Thoits, P. A., & Hewitt, L. N. (2001). Volunteer work and well-being. *Journal of Health and Social Behavior, 42*, 115-131.

Uggen, C., & Janikula, J. (1999). Volunteerism and arrest in the transition to adulthood. *Social Forces, 78*, 331-362.

Van Willigen, M. (1998, June). Doing good, feeling better: The effect of voluntary association membership on individual well-being. Paper presented at the annual meeting of the Society for the Study of Social Problems.

Van Willigen, M. (2000). Differential benefits of volunteering across the life course. *Journal of Gerontology: Social Sciences, 55B*, S1-S11.

Wheeler, J. A., Gorey, K. M., & Greenblatt, B. (1998). The beneficial effects of volunteering for older volunteers and the people they serve: A meta-analysis. *International Journal of Aging and Human Development, 47*, 69-79.

Young, F. W., & Glasgow, N. (1998). Voluntary social participation and health. *Research on Aging, 20*, 339-36.

3

PUBLIC HEALTH, RACE, AND THE AIDS MOVEMENT: THE PROFILE AND CONSEQUENCES OF LATINO GAY MEN'S COMMUNITY INVOLVEMENT

Jesus Ramirez-Valles
University of Illinois at Chicago

Rafael M. Diaz
San Francisco State University

One of the unintended consequences of the AIDS epidemic in the United States is that it opened up spaces for thousands of gay men, and their allies, to mobilize to address their communities' needs, demand access to basic health services, and fight discrimination (Epstein, 1996; Ouellette, Cassel, Maslanka, & Wong, 1995). Largely due to this mobilization, public and private support became available for HIV/AIDS prevention, care, and research. A myriad of new community-based organizations emerged throughout the country to provide prevention, advocacy, testing, and care services to gay and bisexual men. Numerous other new programs or services were added into existing gay-related organizations. Furthermore, this mobilization and the newly created spaces allowed many men to develop a sense of community and a social support system, as well as a feeling of pride and heightened self-esteem (Ouellete et al., 1995; Ramirez-Valles, 2002; Ramirez-Valles & Brown, 2003).

The vast majority of activists and volunteers in the AIDS movement, however, have been middle-class White gay men (Arno, 1988; Kobasa, 1991). Also, the academic literature on social movements and volunteerism around HIV/AIDS has overlooked the experiences of Latino and other minority gay groups. We do not have any systematic information from these groups that could help us assess who is involved, and what are the consequences of such involvement. This had, and still has, negative implications for both ethnic minority communities and public health efforts. The limited involvement in the movement might have hindered minority gay men's political power to influence both the public health agenda and distribution of resources. It also might have precluded gay men of color from getting some of the individual benefits of community involvement, such as access to a social support system and a sense of pride. From a public health viewpoint, the reduced community involvement of gay men of color has hampered efforts to make prevention efforts culturally appropriate and sustainable. This acquires further significance because minority gay men, and young men in particular, are disproportionally affected by the epidemic (Catania et al., 2001; Wolitski, Valdiserri, Denning, & Levine, 2001)

The overall goal of this chapter is to document the community involvement of Latino gay men. Specifically, we first assess the extent of Latino gay men's involvement in gay, Latino, and HIV/AIDS-related organizations across three cities (i.e., New York City, Miami, and Los Angeles). Second, we want to explore the characteristics of those Latino gay men involved in gay, Latino, and HIV/AIDS-related organizations. That is, we identify the factors that may lead to community involvement in this population, in particular, acculturation, experienced homophobia, and experiences with HIV/AIDS. Third, we examine the positive consequences of community involvement in individuals' lives. We test whether community involvement predicts social support and self-esteem among Latino gay men. In this study, we define *community involvement* as individuals' unpaid work on behalf of others, or for a collective good, and in the context of a formal or semiformal organization and social networks, taking place outside the home and the family (Ramirez-Valles, 2002; Schondel, Shields, & Orel, 1992; Smith, 1997; Thoits & Hewitt, 2001; Wilson & Musick, 1997). Our analysis includes participation in three types of organizations as indicators of community involvement: gay, Latino, and Latino gay organizations. As Cantu (2000) rightly agues, most of Latino gay men's participation in HIV/AIDS has taken place in those social spaces.

Who Is Involved?

In his now classic work, *The Volunteers*, Sills (1957) argued that one of the most important factors leading to participation in health-related organizations is the experience of the illness, disease, or condition. Those who suffer the illness, either directly or indirectly through relatives and friends, are likely to get involved as activists or volunteers in organizations or movements related to the illness. Sills' insight was confirmed in the AIDS movement, where gay men, their relatives, and their lesbian sisters came together to create organizations and make demands on the health care system to address the epidemic (Patton, 1989). The experience of the illness thus works as a trigger or motive to act. This motive, then, may be articulated like a "concern for one's community" or "coping with one's troubles," as contemporary research shows (Ramirez-Valles, 2001; Bebbington & Gatter, 1994; Gabard, 1995; Hodgkinson, 1995; Knoke & Wood, 1981; Omoto & Snyder, 1995; Ouellette et al., 1995; Smith, 1994; Snyder & Omoto, 1992). In this study, we explore whether this principle applies to Latino gay men. We test the relationship between HIV/AIDS experience (i.e., having HIV, losing someone to AIDS, and knowing peers with HIV) and being involved in gay, Latino, and HIV/AIDS-related organizations.

Social class position, along with ethnic group membership, also define those who are likely to get involved (Chambre, 1991; Smith, 1997). According to the Independent Sector (1999), volunteering is higher among Caucasians, those with higher education (e.g., college degree), and those with higher yearly incomes (e.g., > $40,000). Latino and African American groups are less likely to volunteer than White groups (Smith, 1997). Similar patterns are found in the AIDS movement. Gay men of color have been less involved in HIV/AIDS volunteer work than their White peers (Ferrer, Ramirez-Valles, Kegeles, & Rebehook, 2002; Omoto & Snyder, 1995; Valentgas, Bynum, & Sierler, 1990). Ethnic differences, nonetheless, are likely due to differences in income and levels of formal education (Hodgkinson, 1995; Smith, 1994, 1997; Wilson & Musick, 1997). Thus, our hypothesis is that among Latino gay men, social class (as measured by experienced poverty) and education are positively related to community involvement.

Likewise, among Latino groups, acculturation into mainstream culture must be accounted for in explaining levels of community involvement (Ramirez-Valles, 2002). Individuals who do not speak English or who recently immigrated to the United States (i.e., at the lower end of acculturation), may be less involved either because organizations do not perceive them as assets, or because they are unaware of opportunities to get involved (Snow, Zurcher, & Ekland-Olson, 1980; Williams & Ortega, 1986).

Homophobia, or the stigma of homosexuality, has also affected gay men's participation in the AIDS movement (Ramirez-Valles, 2002). The HIV/AIDS epidemic heightened the stigma toward homosexuality among certain groups who linked the illness to a sexual orientation or identity. Unfortunately, previous research on social movements or community involvement has overlooked this factor. In this study, we explore whether experiences of homophobia hinder or facilitate involvement in gay, Latino, and HIV/AIDS-related organizations. Experiences of homophobia may prevent involvement because individuals have internalized these experiences as self-hate. Thus, men may be reluctant to participate in issues related to homosexuality or AIDS for fear of being identified by family, coworkers, and friends as homosexuals (Diaz, 1998; Gabard, 1995; Herek, 1999; Kayal, 1994; Snyder, Omoto, & Crain, 1999). Alternatively, experienced homophobia may work as a motive to get involved. It may function in a fashion similar to the experience of the illness as described before. For some men, experiences of homophobia (such as been teased and called names as a child, or been denied a job because of sexual orientation) become grievances and motives to get involved in the fight against this type of discrimination.

The Positive Effects of Community Involvement

Community involvement, either as volunteerism or activism, may create positive changes at the individual level, beyond those it brings about at the community and societal levels (Bellah, Madsen, Sullivan, Swidler, & Tipton, 1996; Sills 1957). Evidence from gay men's involvement in the AIDS movement, though insufficient, indicates that participation enhances self-esteem and social support (Bebbington & Gatter, 1994; Boehmer, 2000; Chambre, 1991; Kobasa, 1990, 1991; Omoto & Snyder, 1995; Omoto, Snyder, & Berghuis, 1993; Ouellette et al., 1995; Snyder & Omoto, 1992; Stewart & Weinstein, 1997; Valentgas et al., 1990; Wolfe, 1994). There is, however, no documentation of such effects among Latino gay men. In a previous analysis, Diaz and colleagues (Diaz, Ayala, Bein, Henne, & Marin, 2001) found community involvement among Latino gay men to be one of the resilience factors for mental-health outcomes. Yet, community involvement has not been analyzed independently. Because of this gap in the literature, we seek to explore the association between community involvement and self-esteem and social support.

Community involvement in gay, Latino, and HIV/AIDS-related organizations may increase self-esteem among Latino gay men because it furnishes interaction with peers (Ramirez-Valles, 2002). As Frable and colleagues (Frable, Wortman, & Joseph, 1997) have shown, these peers may maintain and enhance one's self-concept by providing feedback and a point of reference. Likewise, doing volunteer work or activism creates an identity of being a caring and good person, as well as feelings of self-worth (Bellah et al., 1996; Kobasa, 1990; Marsh, 1992; Moen & Fields, 1999; Ouellette et al., 1995; Turner, Hays, & Coates, 1993; Youniss & Yates, 1997). It is important to note that some research has found these effects even after controlling for self-selection (Thoits & Hewitt, 2001).

Community involvement may also increase social support (Bellah et al., 1996). As Waldo and colleagues found (Waldo, Kegeles, & Hays, 1998), gay men's community involvement is positively associated with social support. Participation provides access to social networks, face-to-face interactions, and a sense of community (Altman et al., 1998; Ramirez-Valles, 1999; Rietschlin, 1998; Smith, 1994, 1997; Youniss & Yates, 1997). This could be a significant outcome for Latino gay men, especially if they are involved in gay Latino-related organizations, because they are frequently alienated from mainstream gay-related organizations (Ramirez-Valles & Brown, 2003).

Methods

Sample

Data came from a three-city study of Latino gay men, *Nuestras Voces* (Our Voices; Diaz, R. M., Principal Investigator). The study collected information from a probability sample of 912 self-identified Latino gay men in New York City ($n = 309$), Miami ($n = 302$), and Los Angeles ($n = 301$) between 1998 and 1999. Potential participants were randomly recruited from a probability sample of social venues where Latino gay men are likely to be found (e.g., bars, discos, special gay events). Face-to-face interviews were conducted by trained interviewers in research facilities. (For further details on the study methodology, see Diaz et al., 2001.) Because of the cross-sectional nature of these data, we cannot explore causal relationships (e.g., between community involvement and acculturation). The quality and comprehensiveness of this data set, however, are the best available for this population today.

Measures

Acculturation. We used two indicators to assess levels of acculturation: (a) time living in the United States (1 = *born in this country*, 3 = *living in the United States more than 10 years*); and (b) language spoken with friends (i.e., *mostly Spanish, mostly English, both equally*). For the analysis, this variable was transformed into two dichotomous variables, one for each language with speaking both languages as a reference.

Education. Levels of formal education were measured in a 4-point scale (1 = *less than high school*, 2= *high school*, 3= *some college*, 4= *college and higher*).

Experienced Poverty. This construct was operationalized by means of 4 items. Items include "How often have you had to move in the last 12 months?," "In the last 12 months, how often did you run out of money for your basic necessities?," "In the last 12 months, how often have you had to borrow money from a friend or relative to get by financially?," and "How often have you had to look for work in the last 12 months?" Responses were rated in a 4-point Likert scale (1 = *never*, 4 = *many times*). The Cronbach alpha is .71.

Experienced Homophobia. Lifetime negative experiences attributed to sexual orientation and/or identity were measured by means of 6 items on a 4-point Likert scale (1 = *never*, 4 = *many times*). Examples of questions asked include "As you were growing up, how often were you made fun of or called names for being homosexual or effeminate?," "As an adult, how often have you been made fun of or called names for being homosexual or effeminate?," and "As you were growing up, how often did you hear that homosexuals are not normal?" The Cronbach alpha is .69

HIV/AIDS Experience. We assessed individuals' experiences with HIV/AIDS through three variables:

1. HIV status (per the latest HIV test).
2. AIDS loss. This variable added three indicators asking about having lost a family member, a lover (or boyfriend), and a friend to AIDS (*yes, no*). A point was added for each positive response, for a possible score ranging from 0 to 3.
3. HIV social network. This variables was measured by a single indicator, "How many of your friends, relatives or boyfriends are currently infected with HIV?" Responses ranged from 1 (*none*) to 7 (*more than 17*).

Self-Esteem. This scale used items comparable to the traditional self-esteem scales. It was made of 7 items in a 4-point Likert scale (e.g., 4 = *definitely yes*, 1 = *definitely no*). Example questions include "Do you like most aspects of your personality?" and "Are you proud of who you are?" The Cronbach alpha is .79.

Social Support. This variable was measured by a 7-item scale with ratings on a 4-point Likert scale. Questions include "How often do you feel alone?," "How often do you feel you lack companionship?" (4 = *never*, 1 = *always*), and "Do you feel there are people you can turn to?" (4 = *definitely yes*, 1= *definitely no*). Higher scores indicate higher levels of social support. The Cronbach alpha is .79.

Community Involvement. To assess the types and levels of involvement, we asked participants three questions: (a) Are you involved in events or organizations that promote the rights of homosexuals?, (b) Are you involved in events or organizations that promote the rights of Latinos?, and (c) Are you involved with Latino gay organizations? Responses were rated on a 4-point Likert scale (1 = *definitely no*, 4 = *definitely yes*), with higher scores indicating higher involvement. An overall involvement score was compiled by adding the 3 items.

Analytical Strategy

To assess the characteristics of those involved and the hypothesized outcomes of community involvement, we estimated multiple regression models. Because of the complexity of the sampling design, we used the Stata *svy* procedures (2001). These procedures allow us to handle probability sampling weights, stratification, and cluster sampling. Thus, all our analysis, including distribution estimates and regression models, account for city and venue effects.

Results

Table 3.1 summarizes the distribution of the study variables. The sample is relatively young, with a mean age of 31. Also, most of the participants in the sample are immigrants (72%). Thirty-four percent of the participants have been in the United States less than 10 years, 38% have resided here for more than 10 years, and only 28% reported that they were born in the United States. Likewise, 36% of the participants are primarily Spanish speakers. The educational attainment of the sample is somewhat limited, as the average formal education is some college. Similarly, the levels of experienced poverty are fairly high. Regarding lifetime experiences of homophobia, the mean falls between once or twice to a few times.

The three indicators of HIV/AIDS experience reveal that the average participant has had some personal experience with HIV/AIDS. Twenty-four percent of the sample reported being HIV positive. The average AIDS-related loss is about 1 (either a family member, boyfriend, or friend), whereas the mean number of HIV positive individuals in the informants' networks falls between 1 and 8. Last, the levels of social support reported are slightly high ($M = 3.23$) and the levels of self-esteem are moderate ($M = 3.59$).

TABLE 3.1
Means, Percentages, Standard Errors, and Confidence Intervals for Study Variables

	Mean / %	S.E.	95% C. I.	
Age	31.20	.61	29.97,	32.40
Acculturation				
Time in United States				
< 10 yrs.	34%	.03		
> 10 yrs.	38%	.02		
All life	28%	.02		
Language				
Spanish speaker	36%	.03		
English speaker	24%	.03		
Education	2.80	.05	2.70,	2.90
Less than high school	10%	.01		
High school	26%	.02		
Some college	39%	.02		
College and more	25%	.02		
Experienced poverty	1.86	.04	1.77,	1.94
Had to move [+]	44%	.01		
Run out of money [+]	61%	.01		
Borrowed money [+]	54%	.01		
Had to look for work [+]	45%	.01		
Experienced homophobia	2.61	.04	2.53,	2.68
HIV/AIDS experience				
HIV status (positive)	24%	.04		
AIDS loss	1.12	.06	.99,	1.24
HIV network	2.52	.10	2.13,	2.72
Social support	3.23	.02	3.18,	3.27
Self-esteem	3.59	.02	3.55,	3.63

Note. [+] At least once or twice in last 12 months.

The percentages, frequencies, and confidence intervals for community involvement across the three cities are presented in Table 3.2. Overall, the levels of involvement (in each indicator and in the global score) are comparable to those found in the general population and other samples of gay men (Ferrer et al., 2002; Smith, 1997). In the total sample, 58% of the participants reported being either definitely or somewhat involved. The lowest levels of community involvement are found in Miami and the highest in New York City. Regarding involvement in gay or homosexual rights organizations, New York City ($M = 2.41$) is significantly higher than Miami ($M = 1.91$) and Los Angeles ($M = 2.05$). Participation in Latino rights organizations is significantly lower in Miami ($M = 1.70$) than in Los Angeles ($M = 2.15$) and New York City ($M = 2.33$). Similarly, participation in Latino gay organizations is significantly lower in Miami ($M = 1.71$) than in Los Angeles ($M = 1.93$) and New York City ($M = 2.15$). Finally, the global community involvement scores corroborate those trends. The score for New York City is significantly higher ($M = 6.88$) than for Los Angeles ($M = 6.12$) and Miami ($M = 5.36$). Los Angeles' score is also significantly higher than Miami's.

TABLE 3.2
Percentages and Means (Confidence Intervals) for Community Involvement
by City

Type of Organization	Miami ($n = 302$)	Los Angeles ($n = 301$)	New York City ($n = 309$)	Total
Gay/homosexual rights	31%[+] 1.91 (1.74, 2.08)	38% 2.05 (1.91, 2.19)	49% 2.41* (2.21, 2.60)	43% 2.21 (2.10, 2.34)
Latino rights	27% 1.70* (1.67, 1.93)	42% 2.15 (2.01, 2.30)	46% 2.33 (2.12, 2.54)	58% 2.20 (2.07, 2.32)
Latino gay organizations	24% 1.71* (1.57, 1.84)	33% 1.93 (1.81, 2.05)	40% 2.15 (1.91, 2.40)	35% 2.01 (2.16, 2.71)
Community involvement score	37% 5.36* (4.96, 5.77)	59% 6.12* (5.78, 6.46)	63% 6.88* (6.28, 7.48)	58% 6.41 (6.06, 6.71)

Note. * $p < .05$. [+]Percentage of those responding definitely yes or somewhat involved.

Who Is Involved?

To assess the characteristics of those Latino gay men involved in gay, Latino, and HIV/AIDS-related organizations, we constructed the regression model shown in Table 3.3. The dependent variable in this model is the community involvement score. The independent variables include age, acculturation, education, experienced poverty, experienced homophobia, and HIV/AIDS experiences (recall that this model controls for city and venue effects). The results of this model suggest that participation takes place regardless of age ($b = -.00$, ns). In terms of acculturation, the only significant predictor is being an English speaker ($b = -1.05$, $p < .05$). Given that being a Spanish speaker is also negatively related to participation ($b = -.42$, ns), these results imply that those who speak both languages equally are more likely to be involved than those who mainly speak either Spanish or English. Education (b = .29, *ns*) and experienced poverty (b = .43, *ns*) are not associated with community involvement. Experienced homophobia, however, is positively associated with involvement (b = .40, p < .05). As Latino gay men's experiences of homophobia increase, so does their community involvement. Likewise, HIV social network is the only HIV/AIDS experience that is positively and significantly associated with community involvement (b = .52, p < .05). As the number of HIV positive individuals in Latino gay men's networks increases, the levels of community involvement also increase. HIV status (b = .18, *ns*) and AIDS loss (b = .09, *ns*) are not significantly related to participation. In summary, our model suggests that acculturation, experienced homophobia, and HIV/AIDS experiences are associated with community involvement in gay, Latino, and HIV/AIDS-related organizations.

TABLE 3.3
Regression Analysis Predicting Community Involvement Among
Latino Gay and Bisexual Men (n = 738)[t]

	b	S.E.	t-test	95% C.I.	
Age	-.00	.02	-.01	-.04,	.04
Acculturation					
Time in United States	.12	.21	.50	-.30,	-.55
Spanish speaker	-.42	.48	-.86	-1.38,	.54
English speaker	-1.05	.40	-2.61*	-1.85,	-.25
Education	.29	.19	1.52.	.09,	.69
Experienced poverty	.43	.29	1.52	-.14,	1.00
Experienced homophobia	.40	.19	2.08*	.02,	.78
HIV/AIDS experience					
HIV status (positive)	.18	.37	.48	-.57,	.92
AIDS loss	.09	.19	.47	-.30,	.48
HIV network	.52	.14	3.73*	.24,	.80

F (10, 72) = 7; p < .05; R^2 = .107

Note. * p < .05. [t] Sample size varies due to missing values.

The Possible Consequences of Community Involvement

In this chapter we analyze two potential outcomes of community involvement in gay, Latino, and HIV/AIDS-related organizations: social support and self-esteem. As stated before, our data do not allow us to assess causality. Thus, the analysis is guided by theory and previous research. We conducted multiple regression analyses to assess whether community involvement predicts social support and self-esteem, controlling for those factors likely to be associated with both outcomes. These factors include age, acculturation, education, experienced poverty, experienced homophobia, and HIV status. As in the previous analyses, these also control for city and venue effects.

TABLE 3.4
Regression Analysis Predicting Social Support Among Latino Gay and Bisexual Men (n= 748) [1]

	b	S.E.	t-test	95% C.I.
Age	-.00	.00	-.67	-.00, .00
Acculturation				
Time in United States	-.10	.03	-3.76*	-.15, -.05
Spanish speaker	.03	.03	.97	.03, .10
English speaker	-.00	.05	-.02	-.09, .09
Education	.01	.03	.38	-.04 .06
Experienced poverty	-.19	.03	-5.50*	-.25, -.12
Experienced homophobia	-.18	.02	-9.62*	-.21, -.14
HIV status (positive)	-.02	.05	-.52	-.11, .07
Community involvement	.02	.01	3.85*	.01 .03

$F(9, 73) = 24.80$; $p < .05$; $R^2 = .22$

Note. $* p < .05$. [1] Sample size varies due to missing values.

Table 3.4 depicts the final regression model predicting social support among Latino gay men. Among the control factors, acculturation (i.e., Time in the United States), experienced poverty, and experienced homophobia are significantly associated with social support. These indicate that as time of residence in the United States ($b = -.10$, $p < .05$), experienced poverty ($b = -.19$, $p < .05$), and experienced homophobia ($b = -.18$, $p < .05$) increase, social support among Latino gay men tends to decrease. After controlling for the effects of these factors, community involvement ($b = .02$; $p < .05$) is significantly associated with social support. The effect is in the expected direction, but very small relative to that of experienced poverty and homophobia. The posthoc analysis exploring moderating (e.g., interaction between homophobia and community involvement) and mediating (e.g., between homophobia and social support) effects of community involvement showed no significant results.

The regression model predicting self-esteem is similar to the one for social support (see Table 3.5). Two indicators of acculturation are significantly and negatively related to self-esteem, time of residence in the United States ($b = -.08$, $p < .05$) and being an English speaker ($b = -.15$, $p < .05$). Likewise, experienced poverty ($b = -.08$, $p < .05$) and experienced homophobia ($b = -.15$, $p < .05$) have a negative effect on self-esteem. After controlling for those variables, community involvement is significantly and positively related to self-esteem ($b = .02$, $p < .05$). Again, the effect is relatively small compared to that of experienced homophobia. We did not find significant evidence for the possible moderating or mediating effects of community involvement.

TABLE 3.5
Regression Analysis Predicting Self-Esteem Among Latino Gay and Bisexual Men (n= 755)[1]

	b	S.E.	t-test	95% C.I.
Age	.00	.00	1.25	-.00, .00
Acculturation				
Time in United States	-.08	.02	-4.34*	-.11,-.04
Spanish speaker	-.02	.04	-.62	-.09, .05
English speaker	-.15	.05	-2.97*	-.25,-.05
Education	-.00	.02	-.16	-.05 .04
Experienced poverty	-.08	.03	-2.40*	-.14,-.01
Experienced homophobia	-.15	.02	-6.62*	-.19,-.10
HIV status (positive)	-.09	.07	-1.27	-.22 .05
Community involvement	.02	.00	3.06*	.01, .03

$F(9, 73) = 15.54; p < .05; R^2 = .177$

Note. * $p < .05$. [1] Sample size varies due to missing values.

Discussion

The literature on the AIDS movement, volunteerism, and social movements, although documenting the antecedents, processes, and outcomes of community involvement (Omoto & Snyder, 2002), still lacks systematic knowledge on gay men's involvement, particularly on gay men of color. It has been our purpose in this chapter to address this gap. Using a probabilistic sample, we assessed the extent and types of community involvement among Latino gay men in three cities, as well as the possible antecedents and consequences of such involvement.

The overall community involvement of Latino gay men, according to our results, is comparable, and perhaps higher, to that found in the general population and among other gay men. For example, in a convenience sample from three cities (Austin, Phoenix, and Albuquerque), Ferrer and colleagues (2002) found rates of volunteer work among Latino and White gay men to be 20% and 26% respectively. The levels of involvement among Latino gay men seem to be similar across types of organizations (e.g., gay rights, Latino rights). This, however, may be the result of the overlap of issues in organizations or in the wording of our questions. Many of the organizations in which Latino gay men are likely to be involved are about both gay and Latino rights. It is necessary to note, however, that we still know little about the specific type of involvement (e.g., member, volunteer, client), its length, and frequency.

When community involvement is compared across cities, we find significant differences. The lowest levels of involvement are found in Miami and the highest in New York City. The levels of involvement in Los Angeles are close to, but lower than, New York City. These differences can be due to both structural and sociocultural factors. Regarding structural factors, it is possible that in Miami there are fewer Latino and/or gay-related organizations than in New York City and Los Angeles. As for sociocultural factors, anecdotal data suggest that the stigma toward AIDS and homosexuality might be more heightened in Miami than in the two other cities. This stigma may prevent some Latino men from being associated with organizations dealing with gay and HIV/AIDS-related issues. Unfortunately, we could not test these hypotheses in our data. Yet, these results raise questions about the relevance of context in describing Latino gay men's involvement. Future research may want to explore how contextual factors, such as number and types of organizations, and local cultural idiosyncrasies may affect levels and types of involvement.

In this study, we were also able to identify the factors that may lead to community involvement. Although we could not assess causality, this is, to our knowledge, the first attempt to decipher antecedents of community involvement in this population using variables that are relevant to gay and Latino gay men (e.g., experienced homophobia, acculturation). We found some evidence suggesting that acculturation, experienced homophobia, and HIV/AIDS experience may determine who gets involved. Acculturation seems to work as a deterrent to community involvement, at least around gay and Latino gay rights issues. Latino gay men who are mostly English speakers are less likely to report participation than bilingual or mostly Spanish speakers. This may be due to a combination of organizational and individual factors. On the one hand, organizations working with Latino men may be addressing, or dealing with, issues relevant to those who speak mostly Spanish and are perhaps recent immigrants. On the other hand, Latino men who speak mostly English, and who most likely were born in the United States, may not be motivated to participate in Latino or Latino gay organizations. They may be involved in mainstream gay organizations. This, however, warrants some caution, as about 72% of our informants were immigrants.

Regarding the effects of experienced homophobia and HIV/AIDS experiences on community involvement, our results revealed that both of them are positively associated with community involvement. This leads us to posit, along with Sills' premise (1957), that these two factors may work as motives, or triggers, to involvement. Latino gay men who personally experienced discrimination due to their sexual orientation may get involved in gay or Latino gay organizations to cope with this distress (Ramirez-Valles & Brown, 2003). Also, some Latino gay men may translate that experience into motives to get involved to change society or help other men deal with experiences of homophobia. Experienced homophobia, however, may become a deterrent to participation when it has been internalized. In this case, some men might not want to be identified with gay or AIDS-related issues (Ramirez-Valles & Brown, 2003). Likewise, HIV/AIDS experience may lead to involvement because individuals want to address the needs created by HIV/AIDS in their communities or social networks, or because involvement works as a coping mechanism for them. Of course, it is quite possible for HIV/AIDS experience to be an outcome of community involvement. We believe, nonetheless, that it can be both antecedent and outcome. That is, some Latino gay men may get involved because they want to help their friends living with HIV, and as they get involved they come in contact with many other individuals living with HIV.

Finally, in the individual level outcomes of community involvement, we found some very modest evidence for its effects on self-esteem and social support. After controlling for demographic variables, experienced homophobia, and HIV status, community involvement was associated with self-esteem and social support. Although this seems consistent with the literature (Omoto & Snyder, 2002; Ramirez-Valles, 2002), we believe further research is needed to corroborate this, given the limitations we encountered. Our data are cross-sectional only, and our measure of community involvement is very restrictive. As noted before, we did not ask about the type, length, and frequency of involvement.

Notwithstanding the limitations, this study is a significant contribution to the literature on the AIDS movement and social movements in general. Given the scarcity of data on gay men and gay men of color, this study is a step toward documenting and understanding community involvement among these groups. Furthermore, our study underscores factors such as homophobia and acculturation, which are relevant for these groups' activism, but have been ignored by mainstream research.

ACKNOWLEDGMENTS

This study was funded by a National Institute of Mental Health grant (R01MH62937-01) to Jesus Ramirez-Valles, and a grant from the National Institute of Child Health and Development (R01HD32776) to Rafael M. Diaz.

References

Altman, D. G., Feighery E., Robinson, T. N., Haydel, F. K., Strausberg, L., Lorig, K., & Killen, J. D. (1998). Psychological factors associated with youth involvement in community activities promoting heart health. *Health Education & Behavior, 25*, 489-500.

Arno, P. S. (1988). The future of volunteerism and the AIDS epidemic. In D. Rogers & E. Ginzberg (Eds.), *The AIDS patient: An action agenda* (pp. 56-70). Boulder, CO; Westview.

Bebbington, A. C., & Gatter, P. N. (1994). Volunteers in an HIV social care organization. *AIDS Care, 6*, 571-585.

Bellah, R. N., Madsen, R., Sullivan, W. M., Swidler, A., & Tipton, S. M. (1996). *Habits of the heart: Individualism and commitment in American life* (Updated ed.). Berkeley: University of California Press.

Boehmer, U. (2000). *The personal and the political: Women's activism in response to the breast cancer and AIDS epidemics.* Albany: State University of New York Press.

Cantu, L. (2000). Entre hombres/between men: Latino masculinities and homosexualities. In P. Nardi (Ed.), *Gay masculinities* (pp: 225-246). Thousand Oaks, CA: Sage.

Catania J. A., Osmond, D., Stall, R. D., Pollack, L., Paul, J. P., Blower, S., Binson, D., Canchola, J. A., Mills, T. C., Fisher, L., Choi, K. H., Porco, T., Turner, C., Blair, J., Henne, J., Bye, L. L., & Coates, T. J. (2001). The continuing HIV epidemic among men who have sex with men. *American Journal of Public Health, 91*(6), 907-914.

Chambre, S. M. (1991). Volunteers as witness: The mobilization of AIDS volunteers in New York City, 1981-1988. *Social Services Review, 65*, 531-547.

Diaz, R. M. (1998). *Latino gay men and HIV: Culture, sexuality, and risk behavior*. New York: Routledge.

Diaz, R. M., Ayala, G., Bein, E., Henne, J., & Marin, B. V. (2001). The impact of homophobia, poverty, and racism on the mental health of gay and bisexual Latino men: Findings from 3 US cities. *American Journal of Public Health, 91*, 927-932.

Epstein, S. (1996). *Impure science: AIDS, activism, and the politics of knowledge.* Berkeley: University of California Press.

Ferrer, L. M., Ramirez-Valles, J., Kegeles, S.M., & Rebehook, G. (2002, July). *Community involvement and HIV/AIDS among young gay/bisexual men.* Paper presented at the XIV International AIDS Conference, Barcelona, Spain.

Frable, D. E. S., Wortman, C., & Joseph, J. (1997). Predicting self-esteem, well-being, and distress in a cohort of gay men: The importance of cultural stigma, personal visibility, community networks, and positive identity. *Journal of Personality, 65*, 599-624.

Gabard, D. L. (1995). Volunteers in AIDS service organizations: Motivations and values. *Health and Human Services Administration, 17*, 317-337.

Herek, G. M. (1999). AIDS and stigma. *American Behavioral Scientist, 42*, 1102-1112.

Hodgkinson, V.A. (1995). Key factors influencing caring, involvement, and community. In P. Schervish, V. Hodgkinson, M. Gates & Associates (Eds.), *Care and community in modern society* (pp. 21-50). San Francisco: Jossey-Bass.

Independent Sector. (1999). *Giving and volunteering in the United States, 1999.* Washington, DC: The Independent Sector.

Kayal, P. M. (1994). Communalization and homophile organization membership: Gay volunteerism before and during AIDS. *Journal of Gay and Lesbian Social Services, 1*, 33-57.

Knoke, D., & Wood, J. R. (1981). *Organized for action: Commitment in voluntary associations.* New Brunswick, NJ: Rutgers University Press.

Kobasa, S. C. O. (1990). AIDS and volunteer associations: Perspectives on social and individual change. *Millbank Quarterly, 68* (Suppl. 2), 280-294.

Kobasa, S. C. O. (1991). AIDS volunteering: Links to the past and future prospects. In D. Nelkin, D. Willis, & S. Parris (Eds.), *A disease of society: Cultural and institutional responses to AIDS* (pp. 172-188). Cambridge, England: Cambridge University Press.

Marsh, H. W. (1992). Extracurricular activities: Beneficial extension of the traditional curriculum or subversion of academic goals. *Journal of Educational Psychology, 84,* 553-562.

Moen, P., & Fields, S. (1999, August). *Retirement and well-being: Does community participation replace paid work?* Paper presented at the American Sociological Association Conference, Chicago, IL.

Omoto, A. M. & Snyder, M. (1995). Sustained helping without obligation: Motivation, longevity of service, and perceived attitude change among AIDS volunteers. *Journal of Personality and Social Psychology, 68,* 671–686.

Omoto, A. M. & Snyder, M. (2002). Considerations of community: The context and process of volunteerism. *American Behavioral Scientist, 45,* 846-867.

Omoto, A. M., Snyder, M., & Berghuis, J. P. (1993). The psychology of volunteerism: A conceptual analysis and a program of action research. In J. B. Pryor & G. D. Reeder (Eds.), *The social psychology of HIV infection* (pp. 333-356). Hillside, NJ: Lawrence Erlbaum Associates.

Ouellette, S. C., Cassel, B. J., Maslanka, H., & Wong, L. M. (1995). GMHC volunteers and the challenges and hopes for the second decade of AIDS. *AIDS Education and Prevention, 7* (Suppl.), 64-79.

Patton, C. (1989). The AIDS industry: Construction of "victims," "volunteers" and "experts." In E. Carter & S. Watney (Eds.), *Taking liberties, AIDS and cultural politics* (pp. 113-126). London: Serpant's Tail.

Ramirez-Valles, J. (1999). Changing women: The narrative construction of personal change through community health work among women in Mexico. *Health Education & Behavior, 26,* 23-40.

Ramirez-Valles, J. (2001). "I was not invited to be a [CHW]... I asked to be one":
Motives for community mobilization among women community health workers in Mexico. *Health Education & Behavior, 28,* 150-165.

Ramirez-Valles, J. (2002). The protective effects of community involvement for HIV risk behavior: A conceptual framework. *Heath Education Research, 17,* 389-403.

Ramirez-Valles, J., & Brown, A. (2003). Latino's community involvement in HIV/AIDS: Organizational and individual perspectives on volunteering. *AIDS Education and Prevention, 15* (Suppl. A), 90-104.

Rietschlin, J. (1998). Voluntary association membership and psychological distress. *Health and Social Behavior, 39,* 348-355.

Schondel, C., Shields, G., & Orel, N. (1992). Development of an instrument to measure volunteers' motivation in working with people with AIDS. *Social Work in Health Care, 17,* 53-71.

Sills, L. D. (1957). *The volunteers: Means and ends in a national organization.* Gencoe: The Free Press.

Smith, D. H. (1994). Determinants of voluntary association participation and volunteering: A literature review. *Nonprofit and Voluntary Sector Quarterly, 23,* 243-263.

Smith, D. H. (1997). Grassroots associations are important: Some theory and a review of the impact literature. *Nonprofit and Voluntary Sector Quarterly, 26,* 269-306.

Snyder, M., & Omoto, A. M. (1992). Who helps and why? The psychology of AIDS volunteerism. In S. Spacapan & S. Oskamp (Eds.), *Helping and being helped: Naturalistic studies* (pp. 213-239). Newbury Park, CA: Sage.

Snyder, M., Omoto A. M., & Crain, L. A. (1999). Punished for their good deeds: Stigmatization of AIDS volunteers. *American Behavioral Scientist, 42,* 1171-1188.

Snow, D. A., Zurcher, L., Jr., & Ekland-Olson, S. (1980). Social networks and social movements: A microstructural approach to differential recruitment. *American Sociological Review, 45,* 787-801.

Stewart, E., & Weinstein, R. S. (1997). Volunteer participation in context: Motivations and political efficacy within three AIDS organizations. *American Journal of Community Psychology, 25*(6), 809-837.

Thoits, P. A., & Hewitt, N. L. (2001). Volunteer work and well being. *Journal of Health and Social Behavior, 42,* 115-131.

Turner, H. A., Hays, R. B., & Coates, T. J. (1993). Determinants of social support among gay men: The context of AIDS. *Journal of Health and Social Behavior, 34,* 37-53.

Valentgas, P., Bynum, C., & Sierler, S. (1990). The buddy volunteer commitment in AIDS care. *American Journal of Public Health, 8,* 1378-1380.

Waldo, C. R., Kegeles, S. M., & Hays, R. B. (1998, July). *Self-acceptance of gay identity decreases sexual risk behavior and increases psychological health in U.S. young gay men.* Paper presented at the 12th World AIDS Conference, Geneva, Switzerland.

Williams, J. A., & Ortega, S. (1986). The multidimensionality of joining. *Journal of Voluntary Action Research, 15,* 35-44.

Wilson, J., & Musick, M. A. (1997). Who cares? Toward an integrated theory of volunteer work. *American Sociological Review, 62,* 694-713.

Wolfe, M. (1994). The AIDS Coalition to Unleash Power (ACT UP): A direct model of community research for AIDS prevention. In J. P. Van Vugt (Ed.), *AIDS prevention and services: Community based research* (pp.217-247). Westport, CT: Begin & Garvey.

Wolitski, R. J., Valdiserri, R. O., Denning, P. H., & Levine, W. C. (2001). Are we headed for a resurgence of the HIV epidemic among men who have sex with men? *American Journal of Public Health, 91,* 883-888.

Youniss, J., & Yates, M. (1997). *Community service and social responsibility in youth.* Chicago: University of Chicago Press.

4

BECOMING (AND REMAINING) A COMMUNITY VOLUNTEER: DOES PERSONALITY MATTER?

Mark H. Davis
Eckerd College

The question of whether personality characteristics influence *helping behavior* has been around for some time and has been answered in various ways. At first, most investigations of helping behavior tended to focus very little on individual characteristics and much more on situational factors that encourage or inhibit prosocial actions. The most well-known of these approaches is arguably the bystander intervention model of Latane and Darley (1970), which identified the presence of others as a factor which, somewhat counterintuitively, frequently reduces the likelihood of receiving help during an emergency. Other early social psychological approaches, although they might have allowed a place for personality characteristics, also tended to emphasize the situation, or internal states produced by the situation, as the primary determinant of helping (e.g., Batson, 1991; Cialdini, Darby, & Vincent, 1973; Piliavin, Dovidio, Gaertner, & Clark, 1981).

When social and personality psychologists eventually began to examine the impact of personality variables on helping, they often did so simply by including individual difference measures within existing research paradigms—and one thing that most of these paradigms had in common was that they typically assessed helping by confronting participants with a sudden and unexpected opportunity to provide assistance to a stranger. As evidence began to accumulate using this approach, the picture that emerged showed that personality traits play, at best, a minor role in producing helping behavior (Gergen, Gergen, & Meter, 1972), a finding seemingly at odds with intuition and personal experience.

Several explanations emerged to account for this unexpected finding. One was that many of these early investigations were probably not especially well-suited for an examination of personality's impact on helping. One way to conceptualize this problem is in terms of the distinction that Snyder and his colleagues (Snyder, 1983; Snyder & Ickes, 1985) have drawn between strong and weak situations. *Strong situations* are those that contain clear features that tend to evoke predictable responses from most individuals; such situations exert a more powerful guiding force on individual behavior, thus reducing the degree of control that individual characteristics such as personality can have. Emergency situations, in which victim distress cues can be vivid, and in which one has to quickly decide whether or not to offer help to a stranger, probably fall into this category. Thus, characteristics of the situation will generally be more important than personality traits in affecting helping in such settings.

If strong situations tend to minimize the effect of personality variables on behavior, weak situations tend to maximize such effects (Snyder & Ickes, 1985). *Weak situations* are those in which clear situational cues and characteristics are absent; as a result, they allow individual characteristics more room to operate. Thus, personality effects on helping behavior may be most apparent in this kind of environment. Importantly, one form of helping that seems to fall into this category is volunteering. Unlike the emergency helping opportunities that occur suddenly and allow little time for deliberation, volunteer work is a form of helping in which the initial decision typically does not take place suddenly, but is the result of a more lengthy decision-making process; as such, the environment in which the initial volunteering decision is made seems more like a weak situation

Efforts to link personality characteristics with volunteering have proven fairly successful. Reviews by Allen and Rushton (1983) and Smith (1994) suggest that volunteers are somewhat more likely than nonvolunteers to report higher levels of empathy, self-efficacy, self-esteem, and emotional stability. More recent empirical work (e.g., Thoits & Hewitt, 2001; Unger & Thumuluri, 1997) is also consistent with this pattern. However, the size of these associations is often modest, leaving open the question of just how important personality really is as an influence on volunteering.

One explanation for the frequently modest correlations found between personality and volunteering may be that other characteristics of the individual often "compete" with personality to account for variance in helping. For example, consider the role played by the varied psychological motives that people have for volunteering. Recent work has identified a number of distinct reasons for volunteering, including, for example, a desire to acquire skills, to meet other people, and to gain self-knowledge (e.g., Clary et al., 1998; Omoto & Snyder, 1995). Thus, independent of any particular personality characteristics that a volunteer may possess, he or she may also be animated by one or more of these motive states.

Or consider another possibility—that, independent of personality or motivation, committed volunteers eventually develop stable *role-identities* as volunteers, and that these identities substantially control subsequent volunteer behavior. Piliavin and her colleagues (e.g., Piliavin & Callero, 1991) have found evidence that one's psychological identity as a volunteer—or more frequently as a particular kind of volunteer such as a blood donor—does indeed predict later volunteer behavior. It seems clear, then, that personality variables are not the only characteristics of the individual that might influence volunteer behavior, and the relatively modest correlations between personality and volunteering may reflect this.

However, I suggest that there is another reason for the frequently low correlations between personality variables and indices of volunteer behavior: the fact that personality's impact on later behavior is often, perhaps always, *mediated* by intervening thoughts, feelings, and expectations. These cognitive and affective responses by the individual are the most proximal causes of volunteer behavior, and any effect that personality exerts is only through them. Unless these intervening variables are also identified and measured, then, researchers often simply assess associations between two variables that are separated from one another by several links in the causal chain. As a consequence, associations between two such distal constructs will necessarily be reduced.

This logic underlies a body of research that my colleagues and I have been investigating for several years. In this work we have pursued two different goals— first, to examine the impact of personality on the initial decision one makes to enter a volunteer setting or not, and second, to examine personality influences on what happens after this initial decision has been made and acted upon. The remainder of this chapter presents and summarizes these research efforts.

Choosing to Encounter Needy Others

Before ever engaging in volunteer work, one must take a simple but crucial step: making the decision to become a volunteer. Thus, one way that personality variables might affect volunteer behavior is by affecting that initial choice. Considerable evidence has in fact accumulated over the past 25 years that, over time, people do tend to select life situations that allow the expression of their characteristic traits and values (Ickes, Snyder, & Garcia, 1997; Snyder & Ickes, 1985). Support for this view has come from investigations using a variety of methodologies and a number of different traits.

Working with several colleagues at Eckerd College, I became interested in testing the proposition that individual differences in a particular personality trait— *empathy*—would influence a specific kind of situational choice—the preferred setting for volunteer work. Unlike most of the previous work that has examined the influence of empathy on helping, our focus was not on the likelihood of offering help when one encounters a needy other, but on the decision to encounter a needy other in the first place. More specifically, we hypothesized that the effect of dispositional empathy on situational choice would be largely mediated by its impact on two intervening variables: the emotional responses that people expect to have during the volunteer activity, and the degree of satisfaction they expect to derive from it. This model appears in Figure 4.1.

The model begins at the far left with two different forms of dispositional empathy: feelings of empathic concern and personal distress. These two emotional responses to distress in others have been identified for decades as particularly important in producing responses to such distress (e.g., Batson, 1991; Davis, 1996). *Dispositional empathic concern* refers to the tendency to have feelings of sympathy, compassion, and concern for the other person; it is an other-oriented emotion. *Dispositional personal distress*, on the other hand, refers to the tendency to have feelings of personal unease, anxiety, and discomfort; it is clearly a self-oriented, rather than other-oriented, emotional response. The Interpersonal Reactivity Index (IRI; Davis, 1980, 1983) provides reliable and valid measures of the degree to which people possess these two characteristics, and that is how we measured them in our research.

FIGURE 4.1

*Model depicting the hypothesized relations between dispositional
empathy, anticipated emotional responses, anticipated satisfaction, and
situational preference*

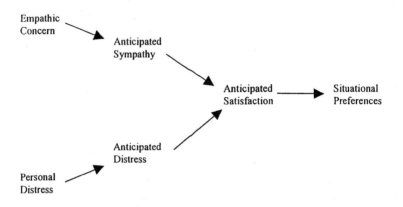

The second step in the model is the degree to which people expect to actually experience sympathy and/or distress in a particular setting. That is, based on what they know about a specific environment, to what degree do they anticipate actually having feelings of empathic concern or personal distress? We hypothesized that one important determinant of such specific expectations would be the person's general empathic tendencies. Thus, dispositional empathic concern should increase expectations of situational sympathy, and dispositional personal distress should increase expectations of situational distress. The rationale for these predictions is fairly simple: As a result of perceiving their own emotional reactions in the past, those who are especially prone to sympathy (or distress) come to know themselves with at least some degree of accuracy, and make predictions based on this knowledge

These anticipated emotional reactions in turn predict the third step of the model: a global expectation of the degree of satisfaction/enjoyment that people would feel in that situation. We predicted that anticipated feelings of distress would diminish expected satisfaction, and anticipated feelings of sympathy would increase expected satisfaction. Finally, we predicted that overall expectations of satisfaction would be the proximal determinant of situational choice—the greater the level of anticipated satisfaction, the greater the likelihood that the person would choose to enter a given situation. Thus, the model argues that dispositional empathy does not directly produce a situational choice, but does so through a series of intervening steps.

Study 1: Hypothetical Choices

In the first study designed to test this model (Davis et al., 1999; Study 1), we recruited 189 college students (82 males; 102 females; 4 who did not answer this question) for an experiment ostensibly concerned with people's perceptions of volunteer work. Each participant completed a questionnaire packet containing several instruments. First, they read short descriptions of 12 hypothetical volunteer activities, each of which was designed to evoke a particular kind of emotional response. Four descriptions were written to make it seem likely that a person doing this work would experience feelings of sympathy (e.g., working one-on-one with abused children to increase self-esteem). Another four descriptions were written to make it seem likely that a person doing this work would experience feelings of distress (e.g., working with head injury survivors who had significant facial disfigurement). Finally, four descriptions were written to make it seem likely that a person doing this work would experience little emotion at all (e.g., deliver and pick up mail). Following each description, the participants indicated the degree to which they would like to participate in each volunteer activity; this constituted the measure of *situational preference*.

After participants had indicated the extent of their desire to participate in each activity, they were asked to go back and rate each activity on items that reflected three dimensions: how much sympathy they expected to feel in each situation; how much distress they expected; and how much enjoyment they expected to derive from the activity. Finally, all participants completed the IRI to measure dispositional empathic concern and personal distress, and the Marlowe-Crowne social desirability scale (Crowne & Marlowe, 1960) to measure a concern for social appropriateness.

To evaluate the model depicted in Fig. 4.1, we carried out a series of path analyses separately, for each of the three kinds of volunteer settings: sympathy-arousing, distress-arousing, and neutral. As a first step in all of these analyses, sex and social desirability were entered as predictors; thus, the effect of these two variables was always removed before the effects of other predictors on the criterion were assessed. The results of these analyses appear in Table 4.1.

When the participants were asked to evaluate the sympathy-arousing volunteer settings, all of the hypothesized associations were supported, in some cases very strongly. Greater dispositional empathic concern was robustly related to anticipated sympathy, and dispositional personal distress was substantially related to anticipated distress. Both of these anticipated emotional states were then associated in the expected directions with anticipated satisfaction, although the negative effect of anticipated distress was not as strong as the effect of anticipated sympathy. Finally, anticipated satisfaction was strongly associated with a desire to enter that situation.

Essentially the same pattern was found when the participants were asked to evaluate the distress-arousing volunteer settings. Dispositional empathy produced greater expectations of each type of emotional response; these anticipated emotions affected anticipated satisfaction in the expected ways, and anticipated satisfaction powerfully affected situational preference.

Things were somewhat different, however, when people were asked to evaluate relatively nonarousing situations. In this case, dispositional empathy lost almost all of its ability to predict anticipated emotions, and anticipated distress

TABLE 4.1

Path Coefficients from the Model Testing the Effect of Dispositional Empathy on Anticipated Emotions,
Anticipated Satisfaction, and Situational Choice: Studies 1 and 2

Path from the Model	Study 1			Study 2		
	Sympathy-Arousing Situations	Distress-Arousing Situations	Neutral Situations	Sympathy-Arousing Situations	Distress-Arousing Situations	Neutral Situations
Empathic concern → Anticipated sympathy	.52**	.37**	-.05	.39**	.45**	.01
Personal distress → Anticipated distress	.33**	.39**	.19*	.13	.08	.17
Anticipated sympathy → Anticipated satisfaction	.41**	.23**	.70**	.31*	.43**	.67**
Anticipated distress → Anticipated satisfaction	-.14+	-.24**	.04	.06	.03	.02
Anticipated satisfaction → Situational Preference	.49**	.64**	.61**	.51**	.73**	.66**

Note. ** $p < .01$. * $p < .05$. + $p < .10$.

became clearly nonsignificant as a predictor of anticipated satisfaction. Thus, as we might expect, if the volunteer work in question is unlikely to evoke much in the way of emotional response, then anticipated emotional responses become much less useful as a way to predict situational preferences.

Study 2: Nonhypothetical Choices

The results of the first study provided good initial support for the model, but they suffer from one obvious problem: All of the judgments we asked people to make were strictly hypothetical. That is, no one in Study 1 believed that the evaluations of the volunteer activities would actually commit him or her to *participate* in them. In the next study, we tried to get around that problem by having undergraduate students participate in a procedure much like the first one, but with one crucial difference. Participants were told that in order to receive the extra credit for being in the experiment, they would not only take part in the laboratory session, but would also need to work for 2 hours in one of the community agencies they would be reading about. Their responses to the questionnaires in the lab session—ratings of anticipated enjoyment and desire to perform the activity—would be used to place them in a volunteer setting. Thus, in contrast to the first study, participants now believed that there would be some consequences for their situational preferences; in actuality, no one was ever required to perform the volunteer work.

In this investigation (Davis et al., 1999; Study 2), 81 undergraduate participants (32 males; 49 females) completed questionnaire packets similar to those employed in the first study. They read short descriptions of 12 hypothetical volunteer activities; as before, four of these were written to evoke sympathy, four to evoke distress, and four to evoke no emotional response. Following each description, the participants indicated the degree to which they would like to participate in each volunteer activity; this again constituted the measure of situational preference.

Participants were then asked to rate each activity in terms of how much sympathy they would expect to feel in each situation, how much distress they would expect, and how much enjoyment they would expect. Finally, all participants again completed the IRI and the Marlowe-Crowne social desirability scale. As in the previous study, a series of path analyses was conducted with sex and social desirability controlled on the first step of all analyses. These results appear in Table 4.1.

When they were asked to evaluate the sympathy-arousing volunteer settings, the results from these participants strongly supported one part of the model, but not the other. Dispositional empathic concern predicted anticipated sympathy, and sympathy predicted anticipated satisfaction, which then was strongly associated with preference for the situation. On the other hand, anticipated distress was not predictable, nor was it predictive of anticipated satisfaction. An essentially identical pattern was found when the distress-arousing settings were considered. Again, the links involving dispositional empathic concern, situational sympathy, and anticipated satisfaction were all strongly significant; as before, anticipated satisfaction was strongly related to situational preference. Again, however, none of the distress paths were significant. Finally, as in Study 1, when nonarousing situations were being evaluated, neither personality measure had any reliable effect on anticipated emotional response.

Taken together, these two studies provided good evidence for two conclusions: first, that those who are dispositionally disposed toward feelings of compassion also tend to anticipate having such feelings in new situations; and second, that this expectation contributes to anticipating greater satisfaction in those situations, along with a greater willingness to enter them. With regard to distress, the evidence from these studies was mixed, making the picture less clear. We were not sure at this point whether feelings of distress really were unimportant in affecting volunteer satisfaction, which seemed intuitively unlikely, or whether the results from Study 2 were an anomaly. To try to answer this question, we took a different tack in the next study.

After the Situational Choice: Emotional Reactions and Satisfaction

The first two studies explored the role of dispositional empathy in affecting the initial decision to encounter needy others. But what happens after this decision has been made and acted upon? What effect does dispositional empathy have on the emotions actually experienced during volunteer work? What effect do these emotions have on satisfaction? To examine these questions, we conducted a third study, this time using actual community volunteers.

Study 3: Real Community Volunteers

Instead of again asking college students to predict their emotions, satisfaction, and willingness to enter various volunteer situations, in Study 3 (Davis et al., 1999; Study 3) we contacted actual volunteers and asked them for retrospective accounts of their volunteer experiences. We did so by working with the Volunteer Action Center (VAC) in Pinellas County, Florida, an agency that helps place potential volunteers with appropriate organizations. The VAC agreed to let us send questionnaires to over 300 people who had contacted them for such help over the previous 5 years. After eliminating those individuals for whom the questionnaires were returned by the post office as undeliverable, we were left with an effective sample population of 233; of these, we received usable responses from 93 people (20 males; 72 females; one who did not respond to this item), producing a response rate of 40%.

All participants completed a questionnaire in which they indicated whether they had ever actually engaged in volunteer work as a result of contacting the VAC; if so, they were then asked a series of questions that tapped the extent to which they had experienced the following during their work: feelings of sympathy, feelings of distress, and feelings of satisfaction. In addition, the questionnaire contained the empathic concern and personal distress scales from the IRI. Regression analyses similar to those employed in the first two studies were then carried out.

Even though the responses in this case were reports of *actual* emotions and *actual* satisfaction rather than expectations, the general pattern remained the same. Those with a dispositional tendency to experience compassion for needy others reported significantly more of such feelings in their volunteer work ($\beta = .59$), and these feelings were significantly associated with greater reported satisfaction ($\beta = .49$). In addition, dispositional distress was significantly related to actual feelings of distress ($\beta = .35$), and these feelings were significantly and negatively related to volunteer satisfaction ($\beta = -.44$). Thus, unlike Study 2, the distress paths again emerged as significant for this sample of actual volunteers, reinforcing support for this portion of the model.

Taken as a whole, then, these three studies offer fairly good support for the view that trait empathy does have an impact on the decision to volunteer, and that this impact is mediated by empathy's effect on a particular set of expectations about the way one is likely to feel during the volunteer work. The first two studies support the idea that empathy affects such expectations—especially for feelings of sympathy—and the third study demonstrates that the expectations people have are probably accurate. That is, not only do people high in empathic concern (or personal distress) expect to feel sympathy (or distress), but it appears that once in the volunteer setting, they actually do have such feelings. These feelings, as predicted, then contribute to the degree of satisfaction experienced (or anticipated) by the volunteer. Anticipated satisfaction then plays a large role in affecting the situational choices that the individual makes.

After the Situational Choice:
Volunteer Involvement and Persistence

There is more to the volunteer experience, of course, than just the subjective experience of emotion and satisfaction. In particular—and of special importance to the volunteer agencies themselves—there is the matter of behavior. Volunteers differ considerably, for example, in their degree of active involvement, as well as in the length of time they maintain that involvement. To examine these issues, we decided to carry out a longitudinal project in which we would identify volunteers during their initial orientation, measure dispositional empathy at that time, and then follow them for the first full year of their service, periodically assessing their emotional reactions, satisfaction, involvement, and persistence.

In preparation for this investigation, we decided to expand our focus by combining our model with an existing model of volunteerism that we found very attractive: Omoto and Snyder's (1995) volunteer process model. In its most general form, the volunteer process model conceptualizes volunteering in terms of three sequential stages: *antecedents* (which, among other things, would include the personality traits we have been emphasizing), *volunteer experiences* (which, among other things, would include an individual's satisfaction with the work), and *consequences* (which, among other things, would include such things as volunteer persistence over time). Because this seemed to be a very reasonable model, we decided to simply elaborate on it by adding a more detailed consideration of what occurs at the stage of volunteer experience (see Fig. 4.2).

FIGURE 4.2
Elaborated Version of the Volunteer Process Model (Omoto &
Snyder, 1995) Incorporating Elements of the Dispositional Empathy Model

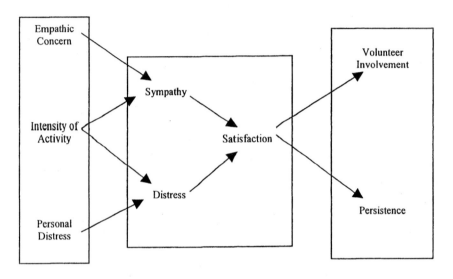

Our elaborated version of this model conceives of at least two kinds of volunteer experience variables that fall into a rough causal sequence: first, emotional experiences such as feelings of sympathy and distress, and second, a global sense of satisfaction with the volunteer work. Consistent with our earlier work, satisfaction is seen as the most proximal determinant of variables that make up the consequences stage—the amount of time one devotes to volunteer work, or how long one persists as a volunteer. In addition, we added one other variable of note to the original volunteer process model at the antecedents stage: the *intensity* of the activity.

What we have tried to capture with this new variable is that situations differ in terms of how emotionally intense and arousing they are to the volunteer, and that this can be considered an antecedent variable just like personality traits. The volunteer's actual experience of arousal or distress would of course fall in the middle of the model, in the volunteer experiences stage; however, the features of the work which make it arousing seem more like an antecedent variable—something that exists before any particular volunteer ever enters that situation, and that continues to exist long after that volunteer is gone.

Study 4: Following New Volunteers Over Time

The participants in this study (Davis, Hall, & Meyer, 2003) were 238 individuals (67 males; 171 females) who began volunteering at one of nine organizations in the Tampa Bay area between July 1996 and September 1997. The organizations were quite varied, and included the St. Petersburg Free Clinic, Big Brothers/Big Sisters, a telephone helpline, and a Guardian ad Litem program. The study was a fully prospective longitudinal investigation. That is, we contacted and recruited volunteers at their initial orientation session, and then contacted them at four additional points during the next year: at 1 month after orientation, 4 months, 8 months, and 12 months.

At the orientation session, participants completed a fairly lengthy questionnaire assessing dispositional empathy, as well as a number of other variables not relevant to this chapter. At each of the follow-up contacts there was a brief, 5-minute phone interview at which time the volunteer experience and consequence data were collected: measures of current sympathy, distress, satisfaction, and weekly time spent volunteering. In addition, participants were asked to describe the nature of their volunteer duties at each contact point; these descriptions were used to code the intensity of the volunteer activity.

A very simple coding system was used for this purpose, placing each activity into one of only two categories: intense or nonintense. Examples of volunteer work characterized as "intense" included child care worker, Big Brother/Big Sister, reading to the blind, rape counselor, hospice worker, and guardian ad litem; examples of "nonintense" activities included such things as grant writer, office aide, typist, cook, lawn care, and food sorter at a food bank.

Space considerations preclude a presentation of the complete analyses resulting from this lengthy investigation. Instead, what follows is a simplified version of the key findings; however, none of the results reported here are inconsistent with the conclusions that result from the more complete and sophisticated analyses. Two points bear special emphasis. First, what Fig. 4.3 displays is simply the *mean correlation* between variables in the model, averaged across all the time periods at which data were collected. For example, the link between dispositional empathic concern (measured at Time 1) and actual feelings of sympathy was assessed four times (Times 2, 3, 4, and 5); Fig. 4.3 presents the average of these four correlations. Second, when the variables in question come from different "stages" of the volunteer process model (i.e., antecedents and experiences; experiences and consequences), then the correlations are calculated between variables at different time points (e.g., personality at Time 1 and sympathy at Times 2 - 5; satisfaction at Time 2 and involvement at Time 3). When the variables in question come from the same stage, then the correlations are calculated between variables at the same time point (e.g., sympathy and satisfaction at Time 3).

Although both of the empathy traits measured at orientation—dispositional empathic concern and personal distress—were positively associated with later emotional responses to volunteer work, only the effect of empathic concern on sympathy was statistically significant. Thus, people who are dispositionally prone to feeling compassion for others did in fact report more of such feelings during the actual volunteer work. This finding replicated again the pattern found in each of the previous three studies, probably the most reliable association we have found in this line of research.

Within the experiences stage, emotional responses did, as predicted, influence overall feelings of satisfaction with the volunteer activity, but only feelings of distress had a significant effect; the greater the degree of distress that volunteers experienced, the less satisfaction they reported. This link between distress and satisfaction is only slightly less reliable than the one between empathic concern and sympathy described earlier; apart from Study 2, this association emerged in each investigation.

FIGURE 4.3
Mean Correlations Among Key Constructs in Study 4

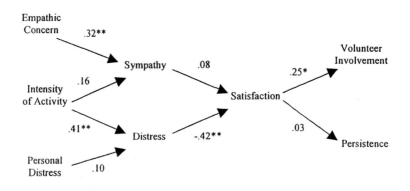

Note. ** *p* < .01.   * *p* < .05.

Finally, satisfaction was associated in the predicted fashion with time spent in the volunteer activity; the more satisfied that volunteers were at one time point, the more hours per week they volunteered at the next time point. Unexpectedly, however, satisfaction had no effect at all on the likelihood of remaining a volunteer at the next time period; being satisfied—or dissatisfied— with one's volunteer work was of no use in predicting persistence.

A number of interesting questions resulted from this investigation, but given space constraints, I focus on only two. The first of these concerns the role played by the volunteers' feelings of distress. As Figure 4.3 reveals, such feelings of distress were the only predictor of satisfaction, and they were substantially related. However, unexpectedly, dispositional personal distress did not have the predicted influence on these feelings.

Instead, the only significant predictor of volunteer distress was the intensity of the volunteer work itself; the more intense the activity, the greater the distress. In contrast, the intensity of the work had no appreciable effect on the feelings of sympathy and compassion experienced by the volunteer. Thus, an interesting pattern emerged. Personality had an impact on one kind of emotional response to volunteer work (sympathy), but not the other; in contrast, characteristics of the situation (intensity) had an impact on distress but not on sympathy.

The second big question that emerged from this study was more perplexing: Why were we not better able to predict volunteer persistence? The elaborated model specified volunteer satisfaction as the most direct influence on volunteer consequences such as amount of time spent volunteering and persistence over time. Although time spent volunteering was associated with earlier satisfaction, volunteer persistence was not. In fact, even when other variables in the study not mentioned thus far are included, the model still did a very poor job of predicting who would persist as a volunteer over the 12-month course of the study. The question is: Why?

In retrospect, the answer may lie in a choice we made at the beginning of the project: The decision to follow completely new volunteers over their first year of work. The vast majority of investigations in this area—even longitudinal ones— have not employed this strategy. Instead, the typical approach is to recruit people who are currently serving as volunteers, regardless of how long they may have been doing so (e.g., Omoto & Snyder, 1995; Penner & Finkelstein, 1998). Although some of the participants in such studies may therefore be relatively recent volunteers, many have been volunteering for months or years at the time the study begins. These "mature" volunteers stand in contrast to the purely "virgin" volunteers that we recruited in this study.

Why would this distinction be important? Our suspicion, after the fact, is that there may be a substantial "shaking out" process that occurs during the first year of volunteering, one that may have relatively little to do with many of the variables that make up our model. That is, forces outside the control of the individual and outside the scope of our model may have played the biggest role in determining whether or not people continue to volunteer. To explore this possibility, we examined one final question that we posed to our participants. When contacted at each time point, we asked first if they were still volunteering; if not, we then asked why they were no longer doing so. We later coded these responses into a variety of categories that appear in Table 4.2.

TABLE 4.2
Volunteers' Reasons for Discontinuing Their Volunteer Service: Study 4

Reason for Discontinuing	Percent Reporting
Dissatisfaction (e.g., conflict with supervisor; not interested; too stressful)	12%
Time conflicts (e.g., work hours changed)	48%
Emergencies	9%
Changed residence	15%
Vacations	7%
Miscellaneous	10%

Of the 238 people in the original sample, 101 reported their reasons for quitting; the rest either did not quit, did not respond to that question, or were unreachable. However, of those who provided answers, the vast majority reflected factors outside the scope of the model. Only 12 of the 101 reported quitting for reasons that seemed relevant to dissatisfaction with the work: "conflict with supervisor," "not interested in the volunteer activity," and "too stressful." By far the biggest reason for discontinuing their volunteer work was "time conflicts"—which typically meant that their hours or responsibilities at their place of employment had changed, making it impossible to continue as a volunteer. Other reasons not reflecting dissatisfaction with the volunteer placement—such as changing residences and vacations—were also common. Although it would not be prudent to place too much weight on these post hoc analyses, they reinforce our belief that much of the variation in persistence across the first year is due to features of the volunteer environment not captured by this model.

Conclusion

So what is the answer to the question posed in the title of this chapter: Does personality matter? One way to answer the question is by focusing on the initial decision to engage in volunteer work. In this case, I think the answer is "yes." At least for the kinds of volunteering we have studied, it seems apparent that people weigh the potential costs and benefits of their actions, including the emotional responses likely to be evoked, as they make their decisions. Our evidence suggests that at least one kind of personality variable—individual differences in empathy—plays a significant role in this strategic decision making.

A second way to answer the question is by focusing on the subjective experiences of volunteers during their volunteer activities; in this case, I think the answer is "at least sometimes." Dispositional empathic concern was associated with feelings of sympathy in both the retrospective study of established volunteers as well as the prospective study of new volunteers. Dispositional personal distress was associated with actual distress in the retrospective but not the prospective investigation. Further, these emotional responses were consistently related to subjective feelings of satisfaction in both studies.

A final way to answer the question is by focusing on volunteer behavior such as involvement and persistence. Here the answer seems less encouraging. Although trait empathy does seem to influence at least some of the subjective responses experienced by volunteers, dispositions appear to play little role in determining how much time will be spent as a volunteer, or if one will persist in volunteering through the end of the first year. Instead, other factors seem to be more important, at least during the first year, in determining the length of volunteer persistence.

So where does that leave us? One useful implication of these findings is that volunteer satisfaction is substantially influenced by the level of emotional distress that volunteers experience in their work. Thus, minimizing this distress may be one of the most effective ways of increasing volunteer satisfaction, which may in turn increase the level of volunteer involvement. Evidence from this study suggests that screening volunteers on the basis of personality or motivation will not help to accomplish this, because those variables were essentially unrelated to actual distress. Instead, attention might better be given to training methods that would prepare volunteers for distressing situations, or provide them with effective coping strategies. In any event, these results suggest that the volunteer experience is heavily shaped by the amount of distress that it contains, and that there is much to be gained by dealing with the reality.

References

Allen, N. J., & Rushton, J. P. (1983). Personality characteristics of community mental health volunteers: A review. *Journal of Voluntary Action Research, 12,* 36-49.

Batson, C. D. (1991). The *altruism question: Toward a social-psychological answer.* Hillsdale, NJ: Lawrence Erlbaum Associates.

Cialdini, R. B., Darby, B. L., & Vincent, J. E. (1973). Transgressions and altruism: A case for hedonism. *Journal of Experimental Social Psychology, 9,* 502-516.

Clary, E. G., Snyder, M., Ridge, R. D., Copeland, J., Stukas, A. A., Haugen, J., & Miene, P. (1998). Understanding and assessing the motivations of volunteers: A functional approach. *Journal of Personality and Social Psychology, 74,* 1516-1530.

Crowne, D. P., & Marlowe, D. (1960). A new scale of social desirability independent of psychopathology. *Journal of Consulting Psychology, 24,* 349-354.

Davis, M. H. (1980). A multidimensional approach to individual differences in empathy. *JSAS Catalog of Selected Documents in Psychology, 10,* 85.

Davis, M. H. (1983). Measuring individual differences in empathy: Evidence for a multidimensional approach. *Journal of Personality and Social Psychology, 44,* 113-126.

Davis, M. H. (1996). *Empathy: A social psychological approach.* Boulder, CO: Westview.

Davis, M. H., Hall, J. A., & Meyer, M. (2003). The first year: Influences on the satisfaction, involvement, and persistence of new community volunteers. *Personality and Social Psychology Bulletin, 29,* 248-260.

Davis, M. H., Mitchell, K. V., Hall, J. A., Lothert, J., Snapp, T., & Meyer, M. (1999). Empathy, expectations, and situational preferences: Personality influences on the decision to participate in volunteer helping behaviors. *Journal of Personality, 67,* 469-503.

Gergen, K. J., Gergen, M. M., & Meter, K. (1972). Individual orientations to prosocial behavior. *Journal of Social Issues, 8,* 105-130.

Ickes, W., Snyder, M., & Garcia, S. (1997). Personality influences on the choice of situations. In R. Hogan, J. Johnson, & S. Briggs (Eds.), *Handbook of personality psychology* (pp. 165-195). New York: Academic.

Latane, B., & Darley, J. M. (1970). *The unresponsive bystander: Why doesn't he help?* New York: Meredith.

Omoto, A. M., & Snyder, M. (1995). Sustained helping without obligation: Motivation, longevity of service, and perceived attitude change among AIDS volunteers. *Journal of Personality and Social Psychology, 68*, 671-686.

Penner, L. A., & Finkelstein, M. A. (1998). Dispositional and structural determinants of volunteerism. *Journal of Personality and Social Psychology, 74*, 525-537.

Piliavin, J. A., & Callero, P. L. (1991). *Giving blood: The development of an altruistic identity*. Baltimore, MD: Johns Hopkins University Press.

Piliavin, J. A., Dovidio, J. F., Gaertner, S. L., & Clark, R. D., III (1981). *Emergency intervention*. New York: Academic.

Smith, D. H. (1994). Determinants of voluntary association participation and volunteering: A literature review. *Nonprofit and Voluntary Sector Quarterly, 23*, 243-263.

Snyder, M. (1983). The influence of individuals on situations: Implications for understanding the links between personality and social behavior. *Journal of Personality, 51*, 497-516.

Snyder, M., & Ickes, W. (1985). Personality and social behavior. In G. Lindzey & E. Aronson (Eds.), *The handbook of social psychology*: (Vol. 2, 3rd. ed., pp. 883-948). New York: Random House.

Thoits, P. A., & Hewitt, L. N. (2001). Volunteer work and well-being. *Journal of Health and Social Behavior, 42*, 115-131.

Unger, L. S., & Thumuluri, L. K. (1997). Trait empathy and continuous helping: The case of voluntarism. *Journal of Social Behavior and Personality, 12*, 785-800.

5

PSYCHOLOGICAL SENSE OF COMMUNITY: CONCEPTUAL ISSUES AND CONNECTIONS TO VOLUNTEERISM-RELATED ACTIVISM

Allen M. Omoto
Anna M. Malsch
Claremont Graduate University

A recurrent theme among commentators and scholars of contemporary American society, as well as politicians of nearly every stripe, has been the seemingly negative changes that have occurred over the past several decades in the American psyche and patterns of social life.   Specifically, declines in community-mindedness and indicators of social and civic engagement have been documented, including reductions in participation in social networks (e.g., bridge clubs, bowling leagues), political processes (e.g., voting, attending public meetings), civic groups (e.g., Parent-Teacher Associations and veterans groups), religious institutions (e.g., church attendance), and volunteerism and philanthropy (e.g., donating time, money; see Putnam, 2000). Reciprocally linked to these declines, meanwhile, have been increases in crime, social disorganization, and restlessness. Although the causes of these changes are numerous, some of the likely suspects that have been identified include an increasingly industrialized, individualized, and mobile society (Glynn, 1986), and shifts to communities that reflect functional and impersonal interests rather than shared values (Durkheim, 1964). In addition, although the principles and values of individualism, freedom, and progress have long been embedded in the ideology of North America (e.g., Curtis, Grabb, & Baer, 1992), increased emphases on them have been identified as potential contributors to the decline (Glynn, 1986). Cumulatively, the changes have resulted in prevalent feelings of loneliness, alienation, and rootlessness (Sarason, 1974) and to weakening of the norms of reciprocity and trust (Putnam, 2000). In short, the *social capital* of the United States has been declining, with potentially pernicious, destabilizing, and destructive consequences predicted to result.

Psychological Sense of Community

Our interests in these issues have less to do with behavioral indicators of social capital (i.e., bowling leagues, church attendance), and more to do with the psychological concomitants, if not foundations, of various forms of social engagement and civic participation. Of special concern in this chapter is the concept of *psychological sense of community*, a construct that has been of enduring interest to psychologists for nearly three decades (Gusfield, 1975; Hill, 1996; Sarason, 1974). In fact, it has been suggested that the subdiscipline of community psychology embrace, if not be defined by, psychological sense of community as its overarching value and concern (see Sarason, 1974). In this view, psychological sense of community is defined as the "sense that one belongs in and is meaningfully a part of a larger collectivity" (p. 1), and includes "perceptions of similarity to others, acknowledged interdependence with others, willingness to maintain interdependence by giving to, or doing for, what one expects from them, and feelings that one is part of a larger dependable and stable structure" (p. 156).

Sense of community has been studied in an impressive array of settings, including neighborhoods (Brodsky, 1996; Brodsky, O'Campo, & Aronson, 1999; Glynn, 1986; Kingston, Mitchell, Florin, & Stevenson, 1999), workplaces (Borroughs & Eby, 1998; Klein & D'Aunno, 1986; Royal & Rossi, 1996), and universities (Lounsbury & DeNeui, 1996). It has been investigated among different populations, including adolescents (Pretty, Conroy, Dugay, Fowler, & Williams, 1996), single mothers (Brodsky, 1996), members of politically constructed groups (Sonn & Fisher, 1996), and individuals on the frontlines of social change and care initiatives (Omoto & Snyder, 2002). Further, many correlates of sense of community have been identified. It tends to increase with age, education, and income (Brodsky et al., 1996), and to be positively related to certain personality variables such as need for affiliation (Davidson, Cotter, & Stovall, 1991). Sense of community has been shown to relate positively to psychological well-being (e.g., happiness; Pretty, Conroy, Dugay, Fowler, & Williams, 1996) and negatively to variables indicative of poorer adjustment (e.g., loneliness and worry; Davidson & Cotter, 1991; Pretty, Conroy, Dugay, Fowler, & Williams, 1996). Finally, sense of community is also related to behavioral indicators of social capital such as church attendance and voting (Brodsky et al., 1999).

As might be anticipated from the broad conceptualization advanced by Sarason (1974), careful reading of the available research reveals that there have been numerous attempts to define, operationalize, and measure sense of community more specifically. Some critical issues that have been broached include whether sense of community is best conceptualized as characterizing a geographical location, individual relationships, common interests, a place, or a process (see Dunham, 1986; Glynn, 1986; Omoto & Snyder, 2002), and the most appropriate level of analysis for measuring sense of community and its effects (see Chavis & Pretty, 1999; Hill, 1996; Puddifoot, 1996).

Traditional definitions of community refer to a specific place (Dunham, 1986) and are illustrative of a *locational, territorial, geographical, or structural* community; a village, small town, or network of individuals living in close proximity to people they know. In fact, most of the theorizing and research on sense of community has been focused on feelings about specific places or geographic entities (see Hill, 1996), or on "community" as a descriptor or characteristic of a locality (Sonn & Fisher, 1998). Even when sense of community is investigated with data taken from individuals, it is generally conceived of as having boundaries. As we have argued elsewhere (Omoto & Snyder, 2002), this type of approach often overlaps with *community as context*, in which localities, institutions, and organizations are seen more as backdrop than cause of social action and organizing. The emphasis on place does not negate the potentially important psychological attachments and processes associated with those locations, nor does it prevent psychological measurement of people's feelings about localities and even organizations (e.g., Hughey, Speer, & Peterson, 1999). However, to our minds it does tend to limit the scope, power, and flexibility of a fully psychological conceptualization of community.

It should come as no surprise, then, that our preference is for a more purely psychological definition of sense of community, one that can transcend geographic or institutional boundaries. Specifically, we are interested in communities that are formed out of shared interests, characteristics, experiences, or opinions, and that are not restricted to individuals in proximity to each other. To identify with or belong to psychological communities, an individual does not need to have direct knowledge or the acquaintanceship of other community members or even disclose community-defining characteristics or status to others. Psychological communities are potentially quite diffuse and are also changeable. Rather than stressing specific physically bounded communities, then, we suggest that it is possible, and perhaps advantageous, to consider sense of community in a completely psychological sense and to focus on what we refer to as *community as process* (Omoto & Snyder, 2002). The meanings, attachments, and consequences of psychological communities and especially their implications for motivating social action are important to explore, in particular for the purposes of this chapter.

This perspective, we believe, is not inconsistent with what is perhaps the only full theoretical discussion of sense of community in the literature (see Hill, 1996). This conceptualization, originally advanced by McMillan and Chavis (1986; and later updated and revised by McMillan, 1996), identifies four critical components of sense of community: membership, influence, integration and fulfillment of needs, and shared emotional connection. *Membership* refers to the boundaries of the community—who is a member and who is not—as well as shared history, common symbols, emotional safety, and personal investment. Membership in a community entails certain rights as well as responsibilities; community membership provides for the attainment of a particular identity, and as a result of membership, social support and acceptance are enjoyed. The *influence* component reflects the interdependence between individuals and the larger community. Specifically, any individual member has the potential to influence the decisions and behaviors of the larger community, but in turn, the community has the power to influence individual members. For example, communities develop certain norms and expectations for behavior, and individual members are expected to follow these norms as long as they are members of the community. *Integration and fulfillment of needs* refers to the benefits of belonging to a community. Some of the obvious needs community membership helps individuals meet are those related to social status and affirmation, especially when derived from shared values and opinions of the group. In addition, the potential for having needs met can serve as a powerful motivating force compelling people to join certain communities or groups. Finally, *shared emotional connection* highlights the bonds that exist among community members.   Sharing time and experiences, especially around significant events related to the merit or status of the community, can produce these emotional connections.   The value and importance of shared history manifests itself in emotional bonds among community members.

In much of the extant research, these or similar components have been measured with respect to a block (Chavis, Hogge, McMillan, & Wandersman, 1986; Chavis & Wandersman, 1990), neighborhood (Pretty, Andrews, & Collett, 1994; Zaff & Devlin, 1998), campus (Lounsbury & DeNeui, 1995), organization or workplace (Borroughs & Eby, 1998; Hughey et al., 1999; Lambert & Hopkins, 1995; Royal & Rossi, 1996, 1999), or town or city (Davidson & Cotter, 1991; Plas & Lewis, 1996). However, in our understanding and further articulation of these components, there seems to be no inherent requirement that they have a geographical referent. All of these dimensions of community can be construed in fundamentally psychological terms and as such, should be applicable to a wide range of possible communities, including those defined by interests, opinions, characteristics, and so on.

Take, as an example, an individual who is a member of the Democratic party. This community is not restricted to a particular location or place, but rather, exists in many different locations and with varying structures within each.   It also is not possible for our hypothetical individual to know all community members across these different locations.   Instead, community membership is defined by a set of common political opinions and identifications. Consistent with the community components already outlined, the individual's membership in the Democratic party may represent an important identity, and affiliation with it may be supported by other (even unseen) members of the community.   The individual is also likely to gain esteem and to experience feelings of success when candidates and positions tied to this community score electoral victories. This person may even adopt symbols of the party such as bumper stickers and t-shirts, and may come to know some of the history and traditions of this community. The individual is likely to have a sense of what it means to adopt Democratic views, and his or her (especially voting) behavior may be affected by party pronouncements and positions. In addition, under some circumstances (e.g., caucuses, meetings, fundraising events), the individual may seek to influence community positions, as well as to attempt to persuade others to join this community. In short, it is possible for people to experience membership, influence, need fulfillment, and emotional connection with diffuse communities such as political parties, with both the components and communities conceptualized in psychological terms.

Distinguishing Psychological Sense of Community From Other Constructs

Having described what we mean by psychological sense of community, we explore some of the connections between sense of community and civic engagement and social action. We have articulated our preference for a purely psychological approach, and we seek now to acquire empirical evidence for the utility of this approach. Specifically, we investigate the ability of psychological sense of community, when construed in terms of a broad and diffuse community, to predict social action and civic engagement.

Before doing so, however, we briefly clarify the conceptual status of psychological sense of community relative to two other extensively researched constructs in psychology: social support and social identity. To be sure, social groupings and their roles in providing assistance and support, in reinforcing norms and values, and in enhancing identities, are relevant to all three of these constructs. However, it is not clear that *group* is functionally synonymous with *community*. It also is not clear that psychological sense of community has the same correlates and effects, especially in terms of civic engagement, as social support, social networks, or social identities. Later, we describe data and analyses that permit us to begin to address these issues.

At a conceptual level, however, we view psychological sense of community as quite different from *social support* (see also Felton & Shinn, 1992; Pretty et al., 1994; Shinn, 1990). Although psychological sense of community may evolve out of and be enhanced by supportive social networks, the key elements involve feelings of belonging, connection, confidence, and esteem that is attached to a psychologically identifiable community or grouping, and not necessarily to particular others and their actions. Social support, on the other hand, is usually linked to the actions of specific others, whether they be family members, friends, professionals, or even strangers who offer aid and advice. Individuals can receive as well as provide social support and can evaluate supportive behaviors in terms of how complete, satisfying, and frequent they are (either as received or given). Fundamentally, social support involves networks of individuals embedded in a larger social system, and the focus is generally on supportive relationships with specific individuals within these networks (Felton & Shinn, 1992). And, whereas an individual's social support network may be embedded within a community (as context, see Omoto & Snyder, 2002), individuals need not be personally acquainted with community members to experience psychological sense of community. Furthermore, perceptions of community support may persist even as individual members come and go.

This distinction is supported by empirical research on psychosocial climate and sense of community. Pretty (1990), for example, found that sense of community involved more than an individual's perceptions of social networks and support. In another study on loneliness among adolescents, Pretty et al. (1994) found that a measure of sense of community (taken from Perkins, Florin, Rich, & Wandersman, 1990) elicited information about respondents' social settings that was unique from the information obtained from measures of social support. In addition, the results of this study revealed that the sense of community measure was more strongly correlated with loneliness than was social support.

We also distinguish between psychological sense of community and a *social identity* associated with membership in a group. Social identity and self-categorization theories (e.g., Tajfel & Turner, 1986; Turner, Hogg, Oakes, Reicher, & Wetherell, 1987) stress the distinctiveness and esteem benefits (i.e., perceived superiority) that occur as a result of natural categorization processes by which individuals divide their social worlds into in-groups and out-groups, or those groups to which they belong and those to which they do not. This categorization process produces a heightening of divisions (including dissimilarities) between and among groups. In addition, the apparently inherent desire to maintain a positive identity leads to the tendency to derogate members of groups other than one's own.

Social identity theory also distinguishes between personal and social identities. *Personal identities* are tied to characteristics that differentiate individuals from other people, whereas *social identities* refer to portions of an individual's self-concept that are derived from membership in specific social groups (see Luhtanen & Crocker, 1992, especially for measurement issues). According to some theorists (Brewer, 2003), individual group members must balance the competing demands of distinguishing themselves from other group members while at the same time blending with them. What is important to note, however, is that personal and social identities both provide scaffolding for feelings of self-worth and esteem.

Thus, both psychological sense of community and social identity emphasize the importance of membership, shared emotional connection, and common symbols among group members. However, unlike social identity theory, our view of psychological sense of community does not require out-group comparisons and derogation to provide esteem benefits. Identifying as a member of the community in and of itself should prove to be psychologically rewarding to individuals and lead to positive self and community evaluations (see also Omoto & Snyder, 2002).

As noted earlier, for social identity theory, identities primarily result from cognitive and perceptual processes of categorizing the self and other people. In our consideration of psychological sense of community, however, we look beyond cognitive and perceptual processes, and include possible affective and motivational bases for community membership. Rather than heightening subgroup or between-group differences, moreover, we suggest that, to the extent that psychological sense of community is broad and inclusive, it should blur distinctions or actually render them less important.

Similar challenges to homogeneous and "us and them" views of community have been offered by others (Wiesenfeld, 1996). In this view, members of communities possess multiple identities, with the community as a whole consisting of interdependent but distinct identities. Thus, the social grouping that defines a community may very well tolerate and appreciate diversity (Wiesenfeld, 1996), as well as provide members with a safe environment to be unique and embrace difference (see McMillan, 1996). This is a very different description of groups and communities than would be found in most of the literature derived from the social identity theoretical tradition.

Investigating Psychological Sense of Community and Volunteerism-Related Activism

Thus, although there are many points of overlap between psychological sense of community, social support, and social identity, we see important conceptual distinctions among these constructs. We now turn our attention to providing empirical evidence bearing on the distinctions we have made, including investigating the relative predictive validity of these constructs. That is, we seek to explore some of the behavioral consequences of these constructs, especially psychological sense of community, for important indicators of social capital—volunteerism and social action. Previous cross-sectional research has demonstrated a positive association between psychological sense of community and civic participation and other prosocial behaviors. For example, a random household survey conducted in three Baltimore City communities revealed that individuals who claimed greater psychological sense of community were more likely to be registered voters and more likely to be active in their neighborhoods (Brodsky et al., 1999). Secondary analyses of data collected as part of an evaluation of a community-based drug and alcohol reduction demonstration project also revealed a positive correlation between psychological sense of community and neighboring behavior (e.g., claims that one will "lend a neighbor some food or a tool;" Kingston et al., 1999). Further, citizen participation in community organizations (Chavis & Wandersman, 1990; Perkins & Long, 2002; Wandersman, 1980, 1981; Wandersman, Florin, Friedman, & Meier, 1987), and political participation (Davidson & Cotter, 1989) have been positively associated with psychological sense of community. Thus, we expected psychological sense of community to predict future volunteerism-related activities, which might also be expected to be related to social support and social identity concerns.

To address these issues, we examined data from an ongoing program of research on AIDS volunteerism (Omoto & Snyder, 1995, 2002; Snyder, Omoto, & Lindsay, 2004; Snyder, Omoto, & Smith, in press). HIV disease and AIDS have had and continue to have a major medical and societal impact around the globe; a critical component of society's response to HIV has been community-based organizations of volunteers involved in caring for people living with HIV/AIDS (PWAs) and in educating the public. AIDS service organizations (ASOs) have developed throughout the United States, and are part of a larger and widespread phenomenon of voluntary helping (Independent Sector, 1999). In ASOs, volunteers provide emotional and social support as "buddies" to PWAs, help with household chores or transportation, staff information and referral hotlines, make educational presentations, and engage in advocacy and social change efforts (see Bebbington & Gatter, 1994; Chambré, 1991; Kayal,

1993; Omoto & Snyder, 1993). Because the cost of caring for PWAs is greatly reduced in areas with volunteer programs (Hellinger, 1993; Kelly, Chu, & Buehler, 1993; Turner, Catania, & Gagnon, 1994), AIDS volunteerism has considerable economic and public health significance. It is, to be sure, a prime example of community involvement and of individuals and organizations engaged in processes of social change and action.

In the context of our concerns with psychological sense of community, we suggest that AIDS volunteerism can be enacted in the service of the broad *community of people affected by HIV and AIDS*. Conceptualized in this way, this community includes not only people living nearby but also far away and includes more people than an individual personally knows. It is a community that includes people living with HIV and those at risk for it, members of their social networks, and volunteers and staff at organizations that provide HIV-related services. (See Bishop, Chertok, & Jason, 1997, for a similar conceptual approach but in a different context.) To the extent that volunteers identify with, are motivated to be part of, and feel immersed in, this community, they should be willing to engage in activities that benefit the community, including frequently involving themselves in a wide range of volunteerism-related activities.

We turn now to data to examine the empirical relationships between sense of community, social support, and social identity, and their relative power to predict future AIDS-related activism and civic participation. In doing so, we take advantage of an existing data set and identify measures that we feel are reasonable proxies for the constructs of interest. That is, the data presented here were not collected with the purposes of this chapter in mind. However, we believe that they are sufficient for an initial attempt to evaluate our predictions, even if they cannot provide a definitive test of our propositions.

Participants and Measures

Prior to completing volunteer orientation and training, new volunteers in two AIDS-service organizations in the Midwest were invited to participate in a study of how community service impacts volunteers and their social networks. A questionnaire utilized in this research covered a wide range of topics; for the current study we examined only a subset of the questionnaire content. Those 197 volunteers who agreed to be in the study completed a pretraining questionnaire which, among other measures, included indicators of psychological sense of community, social support, and social identity. Six months later, these now-active volunteers completed a Time 2 questionnaire that contained a measure of AIDS activism and participation. Participants received $10 for each questionnaire that they completed.

Psychological Sense of Community. Items we felt measured psychological sense of community at Time 1 included questions regarding volunteers' community-related motivations for engaging in their AIDS volunteer work (see Omoto & Snyder, 1995). For example, respondents rated the importance of five reasons for motivating them to volunteer, including "Because of my sense of obligation to communities affected by AIDS," "Because I consider myself an advocate for communities affected by AIDS and AIDS-related issues," and "Because of my concern and worry about communities affected by AIDS." In addition, to capture the extent to which volunteers were immersed in a network affected by HIV and AIDS, we included items that measured the total number of people each participant knew who were HIV-positive and who had died from AIDS-related illnesses.

Social Support. Time 1 items that separately assessed the amount of emotional and psychological support for their AIDS volunteer work that participants thought they would receive from their friends, relationship partner, staff at the ASO, other volunteers at the ASO, their family, and their client were utilized to tap social support. In addition, we included a single item that assessed how "affirmed" participants expected to feel by their experiences as volunteers.

Social Identity. Four Time 1 items that tapped social dominance (see Pratto, Sidanius, Stallworth, & Malle, 1994), such as "Some groups of people are simply not the equals of others," "Some people are just inferior to others," were identified as possibly reflecting in-group favoritism that presumably results from social identifications and related concerns. In addition, we included an item in which participants rated how "superior" they expected to feel as a result of their volunteer experiences. Participants also provided ratings of several different ethnic groups. We used these ratings to create an individualized measure of in-group favoritism by subtracting each participant's average rating of all of the ethnic out-groups from their rating of their own ethnic group.

AIDS-Related Activism and Civic Participation. Because we were interested in the relative predictive abilities of psychological sense of community, social support, and social identity, we created a measure of AIDS-related activism and related activities from items in the Time 2 questionnaire. Specifically, we averaged participant frequency ratings of how often they had done each of four types of activities in the last 6 months: (a) donated money or other material goods to groups and organizations engaged in charitable activities related to AIDS; (b) worked on or helped plan fundraisers, special events, or other activities for an AIDS organization; (c) attended AIDS fundraisers or events that donate their proceeds to AIDS research, care, or service; and (d) engaged in AIDS activism activities (e.g., letter writing to legislators, involvement in public awareness activities).

Sample Characteristics

The sample of volunteers ranged in age from 17 to 78 years (M = 33.04, SD = 12.96) and was primarily female (62%). Most (88%) of the volunteers were White (n = 174), although Asian Americans and African Americans each made up 3% of the sample, 2% were Latino, and the remaining

4% were Native American and "Other." The participants were generally well-educated; 17% ($n = 33$) possessed an advanced degree, 37% ($n = 73$) held a college degree, 35% ($n = 68$) had completed some college, 6% ($n = 12$) had a high school education, 5% ($n = 9$) had received trade/technical training, and 1% ($n = 2$) had less than a high school education. The majority (68%, $n = 134$) of volunteers identified themselves as heterosexual, 26% ($n = 51$) were homosexual, and 6% ($n = 12$) identified themselves as bisexual.

Creation of Composite Measures

Our first aim was to establish the uniqueness and reliability of our measures of psychological sense of community, social support, and social identity. Consequently, we submitted all the items we identified as indicators of these three constructs to a principal components factor analysis with varimax rotation specifying three factors for extraction (total variance accounted for 40.07%). As anticipated, the items intended as indicators of psychological sense of community all loaded on the same factor (13.01% variance accounted for) with only negligible loadings on the other extracted factors. Consequently, we standardized each of the items and combined them into a single composite measure. All but one of the items included to tap social support loaded together on a single factor (12.54% variance). Because the wording of this (family support) item was nearly identical to the other items, we retained it in the social support composite, created by standardizing and summing the items. Finally, all of the items we selected to tap social identity except the measure of in-group favoritism loaded on the same factor (14.52% variance). Owing to our a priori theoretical conceptualization and the fact that this item loaded positively on this factor, we retained it in the composite index of social identity that we created by standardizing the items and averaging them.

Thus, although not all of the items loaded on the anticipated factors, the results of the factor analysis generally confirmed our predictions that the items we selected would cluster into factors that could be labeled to represent psychological sense of community, social support, and social identity (see Table 5.1). Based on these analyses, we created three composite measures, and as might be expected from the factor analysis results, the reliabilities for each of these constructs were comparable and generally acceptable (see Table 5.2).

Table 5.1
Results of Factor Analysis

	Factor loadings		
	Social Identity	Psych. Sense of Community	Social Support
Item			
Sense of obligation to the HIV/AIDS community	-.239	.601	-.038
Advocate for the HIV/AIDS community	.087	.681	.235
Concern and worry for the HIV/AIDS community	-.228	.609	-.133
Get to know members of the HIV/AIDS community	.064	.673	-.133
Help members of the HIV/AIDS community	-.261	.709	.004
Total number of people know who have HIV	.043	.346	.296
Total number of people know who have died from AIDS-related illnesses	.103	. 343	.266
Expected emotional and psychological support from friends	-.311	-.04	.272
Expected emotional and psychological support from relationship partner	.132	-.078	.369
Expected emotional and psychological support from staff at ASO	-.186	.026	.804
Expected emotional and psychological support from other volunteers	-.135	.110	.717
Expected emotional and psychological support from family	.05	.410	.222
Expected emotional and psychological support from client	.158	.149	.677
Expect to feel affirmed by volunteer experiences	.009	.196	.381
Some groups of people are simply not the equals of others	.787	-.024	-.022
This country would be better off if we cared less about ensuring equality between people	.704	-.058	-.106
It is not a problem if some people have more of a chance in life than others	.688	-.096	.096
Some people are just inferior to others	.861	.012	-.011
Expect to feel superior about volunteer experiences	.358	-.151	.088
In-group favoritism index	.227	.095	-.366

Concurrent and Predictive Relationships

After establishing the acceptability of our composite measures, we moved to examine the empirical associations between them. As our conceptual analysis suggests, we would expect some overlap between the different measures. That is, to the extent that psychological sense of community may develop from or be bolstered by experiences of actual social support, we would expect the community and social support composites to be related to each other. Similarly, to the extent that social identifications involve attraction to a group and positive evaluations of an in-group, we would expect a correlation between the social identity and community composites. In addition, because in-group members are probably the individuals most likely to offer assistance, social identity and social support should be related to each other. All of these measures were expected to be related to subsequent AIDS-related activism and civic participation.

To assess these relationships, we computed bivariate Pearson correlations among all of the measures. The correlations, shown in Table 5.2, reveal the expected pattern of relationships. Specifically, psychological sense of community and social support were both significantly and positively related to one another, although the strength of this relationship was only moderate ($r =$ .34, $p < .01$). Surprisingly, neither community nor social support was significantly related to social identity. Finally, in terms of the criterion of interest, both psychological sense of community and social support, but not social identity, predicted later AIDS-related activism and civic participation. In fact, the strengths of association between civic participation and the measures of community and social support were nearly identical.

Table 5.2
Reliabilities and Correlations for Composite Variables

	1	2	3	4
1. Psychological sense of community		-.08	.34**	.23*
2. Social identity			.04	.01
3. Social support				.24*
4. Activism and civic participation				
Reliability	.70	.67	.66	.69

Next, we examined whether psychological sense of community, social support, and social identity were differentially related to later AIDS-related activism and civic participation, and if the contributions of one were redundant with those of another construct. To assess these relationships, we conducted a regression analysis in which the three constructs, all measured at Time 1, were entered simultaneously as predictors of later AIDS-related activism and participation.

This analysis produced a highly significant regression equation ($F =$ 3.49, $p < .01$), with the three predictors accounting for 9% of the variance in activism and civic participation 6 months later. In terms of the individual predictors, social identity was unrelated to later AIDS-related activism and civic participation. Although we had anticipated that stronger social identification would be related to continuing efforts to work on behalf of the group, we found no support for this notion (see Table 5.3).

Table 5.3

Regression Results Predicting Time 2 Activism and Civic Participation

Time 1 Predictor	B	$SE\ B$	β
Social identity	.05	.10	.05
Social support	.21	.10	.20*
Psychological sense of community	.22	.11	.20*

Note. $R^2 = .09$, $p < .01$. *$p < .05$.

It should be recalled that the measures in this study were the best possible indicators that we could find in our data set and were not necessarily designed or written to tap the constructs of interest. Thus, although the social identity construct was reasonably reliable, it may be that our composite was less than optimal as a measure of social identity. Second, the items we used to tap social identity were general in nature and not specifically focused on social identification as a volunteer, a member of AIDS-related causes, or a member in an AIDS service organization. Given that we were attempting to predict participation in AIDS-related activism, fundraising, and ASO activities, we might have preferred a more specific measure of social identity (had one been available). There are many ways to measure social identifications. Social identifications of particular types and strengths may also be related to specific civic participation activities, or more precisely, activities in support of those identifications (see Simon et al., 1998). These speculations about the social identity construct and its measurement should be explored in future research.

Turning to social support, we found a significant positive relationship between it and later activism. Individuals who claimed that they expected to feel emotionally and psychologically supported by members of their social networks and to feel personally affirmed by their volunteerism were more likely to involve themselves in a range of later AIDS-related activities. We do not have any way of verifying the extent to which participants' expectations of support were fulfilled by members of their social networks; that is, we do not have appropriate process measures to help us explain the mechanisms at work in producing this result. However, to the extent that individuals believe that their social networks will be supportive of their volunteer efforts, they engaged in more activities later on. In other research, we have found that participants who receive relatively unexpected negative feedback from social network members for AIDS-related volunteering, are more likely to drop out of these activities (see Snyder, Omoto, & Crain, 1999), and even that drop out is more likely among volunteers who have greater initial and general social support (Omoto & Snyder, 1995). Thus, it seems reasonable to suggest that the participants in this study were relatively accurate in their expectations for volunteerism-related support. Expecting, and perhaps having, more support made it easier for them to expand the frequency of their AIDS-related activism and civic participation over time.

The results for psychological sense of community revealed it to be a unique and independent predictor of later AIDS-related activism and civic participation. As expected, AIDS volunteers who reported getting involved to enhance community connections and help meet current community needs, and who also knew more people personally affected by HIV disease, engaged in more AIDS-related activities 6 months later. Although not possible to test with the data on hand, a number of reasons indicate why psychological sense of community might lead to increased civic participation and volunteerism-related activities (for further elaboration, see Omoto & Snyder, 2002). For example, it may enhance feelings of personal efficacy and support, as well as heighten feelings of responsibility to help others. To the extent that individuals feel they are members of a broad and diffuse community, moreover, they may perceive that greater collective material and psychological resources are available to be utilized. In addition, feelings of reciprocity for past help received should be made salient by community connections. As individuals engage in social action, they may discover other and new community needs and avenues for service. For the volunteers in our sample that would have meant making more donations, participating in fundraisers and special events, and engaging in AIDS-related activism, or precisely the pattern of results that was found. In future work, we plan to explore some of these explanations, as well as to continue efforts to develop an adequate measure of psychological sense of community.

Finally, it is important to note that the effects of psychological sense of community were independent of the influences of social identity and social support. That is, although these constructs share conceptual and empirical overlap, both social support and sense of community were significant individual predictors of subsequent AIDS-related activism and civic participation.

Discussion and Conclusions

In this chapter, we described psychological sense of community as a broad, inclusive, and diffuse construct. Our perspective departs from traditional, geographically based definitions of community and emphasizes the psychological nature of the communities in question. In fact, we found evidence for the utility of this conceptualization as it applies to the community affected by HIV and AIDS. Members of this community may not personally know one another or have frequent interaction, yet their sense that they belong to this community had important implications for predicting later AIDS-related activism and civic participation.

Although we make no claim that the results of this investigation provide a conclusive test of the relative predictive power of psychological sense of community, social support, and social identity for understanding involvement in activism activities, we find the results intriguing and worthy of more focused empirical pursuit. The constructs of interest in this investigation have not always been clearly defined or distinguished from each other. Our conceptual analysis revealed important differences between them, however, and our data analyses further bolstered our points. Psychological sense of community, social support, and social identity share features in common. As illustrated by our findings, however, that does not mean that they cannot uniquely predict important outcomes of interest. Although our data were collected in the context of AIDS volunteerism, we have no reason to expect the results would differ in other social contexts.

Future research should continue to explore the links and distinctions between psychological sense of community, social support, and social identity. For example, a core component of all three constructs involves the fulfillment of needs, especially social needs related to belonging, affirmation, and responsiveness (e.g., Baumeister & Leary, 1995). However, it is possible that key differences exist between them in their mechanisms, correlates, and consequences. As revealed by our results, for example, they seem not to be equally important in predicting activism and related activities of volunteers.

The results also suggest that more research on psychological sense of community is warranted, although with an accompanying need for investigators to be clear about the construct they are studying. Many researchers use the term psychological sense of community when they are actually conceptualizing and measuring people's beliefs about a geographical community. Similarly, some advocate for a community-level conceptualization of this construct. We are not advocating for any single ascendant conceptualization, but rather, for greater clarity in what construct is being studied and recognition of the potentially important theoretical and empirical distinctions among community constructs. Our findings lend credence to a purely psychological conceptualization, not necessarily with reference to an identifiable area or institution, measured at an individual-level. It seems reasonable, therefore, to devote future theorizing and research to understanding communities based on shared experiences and interests (e.g., the community affected by HIV/AIDS) and communities with inclusive membership that extend beyond traditional boundaries of region, ethnicity, and nationality. Indeed, with communication and technological advances (e.g., the Internet), psychologically meaningful communities that literally cut across the world are being formed and sustained everyday.

In addition, although our investigation revealed that psychological sense of community predicted later domain-relevant activism and civic participation, other prosocial behaviors and outcomes may follow an enhanced sense of community. In short, important knowledge may be gained by adopting a relatively encompassing and psychological definition of community and examining its relations with a diverse range of behavioral indicators of social capital.

Quality of life and the well-being of both communities and individuals may depend importantly on psychological sense of community and the connections that people share. Whereas some have decried the breakdown of social capital in contemporary society, along with decreases in its psychological concomitants, we feel optimistic that this apparent trend can be reversed. Specifically, based on our results, we suggest that one way to build social capital would be by intervening to increase people's sense of community. This suggestion derives from the reciprocal relationship between sense of community and behaviors indicative of social capital (e.g., Putnam, 2000), as well as our findings that psychological sense of community predicts subsequent volunteerism and social action.

It is likely impossible to legislate social capital behaviors. Even if it were possible, the effects of such programs, as suggested by research on service learning programs (see Stukas, Snyder, & Clary, 1999), may be inconsistent. Certain conditions must be met for individuals who are induced to engage in service activities to develop more positive views of their communities and its members (e.g., Yates & Youniss, 1999). Rather, in our view, it may be easier and more appropriate to intervene so as to affect psychological sense of community.

A strong tradition already exists in many cultures, including among North American countries, whereby people should give back to society and engage in prosocial actions (see Curtis et al., 1992). The question does not seem to be *do* people believe in the value of doing social good, but rather, *why* do they not act on their beliefs (see Snyder, Omoto, & Smith, in press)? One strategy for motivating action might be to bolster people's psychological sense of community and to call attention to the responsibility of community members to mobilize and work on behalf of other community members. As our data analyses indicate, to the extent that individuals experience psychological sense of community, they are likely to engage in more frequent activism and civic actions in the future. In the end, then, knowledge gained from research on psychological sense of community and interventions designed to create it can be put to use in making more effective social programs geared toward enhancing quality of life, ameliorating social problems, and increasing general civic participation.

ACKNOWLEDGEMENTS

The preparation of this chapter and the research described in it were supported by grants from the National Institute of Mental Health to Allen M. Omoto and to Mark Snyder (University of Minnesota). We thank Mark Snyder for his helpful comments on an earlier draft of this chapter.

References

Baumeister, R. F. & Leary, M. R. (1995). The need to belong: Desire for interpersonal attachments as a fundamental human motivation. *Psychological Bulletin, 117*, 497-529.

Bebbington, A. C., & Gatter, P. N. (1994). Volunteers in an HIV social care organization. *AIDS Care, 6*, 571-585.

Bishop, P. D., Chertok, F., & Jason, L. A. (1997). Measuring sense of community: Beyond Local boundaries. *Journal of Primary Prevention, 18*, 193-212.

Borroughs, S. M. & Eby, L. T. (1998). Psychological sense of community at work: A measurement system and explanatory framework. *Journal of Community Psychology, 26,* 509-532.

Brewer, M. B. (2003). Optimal distinctiveness, social identity, and the self. In M. R. Leary & J. P. Tangney (Eds.), *Handbook of self and identity* (pp. 480-491). New York: Guilford.

Brodsky, A. E. (1996). Resilient single mothers in risky neighborhoods: Negative psychological sense of community. *Journal of Community Psychology, 24*, 347-363.

Brodksy, A. E., O'Campo, P. J., Aronson, R. E. (1999). PSOC in community context: Multi-level correlates of a measure of psychological sense of community in low-income, urban neighborhoods. *Journal of Community Psychology, 27*, 659-679.

Chambré, S. M. (1991). The volunteer response to the AIDS epidemic in New York City: Implications for research on volunteerism. *Nonprofit and Voluntary Sector Quarterly, 20*, 267-287.

Chavis, D. M., Hogge, J., McMillan, D., & Wandersman, A. (1986). Sense of community through Brunswick's lens: A first look. *Journal of Community Psychology, 14,* 24-40.

Chavis, D. M., & Pretty, G. .M. H. (1999). Sense of community: Advances in measurement and application. *Journal of Community Psychology, 27,* 635-642.

Chavis, D. M., & Wandersman, A. (1990). Sense of community in the urban environment: A catalyst for participation and community development. *American Journal of Community Psychology, 18,* 55-81.

Curtis, J. E., Grabb, E. G., & Baer, D. E. (1992). Voluntary association membership in fifteen countries: A comparative analysis. *American Sociological Review, 57*, 139-152.

Davidson, W. B., & Cotter, P. R. (1989). Sense of community and political participation. *Journal of Community Psychology, 17*, 119-125.

Davidson, W. B., & Cotter, P. R. (1991). The relationship between sense of community and subjective well-being: A first look. *Journal of Community Psychology, 19*, 246-253.

Davidson, W., Cotter, P. R., & Stovall, J. (1991). Social predisposition for the development of sense of community. *Psychological Reports, 68*, 817-818.

Dunham, H. W. (1986). The community today: Place or process? *Journal of Community Psychology, 14,* 399-404.

Durkheim, E. (1964). *The division of labor in society*. New York: Free Press of Glencoe.

Felton, B., & Shinn, M. (1992). Social integration and social support: Moving "social support" beyond the individual level. *Journal of Community Psychology, 20*, 103-115.

Glynn, T. J. (1986). Neighborhood and sense of community. *Journal of Community Psychology, 14*, 341-352.

Gusfield, J. R. (1975). *Community: A critical response*. New York: Harper.

Hellinger, F. J. (1993). The lifetime cost of treating a person with HIV. *Journal of the American Medical Association, 270*, 474-478.

Hill, J. L. (1996). Psychological sense of community: Suggestions for future research. *Journal of Community Psychology, 24*, 431-438.

Hughey, J., Speer, P. W., & Peterson, N. A. (1999). Sense of community in community organizations: Structure and evidence of validity. *Journal of Community Psychology, 27*, 97-113.

Independent Sector. (1999). *Giving and volunteering in the United States: Findings from a national survey*. Washington, DC: Author.

Kayal, P. M. (1993). *Bearing witness: Gay men's health crisis and the politics of AIDS*. Boulder, CO: Westview.

Kelly, J. J., Chu, S. Y., & Buehler, J. W. (1993). AIDS deaths shift from hospital to home. *American Journal of Public Health, 83*, 1433-1437.

Kingston, S., Mitchell, R., Florin, P., & Stevenson, J. (1999). Sense of community in neighborhoods as a multi-level construct. *Journal of Community Psychology, 27*, 684-394.

Klein, K. J., & D'Aunno, T. A. (1986). Psychological sense of community in the workplace. *Journal of Community Psychology, 14*, 365-377.

Lambert, S. J., & Hopkins, K. (1995). Occupational conditions and workers' sense of community: Variations by gender and race. *American Journal of Community Psychology, 23*, 151-179.

Lounsbury, J. W., & DeNeui, D. (1995). Psychological sense of community on campus. *College Student Journal, 29*(3), 270-277.

Lounsbury, J. W. & DeNeui, D. (1996). Collegiate psychological sense of community in relation to size of college/university and extraversion. *Journal of Community Psychology, 24*, 381-394.

Luhtanen, R., & Crocker, J (1992). A collective self-esteem scale: Self-evaluation of one's social identity. *Personality & Social Psychology Bulletin, 18*, 302-318.

McMillan, D. W. (1996). Sense of community. *Journal of Community Psychology, 24*, 315-325.

McMillan, D. W., & Chavis, D. M. (1986). Sense of community: A definition and theory. *Journal of Community Psychology, 14*, 6-24.

Omoto, A. M., & Synder, M. (1993). AIDS volunteers and their motivations: Theoretical issues and practical concerns. *Nonprofit Management and Leadership, 4*, 157-176.

Psychological Sense of Community 101

Omoto, A. M., & Snyder, M. (1995). Sustained helping without obligation: Motivation, longevity of service, and perceived attitude change among AIDS volunteers. *Journal of Personality and Social Psychology, 68,* 671-686.

Omoto, A. M., & Snyder, M. (2002). Considerations of community: The context and process of volunteerism. *American Behavioral Scientist, 45,* 846-867.

Perkins, D. D., Florin, P., Rich, R. C., Wandersman, A. (1990). Participation and the social land physical environment of residential blocks: Crime and community context. *American Journal of Community Psychology, 18,* 83-115.

Perkins, D. D., & Long, D. A. (2002). Neighborhood sense of community and social capital: A multi-level analysis. In A. Fisher, C. Sonn, & B. Bishop (Eds.), *Psychological sense of community: Research, applications, and implications* (pp. 291-318). New York: Kluwer.

Plas, J. M., & Lewis, S. E. (1996). Environmental factors and sense of community in a planned town. *American Journal of Community Psychology, 24,* 109-143.

Pratto, F., Sidanius, J., Stallworth, L. M., & Malle, B. F. (1994). Social dominance orientation: A personality variable predicting social and political attitudes. *Journal of Personality and Social Psychology, 67,* 741-763.

Pretty, G. M. H. (1990). Relating psychological sense of community to social climate characteristics. *Journal of Community Psychology, 18,* 60-65.

Pretty, G. M. H., Andrewes, L., & Collett, C. (1994). Exploring adolescents' sense of community and its relationship to loneliness. *Journal of Community Psychology, 22,* 346-358.

Pretty, G. M. H., Conroy, C., Dugay, J., Fowler, K., & Williams, D. (1996). Sense of community and its relevance to adolescents of all ages. *Journal of Community, 24,* 365-379.

Puddifoot, J. E. (1996). Some initial considerations in the measurement of community identity. *Journal of Community Psychology, 24,* 327-336.

Putnam, R. D. (2000). *Bowling alone: The collapse and revival of American community.* New York: Touchstone.

Royal, M. A., & Rossi, R. J. (1996). Individual-level correlates of sense of community: Findings from workplace and school. *Journal of Community Psychology, 24,* 395-416.

Royal, M. A., & Rossi, R. J. (1999). Predictors of within-school differences in teacher's sense of community. *Journal of Educational Research, 92,* 259-266.

Sarason, S. B. (1974). *The psychological sense of community: Prospects for a community psychology.* San Francisco: Jossey-Bass.

Shinn, M. (1990).   Mixing and matching: Levels of conceptualization, measurement, and statistical analyses in community research. In P. Tolan, C. Keys, F. Chertok, & L. Jason (Eds.), *Researching community psychology* (pp. 111-126). Washington, DC: American Psychological Association.

Simon, B., Loewy, M., Stürmer, S., Weber, U., Freytag, P., Habig, C., Kampmeier, C., & Spahlinger, P. (1998).   Collective action and social movement participation. *Journal of Personality and Social Psychology, 74*, 646-658.

Snyder, M., Omoto, A. M., & Crain, L. A. (1999). Punished for their good deeds: Stigmatization of AIDS volunteers. *American Behavioral Scientist, 42*, 1175-1192.

Snyder, M., Omoto, A. M., & Lindsay, J. J. (2004). Sacrificing time and effort for the good of others: The benefits and costs of volunteerism. In A. G. Miller (Ed.), *The social psychology of good and evil* (pp. 444-468). New York: Guilford.

Snyder, M., Omoto, A. M., & Smith, D. M. (in press). The role of persuasion strategies in motivating individual and collective action. In E. Borgida, J. L. Sullivan, & E. Riedel (Eds.), *The political psychology of democratic citizenship*, Cambridge, England: Cambridge University Press.

Sonn, C. C., & Fisher, A. T. (1996). Psychological sense of community in a politically constructed group.   *Journal of Community Psychology, 24,* 417-430.

Sonn, C. C., & Fisher, A. T. (1998).   Sense of community: Community resilient responses to oppression and change. *Journal of Community Psychology, 26*, 457-472.

Stukas, A. A., Snyder, M., & Clary, E. G. (1999). The effects of "mandatory volunteerism" on intentions to volunteer. *Psychological Science, 10*, 59-64.

Tajfel, H., & Turner, J. C. (1986). The social identity theory of intergroup behavior. In S. Worchel & W. G. Austin (Eds), *Psychology of intergroup relations* (2nd ed., pp. 7-24), Chicago: Nelson-Hall.

Turner, H. A., Catania, J. A., & Gagnon, J. (1994). The prevalence of informal caregiving to persons with AIDS in the United States: Caregiver characteristics and their implications. *Social Science Medicine, 38*, 1543-1552.

Turner, J. C., Hogg, M. A., Oakes, P. J., Reicher, S. D., & Wetherell, M. S. (1987). *Rediscovering the social group: A self-categorization theory.* Oxford, UK:Basil Blackwell.

Wandersman, A. (1980). Community and individual difference characteristics as influences on initial participation. *American Journal of Community Psychology, 8,* 217-228.

Wandersman, A. (1981). A framework of participation in community organizations. *Journal of Applied Behavioral Science, 17,* 27-58.

Wandersman, A., Florin, P., Friedmann, R. R., & Meier, R. B. (1987). Who participates and who does not, and why? An analysis of voluntary neighborhood organizations in the United States and Israel. *Sociological Forum, 2,* 534-555.

Wiesenfeld, E. (1996). The concept of "we": A community social psychology myth? *Journal of Community Psychology, 24,* 337-345.

Yates, M., & Youniss, J. (Eds.). (1999). *Roots of civic identity: International perspectives on community service and activism in youth.* Hollywood, CA: Covenant House California.

Zaff, J., & Devlin, A. S. (1998). Sense of community in housing for the elderly. *Journal of Community Psychology, 26,* 381-397.

6

A BENEFIT-AND-COST APPROACH TO UNDERSTANDING SOCIAL PARTICIPATION AND VOLUNTEERISM IN MULTILEVEL ORGANIZATIONS

Matthew J. Chinman
RAND, Santa Monica, CA.

Abraham Wandersman
University of South Carolina

Robert M. Goodman
Tulane University

Local block or neighborhood organizations, substance abuse prevention community coalitions, and AIDS volunteer groups all take advantage of the great voluntary human capital that exists in this country to address social problems. Although these efforts benefit the community, what do volunteers receive in return and how does this influence their ongoing participation? Like any organization, voluntary organizations need to continually replenish their resources in order to remain viable. The most important resources these organizations have are their volunteers. Thus, increasing the number of volunteers and their amount of participation would provide these organizations with more resources to achieve their goals. One way to increase participation is to maximize the benefits and minimize the costs volunteers experience as a result of their participation.

In this chapter, after a brief overview of the benefits-and-costs approach, we discuss two different sets of analyses to assess benefits and costs in multilayer organizations: community coalitions. Examining data from these organizations can be challenging as the empirical relationships are often affected by the climate of the subgroups in which participants belong (e.g., coalition committees), the organization that the individual represents, and the individuals themselves. Our approach has shown that accounting for the effects of groups and individual simultaneously yields more accurate findings.

We demonstrate that by directly assessing the benefits and costs of participation, we can use this information to promote organizational viability across several types of groups. The benefit-and-cost approach is based on theories from several disciplines: social exchange (psychology), resource mobilization (sociology), and political economy (political science). There are other approaches to understanding voluntary participation, for example, the social psychological perspective of Clary et al. (1998). This chapter is our attempt to present an additional approach that is face valid, easy to understand and implement, and has demonstrated practical utility.

Background on Benefits and Costs

Olson introduced several ideas that facilitated research on benefits, costs, and participation (Moe, 1980; Olson, 1965), challenging the idea that individuals join and participate in large voluntary organizations only because they believe in the goals of those organizations. He proposed that people join and contribute in order to obtain certain economic benefits, and organizations that only provide *collective goods* would yield suboptimal participation by many members. Collective goods are benefits that people obtain that are not contingent upon their own participation, for example, the benefit from the existence of a public park without helping to build it. When individuals can gain collective goods, Olson argued that it is in their economic self-interest not to participate (called the *free rider problem*). One of Olson's solutions was to provide *selective incentives*, which are contingent upon members' participation and may not even relate to the goals of the organization. For example, an individual who may not be concerned about the "right to bear arms" may participate in the National Rifle Association because it offers reduced life insurance rates. It is an exchange: Leaders provide certain benefits to the members, and in return, members donate a share of their own personal resources (financial or participatory) that are used by the organization to pursue its own goals (Kanter, 1968; Knoke, 1990; Knoke & Wood, 1981). According to Clark and Wilson (1961), the incentive system is the primary variable affecting organizational behavior.

Benefit-and-Cost Categories

The typical approach of measuring benefits and costs with individual paper-and-pencil survey items can be unwieldy. Creating summary categories can help to link benefits and costs more concisely with other variables of interest, such as participation.

Benefits. Clark and Wilson (1961) were the first to create categories for benefits: Material, Solidary, and Purposive. *Material benefits* are tangible rewards that are associated with a monetary value (e.g., receiving information about community services, events, county government, etc.). *Solidary benefits* are the intangible social rewards of group membership (e.g., gaining personal recognition and respect from others). *Purposive benefits* are also intangible and relate to the goals of the organization (e.g., making the community a safer place to live). Whereas Clark and

Wilson created these categories conceptually, other researchers have used factor and principal component analyses and found similar categories, albeit with somewhat different labels. Therefore, the Clark and Wilson framework appears to be useful in organizing the various names given to benefit factors by these researchers (see Table 6.1). Although there are certain categories that are more narrowly defined (e.g., lobbying), the table shows that the three domains—Material, Solidary, and Purposive—continue to be relevant for benefit factors across a wide range of topic areas.

Reconciling the different labels and numbers of factors present in this literature continues to be hampered by: (a) the lack of clarity in this research in the methods used to derive the final number of factors or components; (b) variation in the number of items used in different studies; and (c) variation in the type of organization studied (e.g., coalitions vs. block and neighborhood associations) (Butterfoss, 1993; Clarke, Price, Stewart, & Krause, 1978; Friedman, Florin, Wandersman, & Meier, 1988; Knoke & Adams, 1987; Prestby, Wandersman, Florin, Rich, & Chavis, 1990; Wandersman, Florin, Friedman, & Meier, 1987). Whereas the literature consistently points to two or three benefit factors or components for smaller associations, the results of Butterfoss (1993) suggest that a more global assessment of benefits (one overall benefit factor was found) is more relevant for coalition members.

Costs. Costs can be viewed as the negative consequences associated with participating in a group. Kanter (1968) was one of the first authors to mention "costs" as associated with participation in a group, stating, "For the actor there is a 'profit' associated with continued participation and a 'cost' associated with leaving" (p. 504). Rich (1980) discussed costs that leaders incur as time and energy, opportunities forgone, and material resources that are used. Although there is less research on costs, they can be just as important as benefits. Minimizing members' costs may be as effective in enhancing participation as providing more benefits. The relatively small amount of research conducted on the costs of volunteer participation has shown that the bimotivational model seems to be the most relevant for voluntary organizations (Norton, Wandersman, & Goldman, 1993; Prestby, et al., 1990; Wandersman et al., 1987). These costs seem to involve what members have to give up personally as a result of their participation (Material) and social and organizational conflict with other members (a combination of Solidary and Purposive categories).

Research on Benefits and Costs

Our literature review (Chinman & Wandersman, 1999) demonstrates that a direct assessment of the benefits and the costs are related to participation, although differently in different organizations. For example, whereas the research involving neighborhood groups shows that less active members and nonmembers perceive

TABLE 6.1
Organization of Benefit Factors

Authors	Benefits			Factor types		
	Material*	Solidary*	Solidary + Purposive	Purposive*	Specific
Butterfoss (1993) @ Time 1	-	-	-	-	One factor
Butterfoss (1993) @ Time 2	-	-	-	-	One factor
Clarke et al. (1978)	Personal-Instrumental	Social		Democratic-political	Partisan
Friedman et al. (1988)	Personal gains	-		Helping others	-
Knoke (1988); Knoke & Adams (1987)	Material, Information, Occupational	Social	-	Normative	Lobbying
Norton et al. (1993)	Personal	-	Social-purposive	-	-
Snyder & Omoto (1992); Omoto & Snyder (1995); Snyder (1993)	Esteem enhancement; Personal development; Understanding of AIDS issues	-	-	Community concerns; Acting on personal values	-
Presby et al. (1990)	Personal	-	Social-communal	-	-
Rich (1980)	Protect property values	Obligation to friends		Civic duty, devotion to neighbor.	-
Schmitz & Schomaker (1994)	Material, Personal growth and development	-	Social and political consequences	Goal attainment/ mission support	-
Wandersman et al. (1987)	Personal		Helping others		

TABLE 6.1 Continued

Authors	Factor types				
	Material*	Solidary*	Solidary + Purposive	Purposive*	Specific
		Costs			
Butterfoss (1993) @ Time1	Personal	-	Social/ organizational	-	-
Butterfoss (1993) @ Time 2	Personal	Social	-	Purposive	-
Friedman et al. (1988)	Personal	-	-	Organizational frustration	-
Norton et al. (1993)	Personal	-	Social-organizational	-	-
Prestby et al. (1990)	Personal	-	Social-organizational	-	-
Rich (1980)	-	-	-	Production, Maintenance	-
Schmitz & Schomaker (1994)	Material	Potential conflict	Social & political consequences	-	-
Wandersman et al. (1987)	Personal	-	-	Organizational frustration	-

Note. *From the original work of Clark and Wilson (1961).

more costs or barriers (Prestby et al., 1990; Wandersman et al., 1987), active members of the Alliance for the Mentally Ill (a national network of self-help groups for families of those with a mental illness) report more costs (Norton et al., 1993). Despite these differences, some general conclusions can be drawn: A relationship between participation and benefits exists across several types of organizations. More specifically, (a) Purposive and Social benefits seem to be the most important benefits experienced by voluntary group members, (b) greater participation is associated with members experiencing greater benefits, and (c) activity level is a more accurate measure of participation than membership (member vs. nonmembers). Similarly, a relationship between participation and costs also exists across several types of organizations; however, the relationship is more complex. Higher costs are associated with greater participation in some organizations and with less participation in others. Although it seems counterintuitive to think that a member would participate more due to experiencing more costs, it is probable that with greater participation comes more frustrations and therefore more costs. Although members who participate a great deal may experience costs, the results show that they also experience a greater amount of benefits.

Assessing Benefits and Costs in Multilayer Organizations

This chapter provides an opportunity to report new analyses of the benefits and costs experienced by the members of four multilayer organizations: community coalitions. Given that data analytic strategies usually employed with these types of organizations may not be appropriate, we offer statistical techniques that specifically address the issues inherent in multilevel organizations. We first offer a brief overview of community-based coalitions and the study's backgrounds.

Community Coalitions. These groups are common public health promotion mechanisms, simultaneously intervening on multiple levels (individual, organizational, policy) and sectors (parents, youth, criminal justice, education) needed to have an impact on community health status (Butterfoss, Goodman, & Wandersman, 1993). Although there are several conceptualizations (Allensworth & Patton, 1990; Boissevain, 1974; Butterfoss et al., 1993; Stevenson, Pearce, & Porter, 1985), most state that coalitions are interorganizational, cooperative affiliations that bring people and groups together for a common purpose. The main strengths of the community coalition are their ability to marshal large numbers of individuals and demonstrate broad community support, reduce duplication of efforts, address multiple issues at once, and provide a forum for sharing different perspectives on how to solve community problems. Coalitions typically pass through developmental stages: *formation, implementation,* and *maintenance* (Butterfoss, Goodman, & Wandersman, 1993). Formation involves creating the coalition structure and training its members; implementation involves planning and putting those plans into action; maintenance involves monitoring and refining ongoing implementation.

Study Background. The data presented here come from the members of four community-based coalitions designed to prevent substance abuse in four urban and rural regions in South Carolina: Florence, Spartanburg, Union/Cherokee Counties, and the Midlands (three county area including the city of Columbia). These coalitions were funded by the Center for Substance Abuse Prevention as part of the Community Partnership initiative in the 1990s. All four coalitions received 5 years of funding, around the same time, that were to be used to conduct a needs assessment, develop a plan, and then implement prevention programs. To accomplish these tasks, each coalition created several committees, consisting of community volunteers representing different sectors of the community (e.g., youth, parents, public awareness/media, criminal justice, etc.). Each coalition had a small paid staff to support the work of the committees. A total of 36 committees operated across the four coalitions representing 12 types of community sectors.

The baseline of the survey instrument used for these analyses was administered in a group format at coalition committee meetings—at the fourth meeting for the Midlands coalition and at the sixth meeting for the other three—to allow a sense of "groupness" to form. The coalitions were considered to be at the "formation" stage of coalition development. Those not in attendance were contacted by mail. A follow-up administration of this survey was administered 1 year later (implementation stage), but only the baseline data is considered in these analyses.

Coalition Survey. The evaluation team constructed the survey adapting existing scales (Cammann, Fishman, Jenkins, & Klesh, 1983; Florin, Chavis, Wandersman, & Rich, 1992; Florin, Mitchell, & Stevenson, 1993; Prestby et al., 1990). The 137-item survey assessed committee climate, formalized roles and rules, leadership roles, staff-volunteer relations, member satisfaction, member expectations, member training, communication patterns, decision-making processes, problem solving and conflict resolution, community linkages, member participation in coalition activities, and member benefits and costs.

Here we focus on the member benefits, costs, and participation items. There were 12 benefit items and 11 cost items. Respondents were asked how much they experienced each benefit/cost as a result of the committee participation (4 = *very much* to 1 = *not at all*). Items addressed the three Clark and Wilson domains of benefits and costs, namely the Material, Solidary, and Purposive domains discussed earlier (see Table 6.2 for a complete list of items, organized by domain). Five items assessed participation. The first, the number of meetings attended, was in a 5-point Likert format (1 = *zero to two*, 2 = *three to five*, 3 = *six to eight*, 4 = *nine to eleven*, 5 = *twelve or more*). The second, the number of hours worked outside of meetings, was also in a 5-point Likert format (1 = *less than one hour*, 2 = *one to two hours*, 3 = *three to four hours*, 4 = *five to eight hours*, 5 = *over eight hours*). Three items were in a "yes/no" format: talk at meetings, perform work outside meetings, and help organize activities for the committee.

TABLE 6.2
Benefit and Cost Items*

Benefit Items	Cost Items
	Material
Learn new skills	Find caregivers for family members
Receive information about community services, events, county government, etc.	Demands too much of my personal time
Learn more about alcohol and other drug abuse	Takes too much of my time from agency or organizational commitments
Supports my decision to not abuse alcohol and other drugs	Adds unwanted job responsibilities
Provides an opportunity to improve the way I do my job	Have to go to meetings/events at inconvenient times
Provides a chance to explore new job opportunities	
	Solidary
Gain support by working with other members of the community	Have to give up activities with family and friends
Gain personal recognition and respect from others	Feel unwelcome or not like part of the committee
	Purposive
Receive satisfaction by being involved in an important project	Conflicts between the mission of my organization or agency and the committee's work
Fulfill a sense of responsibility to contribute to the community	Disagree personally with the goals or activities of the committee
Help people at risk for alcohol and other drug abuse	Feel that the committee never gets anything accomplished
Make the community a safer place to live	Feel that the committee cannot really do much to solve the problems of alcohol and other drug abuse

Note. *4 = experienced very much to 1 = not experienced at all.

Survey Respondents. The response rates for the four partnerships were 77.6% (128/165) for the Spartanburg partnership, 74.6% (208/279) for Union/Cherokee, 98.0% (98/100) for Florence, and 87.7% (206/235) for the Midlands, for a total of 82.2% (640/779). Table 6.3 shows the demographic information of the entire sample. Almost all the respondents have lived in their respective counties for at least 1 year (91.1%), and over one half (59.5%) have lived in their area for at least 11 years. Most of the sample is White (73.0%) and African American (23.9%), and over half (60.3%) the respondents were 30 to 49 years old, with those 29 and under accounting for an additional 22.7% of the sample. Most respondents (48.3%) reported having one or two children, or no children (39.7%); over three quarters

(75.2%) of the sample has a college degree, whereas 20.3% graduated from vocational or high school. The sample was evenly split by gender.

TABLE 6.3
Demographic Data

Demographics	Range	Percentage (%) (n = 640)
Partnership	Midlands	32.2
	Florence	14.7
	Spartanburg	20.0
	Union/Cherokee	32.5
Number of years lived in county	0-.9 yrs.	7.0
	1-5 yrs.	20.2
	6-10 yrs.	11.4
	11-20 yrs.	24.7
	21+ yrs.	34.8
Gender	Male	49.1
	Female	49.7
Age	Under 20	13.0
	20-29	9.7
	30-39	28.6
	40-49	31.7
	50-59	10.5
	60+	5.4
Race	African American	23.9
	White	73.0
	Other	1.6
Children in household	None or N/A	39.7
	One	24.5
	Two	23.8
	Three	7.5
	Four or more	2.8
Education level	Eighth grade or less	1.9
	High/vocational school	20.3
	College	36.9
	Graduate School	38.3
Employment status	Full-time	71.3
	Part-time	9.0
	Student	10.5
	Homemaker	2.0
	Volunteer	1.3
	Other	4.8

Analysis Set 1: Organizational Representatives Versus Members Who Only Represent Themselves

Unlike neighborhood groups in which members tend to represent themselves, member participation in community coalitions also usually involves considering the benefits and costs for the host organization they represent (e.g., their employing organization). The benefits and costs described earlier are related to volunteers' perceptions about themselves (e.g., "What benefits and costs do I experience?"). Reconciling the personal and organizational benefits and costs may be difficult for coalition members whose needs are different from those of their sponsoring organization. Therefore, the challenge for coalition leaders is to provide benefits and minimize costs so that both the members and their sponsoring organizations, consider their participation beneficial. Benefits and costs at these two levels may influence member participation differently. Although researchers have studied both types of benefits and costs, none to our knowledge have examined their respective effects on participation simultaneously. In these analyses, we compare the experience of benefits and costs between coalition members who represented other agencies and members who represented only themselves. We also compared these two groups of members on their levels of participation.

Benefit-and-Cost Scales. Separate principal components analyses (PCA) were conducted on the benefit-and-cost items using the baseline survey data. The scree plot of the eigenvalues (Catell, 1966) showed that one linear combination including all the benefit items accounts for most of the variance, with the varimax-rotated factor pattern scores ranging from .55 to .72. Combining the benefit items into a single scale resulted in a Cronbach alpha equal to .88. The cost items behaved similarly, with the varimax-rotated factor pattern scores ranging from .43 to .73 and a single scale Cronbach alpha equal to .78.

Participation Scale. In order to operationally define participation, we attempted to form a scale using the five participation questions already described. However, PCA and Cronbach alpha analyses showed that the following three items formed the most cohesive and reliable participation scale: Number of hours worked outside of meetings (in a 5-point Likert format) and the three items in a "yes/no" format (talk at meetings, perform work outside meetings, help organize activities for the committee) were used to form the participation scale and had a final Cronbach alpha equal to .75.

Benefit, Cost, and Participation Analyses. First, a one-way between-subjects MANOVA was conducted on the benefit and cost scales formed from the baseline data to assess the difference between those who represented another agency and those who represented only themselves (the variable was called *Sponsor*). The MANOVA was significant, $F(2, 557) = 25.3986, p = .0001, \eta^2 = .084$. Individual univariate F-tests (at alpha = .025 level to hold the overall experimentwise alpha = .05) of *Sponsor* were significant for the benefit scale, $F(1, 558) = 13.01, p = .0003$, and for the cost scale, $F(1, 558) = 20.96, p = .0001$. These results indicate that those who represent another organization perceive more benefits ($M = 3.25, SD = 0.47$) than those who represent themselves ($M = 3.10, SD = 0.54$) and more costs ($M = 1.71, SD = 0.45$) than their counterparts who represent only themselves ($M = 1.54, SD = 0.43$). The variable *Sponsor* was crossed with each one of the demographic variables in four separate Chi square analyses. All four were not significant, meaning that the two levels of the variable *Sponsor* were equally represented by Education, Race, Gender, and Age.

Next, the two groups were compared in terms of their participation in coalition activities. An independent groups t test was conducted on the participation scale and was significant, $t(483.8) = -3.43$, $p = .0007$. (The degrees of freedom are not an integer because the variances of the two groups were not equal. As a result, the t test is estimated.) Those who represented another agency ($M = 2.80$, $SD = 1.28$) participated more than those who represented themselves ($M = 2.44$, $SD = 1.16$).

Analysis Set 2: Examining Correlations Simultaneously at the Individual and Group Levels

A committee member's individual perceptions of the benefits and costs may also be affected by his or her group membership. Therefore, examining only the individual level results may be overlooking important information about group level effects (Florin, Giamartino, Kenny, & Wandersman, 1988; Kenny & La Voie, 1985). Also, researchers often assess theories on one level by using measurement techniques designed for a different level (Klein, Dansereau, & Hall, 1994; Shinn, 1990). Shinn (1990) states that "the level of conceptualization may differ from the level at which data are collected—the level of measurement or the level of phenomenon—and the level to which data are assigned for statistical analysis" (p. 114). For example, variables such as *cohesiveness* and *climate* are usually examined by assessing individuals, not taking into account that these individuals also belong to a group. This issue is especially relevant for coalition data because the members belong to various committees, and the committees are comprised of coalition members. Therefore, the "climate" of the committee may be exerting influence on the members' benefit and cost responses.

To assess these group-level effects more accurately, Kenny and La Voie (1985) developed a technique in which the effects of the two levels (individuals and committees) can be separated and examined simultaneously. The technique involves first examining group-level correlations to assess whether group-level effects exist in the data. To do this, Kenny and La Voie (1985) recommend using an intraclass correlation to assess the effect of random variables such as *group*. The intraclass correlation represents the proportion of variance within individuals' scores that is due to group membership. If the intraclass correlations are not significantly different from zero, there is no difference between committees in the way members perceive benefits, costs, and participation. In other words, committee members are *not* more similar to their fellow committee members than they are to members of other committees.

Benefit Analyses. Intraclass correlations were conducted between each benefit item and the total scale and the participation scale (see Table 6.4). The intraclass correlations for 10 out of the 12 benefits (and the benefit scale) with participation were significant at .05. Thus, it seems that variance is present at both the individual and group levels simultaneously, and Kenny and La Voie (1985) recommend that, in this case, correlations be computed at both levels in order to investigate all the information found in the data.

TABLE 6.4
Correlations of Benefit Items With Participation Scale

Benefit Items	Intraclass Correlation	*p* Value	Individual (Standard Correlation)	Adjusted Individual	Group	Adjusted Group
Total benefits	.12	.001	.33	.28	.55	.73
Learn new skills	.05	.015	.35	.33	.45	.61
Receive information about community services, events, county government, etc.	.07	.001	.16	.16	.19	.21
Learn more about alcohol and other drug abuse	.13	.001	.18	.12	.40	.56
Supports my decision to not abuse alcohol and other drugs	.10	.001	.13	.05	.48	.76
Provides an opportunity to improve the way I do my job	.02	.126	.27	.25	.38	--[a]
Provides a chance to explore new job opportunities	.07	.001	.20	.15	.47	.75
Gain support by working with other members of the community	.04	.037	.20	.17	.39	.71
Gain personal recognition and respect from others	.11	.001	.26	.20	.52	.74
Receive satisfaction by being involved in an important project	.14	.001	.24	.22	.32	.37
Fulfill a sense of responsibility to contribute to the community	.12	.001	.23	.19	.41	.55
Help people at risk for alcohol and other drug abuse	.01	.366	.19	.14	.53	--[a]
Make the community a safer place to live	.08	.001	.14	.11	.28	.42

Note. [a]Kenny and LaVoie (1985) recommend that adjusted group correlations be computed only when both variables have significant intraclass correlations.

First, the individual level correlations were adjusted for the effect of *group* or *committee*. For each benefit item-participation correlation, the group mean is subtracted, and then the group-adjusted scores are correlated. The resulting correlations can be viewed as partial correlations, with the effect of *group* partialled out. Almost all of the correlations of the benefit items (and the benefits scale) with participation decreased when moving from the individual ignoring group correlation, to the individual adjusted for group correlations. This indicates that when the effect of group is taken out, less of a correlation exists between most benefits and participation.

Next, the group correlations were adjusted for the effect of *individuals*. This is an indirect correlation because it estimates the relationship between latent measures. Kenny and La Voie (1985) recommend that these adjusted group correlations should be computed only when both measures have significant intraclass correlations. Participation had an intraclass correlation of .13, $F(46, 482)$ = 2.610, p = .001, and adjusted group correlations were only conducted on the benefits that had a significant intraclass correlation (all except "Provides an opportunity to improve the way I do my job" and "Help people at risk for alcohol and other drug abuse"). Compared to the individual adjusted correlations, the group-adjusted correlations for all of the benefit items (and the benefit scale) are larger. This indicates that simply analyzing this data at the individual level is inappropriate, and that processes occurring within the committee affect the magnitude of the individual relationships between many of the benefits and participation.

Cost Analyses. There were less group effects in the costs. When computed with all the costs, the intraclass correlation of participation was .11, $F(46, 453) = 2.353$, p = .001, and was significant. Of the cost items that had significant intraclass correlations, only four cost items had any group effects. These items had adjusted group correlations that were two to five times greater than the individual adjusted correlations (see Table 6.5 for a listing of intraclass correlations and p values). This indicates that, for these four costs, the processes occurring within the committee influence the magnitude of costs experienced by its members.

Summary and Conclusions

Organizational Representatives Versus Members Who Only Represent Themselves

Benefit and Cost Scales. Both those members who represented another organization and those who represented only themselves perceived the overall benefits in the range between "Very much of a benefit" and "Somewhat of a benefit" and perceived the overall costs in the range between "Not at all a cost" and "Not very much of a cost." Despite these similarities, those who represented another organization perceived greater benefits and greater costs, and participated more than those who only represented themselves. Organizational representatives must consider both themselves and their sponsoring agency when serving on a volunteer committee, and therefore may have more reasons to participate. Members who have more reasons to participate may have more likely been satisfied

TABLE 6.5
Correlations of Cost Items and Benefit/Cost Ratio With Participation

Cost Items	Intraclass Correlation	p Value	Individual (Standard Correlation)	Adjusted Individual	Group	Adjusted Group
Total Costs	.09	.001	-.05	-.05	-.03	-.01
Find caregivers for family members	.01	.276	.14	.10	.37	—[a]
Demands too much of my personal time	-.02	.861	-.00	-.00	.03	—[a]
Takes too much of my time from agency or organizational commitments	.07	.002	-.03	-.02	-.10	-.18
Adds unwanted job responsibilities	.01	.353	-.02	.01	-.21	—[a]
Have to go to meetings/events at inconvenient times	.00	.411	-.06	-.08	.02	—[a]
Have to give up activities with family and friends	.15	.001	.07	.02	.22	.34
Feel unwelcome or not like part of the committee	.23	.001	-.07	-.13	.12	.25
Conflicts between the mission of my organization or agency and the committee's work	.01	.236	-.03	-.08	.30	—[a]
Disagree personally with the goals or activities of the committee	.01	.252	.00	-.00	.05	—[a]
Feel that the committee never gets anything accomplished	.26	.001	-.07	-.04	-.16	-.21
Feel that the committee cannot really do much to solve the problems of alcohol and other drug abuse	.21	.001	-.08	-.08	-.08	-.08

Note. [a]Kenny and LaVoie (1985) recommend that adjusted group correlations be computed only when both variables have significant intraclass correlations.

by the benefits that were offered. It is possible that organizational representatives perceived more costs because they had the extra responsibilities of coordinating their committee membership with their duties at their sponsoring agency. These results are strengthened by the fact that they cut across, or are independent of, Age, Race, Gender, and Education.

Examining Correlations Simultaneously at the Individual and Group Levels

Benefits. In the present study, many of the benefit items and the benefit scale had some "group effect" that affected the relationship between the benefits and level of participation. The relationship between participation and the following items seemed to be present only at the individual level:

- Receive information about community services, events, county government, etc.
- Receive satisfaction by being involved in an important project.
- Provides an opportunity to improve the way I do my job.
- Help people at risk for alcohol and other drug abuse.

These items fall into Clark and Wilson's (1961) Material and Purposive categories. The following items that had the largest group effects can be classified as Solidary benefits:

- Supports my decision to not abuse alcohol and other drugs.
- Gain support by working with other members of the community.
- Gain personal recognition and respect from others.

Therefore, items that involve group interactions such as gaining support and recognition from a group show significant group effects in their relationship to participation. In addition, the Material item "Provides a chance to explore new job opportunities" also had a large group effect. Although it is a Material benefit, exploring new job opportunities often involves networking with others (a social function), something that is readily available at committee meetings. Items that can be classified as Material and Purposive benefit items have either individual or smaller group effects.

Costs. Overall, the cost items have less of a relationship with participation, and the cost scale has almost a zero group effect. In addition, the items that do show some group effect are difficult to interpret. The item "Feel unwelcome or not like part of the committee" had a negative, individual-level correlation with participation, but had a positive, group-adjusted correlation with participation. The item "Have to give up activities with family and friends" had a small positive, individual-level correlation with participation, and its group-adjusted correlation was larger and positive. The items "Takes too much time from my agency or organizational commitments" and "Feel that the committee never gets anything accomplished" had small negative, individual-level correlations that became more negative when adjusted for group. For the latter item, it seems reasonable that a group process is, in part, mediating the relationship between the item and participation. The item addresses a group issue, in other words, how much the group is accomplishing. However, the results of the former item are surprising, as this item seems to address an individual's time commitments. One possibility is that members may not have participated in the coalition enough (given that the assessment was done after a handful of initial committee meetings) to fully experience costs.

Practical Implications of Benefits and Costs

The relationship between benefits and costs and participation is a powerful tool that leaders of voluntary groups can use to increase the level of participation of their volunteers through "incentive/cost management," thereby enhancing organizational viability. *Incentive/cost management* (Prestby et al., 1990) describes efforts taken by coalition staff to create a benefit-to-cost ratio that members find favorable enough to continue their participation. This usually involves attempts to provide benefits that members want, while minimizing the costs that they do not want. The results of the two analyses described offer suggestions for how to conduct incentive/cost management efforts.

- Coalition leaders may want to engage in incentive management in different ways during the formation stage of development, depending on the type of benefit. In order to provide Solidary types of benefits, coalition leaders may want to develop the entire group. Using a "group" method takes advantage of the group process that is affecting the relationship between the benefit in question and participation. For example, coalition leaders may model how to provide support and recognition during a committee meeting. On the other hand, in order to provide benefit items that have an individual relationship with participation, one may only need individual-level action. For example, handing out information about alcohol, tobacco, and other drugs is an individual-level action, and that may be all that is required to provide that benefit successfully.
- Examining the Solidary benefits' relationship to participation using only the individual-level correlations, one may conclude that social relationships mediate members' level of participation. However, conceptualizing this issue using only individual-level findings may lead to inappropriate action. Although coalition leaders may attempt to improve social relations among members by working out a conflict between two members, the group-level results suggest that attention to the whole group process is also an important mediating factor in the relationship between Solidary benefits and participation.
- In contrast, these results suggest that leaders should engage in cost management at the individual level while in the formation stage of coalition development. Leaders can do this on an individual level by learning what *each member* perceives to be a cost during this early stage. As the coalition

develops and the committees become more cohesive, it is possible that the cost items will show more of a group effect. Then the leaders' cost management strategies should change to meet these different needs.

- The coalition volunteers who also represent other related agencies are important members. They provide a link between the coalition and the agencies that the coalition needs to impact in order to build enough social capital (Smith, 1995) to address community issues successfully. Although they may participate and receive more benefits in the early stages of coalition development, coalition leaders should take care to prevent burnout among these members. One way to do this could be through the creation of incentive/cost management strategies specifically for this type of member. This may involve specifically offering benefits and minimizing costs that appeal not only to the individual members, but to their host organization as well. Emphasizing this point can be an important marketing strategy for recruiting member organizations. Of course, an organization's participation can engender costs as well, for example, taking employee time away from organization activities.

In addition, there are several other ways to use the benefit and cost approach to improve participation of volunteers. For example, when recruiting volunteers, emphasize all types of benefits to be gained by joining, not only the ones gained by working on the goals of the group (e.g., "We also have fun while trying to create a neighborhood watch program."). If one group cannot provide all the benefits that members desire, linking with other groups can be a way to supplement the available benefits. Compromising efficiency on working toward the stated goals in order to provide other benefits (e.g., time for socializing and networking) can strengthen the organization, enhancing its ability to achieve its goals in the future. Finally, organizations often have less success in retaining volunteer members for longer periods of time, especially after the completion of a specific project (e.g., blocking the construction of a highway through the neighborhood). If members leave at this point, within our framework it can be argued that these members have stopped receiving the Purposive benefits that kept them participating. If the organization is still interested in remaining intact, to retain these members organization leaders ought to provide other types of benefits (i.e., Social, Material) or pursue additional goals that will yield Purposive benefits that interest members (e.g., establishing a neighborhood watch).

In order to implement successful incentive/cost management approaches, coalition leaders need to know which benefits and costs their members are experiencing. Therefore, it is important that, after people join, coalitions repeatedly assess the benefits and costs that will keep their members participating, and then assign them tasks based on those data (e.g., John was interested in networking, so the coalition placed him in charge of working with the Chamber of Commerce). We assisted these coalitions in doing this by arranging the benefit and cost data into tabular form for each committee, called Committee Profiles. We then gave the staff a *Committee Profiles Handbook,* which contained explanations of the data and suggested activities the committees could implement to improve, depending on where they fell. For example, if a committee profile showed that the members were not experiencing many benefits, the staff and the chairperson could then look at the benefits section in the handbook and implement the suggested activities found there. Finally, we conducted a workshop for project staff to train them to offer feedback regarding the committee profile information to their respective committees. The staff and voluntary chairpersons then used this information to enhance member participation.

Some Future Research Directions

Focus on the Importance of Benefits and Costs. Much of the research on benefits and costs asks respondents to rate the degree to which they *experience* various benefits and costs. Although important, this strategy should also be combined with asking respondents how *important* each item is in their decision to participate. In the previous research, it is assumed that the items that respondents experience most are also the items that influence the respondents' decision to participate the most; however, this may not be true. Respondents may be influenced by a benefit or a cost that they do not experience that much, or conversely, they may be influenced very little by a benefit or a cost that they experience a great deal. Future research should study both types of questions at the same time in order to clarify which benefits and costs are the most influential.

Methodological Issues. Some of the shortcomings of the current literature should be rectified. Agreeing on a consistent set of items would allow researchers to compare items and categories of items across groups and determine which ones are relevant for different types of organizations. Similarly, using the same set of items would allow researchers to better answer questions about the number of factors that would best represent the benefit and cost items. Better reporting of extrapolation techniques would help to clarify the factor questions.

Most studies assessed organizations at one point in time. However, voluntary organizations are fluid entities, with members and leaders constantly joining and quitting. In addition, organizations go through phases in which different tasks are the focus of the members' efforts at different points in time during the development of the organization. Future research should assess how members' perceptions of the benefits and costs, and their relationship to participation and empowerment, changes as an organization matures. Gaining a longitudinal perspective would allow leaders to adjust their incentive/cost management approaches over time.

In conclusion, the research and practical value of benefits and costs has been established. The benefit-and-cost approach is straightforward and easily understood by organization leaders and members and has empirical support. We provided several examples that demonstrate how practitioners in the field can use the benefit-and-cost approach to enhance organization viability.

References

Allensworth, D., & Patton, W. (1990). Promoting school health through coalition building. *The Eta Sigma Gamma Monograph Series, 7.*

Boissevain, J. (1974). *Friend of friends.* Oxford: Basil Blackwell.

Butterfoss, F. D. (1993). *Coalitions for alcohol and other drug abuse: Factors predicting effectiveness.* Unpublished doctoral dissertation, University of South Carolina, Columbia.

Butterfoss, F. D., Goodman, R. M., & Wandersman, A. (1993). Community coalitions for prevention and health promotion. *Health Education Research, 8,* 315-330.

Butterfoss, F. D., Goodman, R. M., & Wandersman, A. (1996). Community coalitions for prevention and health promotion: Factors predicting satisfaction, participation, and planning. *Health Education Quarterly, 23,* 65-79.

Cammann, C., Fishman, S., Jenkins, T., & Klesh, L. (1983). Attitudes and perceptions of organizational members. In S. Seashore, E. Lawler, P. Mirvis, & C. Cammann (Eds.), *Assessing organizational change* (pp. 71-138). New York: Wiley.

Catell, R. B. (1966). The scree test for the number of factors. *Multivariate Behavioral Research, 1,* 245-276.

Chinman, M., & Wandersman A. (1999). The benefits and costs of volunteering in community organizations: Review and practical implications. *Nonprofit and Voluntary Sector Quarterly 28,* 46-64.

Clark, P. B., & Wilson, J. Q. (1961). Incentive systems: A theory of organizations. *Administrative Science Quarterly, 6,* 129-166.

Clarke, H. D., Price, R. G., Stewart, M. C., & Krause, R. (1978). Motivational patterns and differential participation in a Canadian party: The Ontario Liberals. *American Journal of Political Science, 22,* 130-151.

Clary, E. G., Ridge, R. D., Stukas, A. A., Snyder, M., Copeland, J., Haugen, J., & Miene, P. (1998). Understanding and assessing the motivations of volunteers: A functional approach. *Journal of Personality and Social Psychology, 74,* 1516-1530.

Florin, P., Chavis, D., Wandersman, A., & Rich, R. (1992). A systems approach to understanding and enhancing grassroots organizations: The Block Booster Project. In R. Levine & H. Fitzgerald (Eds.), *Analysis of dynamic psychological systems* (Vol. 2, pp. 215-243). New York: Plenum.

Florin, P., Mitchell, R., & Stevenson, J. (1993). Identifying training and technical assistance needs in community coalitions: A developmental approach. *Health Education Research, 20,* 331-344.

Florin, P., Giamartino, G. A., Kenny, D. A., & Wandersman, A. (1988). Levels of analysis and effects: Clarifying group influence and climate by separating individual and group effects. *Journal of Applied Social Psychology, 20,* 881-900.

Friedman, R. R., Florin, P., Wandersman, A., & Meier, R. (1988). Local action on behalf of local collectives in the U.S. and Israel: How different are leaders from members in voluntary associations? *Journal of Voluntary Action Research, 17*, 36-54.

Kanter, R. M. (1968). Commitment and social organizations: A study of commitment mechanisms in utopian communities. *American Sociological Review, 33*, 499-517.

Kenny, D. A., & La Voie, L. (1985). Separating individual and group effects. *Journal of Personality and Social Psychology, 48*, 339-348.

Klein, K. J., Dansereau, F., & Hall, R. J. (1994). Level issues in theory development, data collection, and analysis. *Academy of Management Review, 19*, 195-229.

Knoke, D. (1988). Incentives in collective action organizations. *American Sociological Review, 53*, 311-329.

Knoke, D. (1990). *Organizing for collective action: The political economies of associations*. New York: Aline de Grunter.

Knoke, D., & Adams, R. E. (1987). The incentive systems of associations. *Research in the Sociology of Organizations, 5*, 285-309.

Knoke, D., & Wood, J. R. (1981). *Organized for action: Commitment in voluntary organizations*. New Brunswick, NJ: Rutgers University Press.

Moe, T. M. (1980). *The organization of interests*. Chicago: University of Chicago Press.

Norton, S., Wandersman, A., & Goldman, C. R. (1993). Perceived costs and benefits of membership in a self-help group: Comparisons of members and nonmembers of the Alliance for the Mentally Ill. *Community Mental Health Journal, 29*, 143-160.

Olson, M., Jr. (1965). *The logic of collective action*. Cambridge, MA: Harvard University Press.

Omoto, A. M. & Snyder, M. (1995). Sustained helping without obligation: Motivation, longevity of service, and perceived attitude change among AIDS volunteers. *Journal of Personality and Social Psychology, 68*, 671-686.

Prestby, J. E., Wandersman, A., Florin, P., Rich, R., & Chavis, D. (1990). Benefits, costs, incentive management and participation in voluntary organizations: A means to understanding and promoting empowerment. *American Journal of Community Psychology, 18*, 117-149.

Rich, R. C. (1980). The dynamics of leadership in neighborhood organizations. *Social Science Quarterly, 60*(4), 570-587.

Schmitz, C. C. & Schomaker, P. (1994). *Survey of individual members and member organizations on the costs and benefits of belonging to a community-based public health (CBPH) consortium*. Unpublished Survey Report, Cluster Evaluation Team. Minneapolis: University of Minnesota, Center for Urban and Regional Affairs.

Shinn, M. (1990). Mixing and matching: Levels of conceptualization, measurement, and statistical analysis in community research. In P. Toon, C. Keys, F. Chertok, & L. Jason (Eds.), *Researching community psychology: Issues of theory and methods* (pp. 111-126). Washington, DC: American Psychological Association.

Smith, S. R. (1995). *Social capital, community coalitions and the role of institutions.* Unpublished manuscript.

Snyder, M. (1993). Basic research and practical problems: The promise of a "functional" personality and social psychology. *Personality and Social Psychology Bulletin, 19,* 251-264.

Snyder, M., & Omoto, A. M. (1992). Who helps and why? The psychology of AIDS volunteerism. In S. Spacapan & S. Oskamp (Eds.), *Helping and being helped: Naturalistic studies* (pp. 213-239). Newbury Park, CA: Sage.

Stevenson, W., Pearce, J., & Porter, L. (1985). The concept of coalitions in organization theory and research. *Academy of Management Review, 10,* 256-268.

Wandersman, A., Florin, P., Friedman, R. R., & Meier, R. (1987). Who participates, who does not, and why? An analysis of voluntary neighborhood organizations in the United States and Israel. *Sociological Forum, 2,* 534-555.

7

SOCIAL CAPITAL IN DEMOCRATIC TRANSITION: CIVIL SOCIETY IN SOUTH AFRICA

Bert Klandermans
Free University, Amsterdam, The Netherlands

Marlene Roefs
Johan Olivier
Human Science Research Council, Pretoria, South Africa

South Africa's transition to democracy triggered a lively debate about civil society in that country (Marais, 1998; Muthien & Olivier, 1999). Among the issues that fueled the debate were questions such as: What is civil society like? What role did it play in the past? What should its role be in the future? In the literature, civil society is described as a realm distinct from, yet interacting with, the state, consisting of numerous associations organized around specific issues, and seeking to form links with other interest groups (Diamond, 1997; Schmitter, 1995). Civil society is conceived of as an intermediary between citizens and the state, and in that regard it is thought to be of crucial significance for the sustainability of democracy. In the mediation process, the social capital accumulated in these voluntary associations is employed in negotiations and bargaining with the state around policy concerns and interests of the citizens involved (Camerer, 1992). Social capital encompasses the combined efforts of citizens to uphold the network of voluntary associations in a society, but in addition, other important elements are the social trust, the flow of information, and the norms and sanctions that are needed to hold the network together (Mondak, 1998).

Not every voluntary association is part of civil society. Although one can find more and less inclusive approaches in the literature (see Hyden, 1998, for an overview), we propose to take the functions of civil society as our point of departure. Reviewing the literature, we conclude that supposedly civil society both facilitates and monitors the functioning of the state. On the one hand, civil society organizations (CSOs) act as vehicles for political participation. They incorporate the public in political decision-making processes, by informing, organizing, and involving them in politics. At the same time, CSOs monitor politics and government by keeping a critical eye on the authorities and pressurizing them with their capacity to mobilize citizens in support of collective action. CSOs also foster feelings of belongingness and embeddedness; they make people feel like respected members of respected organizations. Despite its crucial role in the maintenance of democratic relations, civil society does not replace the state or overtake the functions of the state as the agent of development of society as a whole. Rather, it provides an important link between citizens and the state, and ensures accountability on the part of the state, no more and no less (Foweraker & Landman, 2000).

Thus defined, voluntary organizations that typically qualify as CSOs include interest-based organizations such as labor unions, consumer organizations, professional associations, and commercial associations; nongovernmental organizations; social movement organizations; cultural and religious organizations; ethnic and communal organizations; and civic organizations such as community, neighborhood, and tenant organizations. Both Diamond (1997) and Bothwell (1995) also include independent organizations devoted to education and communication (schools and free press).

The question that concerns us here is what makes people contribute to the social capital accumulated in these voluntary associations. In the literature, we encounter both explanations accounting for the differences in participation between countries and the changes over time, and explanations accounting for the differences between individual citizens within the same country. Explanations at the country level refer to economic, religious, and political variables (Curtis, Baer, & Grabb, 2001; Schofer & Fourcade-Gourinchas, 2001). Levels of participation in voluntary associations are higher in countries that are economically better off, and in countries that are predominantly Protestant or mixed Christian. The reasoning behind these findings is the following: As societies grow wealthier, they become more heterogeneous and specialized and people accumulate more material resources. The first factor makes for a greater variety of voluntary associations, the latter for more people who can afford to participate. Protestant religions are supposed to be more participation-oriented than Catholicism with its hierarchical and elitist church organization. With regard to the political factors the story is more complicated. First, evidence suggests that long-established democracies show more associational involvement. This confirms, of course, the assumed functional relationship between the existence of healthy CSOs and the quality of democratic institutions. Secondly, evidence suggests that the type of democracy makes a difference. Curtis et al. (2001) report analyses showing that liberal and social democracies are favored more for associational involvement than traditional corporatist societies. Working with the same data, Schofer and Fourcade-Gourinchas (2001) propose that two factors, *statism* and *corporateness*, explain differences between countries. As for the former, levels of participation tend to be higher in societies with a decentralized, responsive state apparatus; for the latter, levels of participation tend to be higher in societies where social actors are incorporated in state institutions to a higher degree. The last finding seems to contradict Curtis et al.'s conclusion with regard to type of democracy, but evidence presented by Schofer and Fourcade-Gourinchas suggests that low levels of statism foster participation in new social movements (environmental associations, Third World development associations, women's organizations, and peace organizations), whereas high levels of corporateness foster participation in old social movements (trade unions, political parties, and professional associations). As for the changes in associational involvement over time,

Schofer and Fourcade-Gourinchas hold that, in the world society, a convergence can be observed "around 'American-style' visions of associational life resulting in higher levels of association over time and more emphasis on 'new' social movement membership" (p. 822). Finally, Curtis et al. investigated both regular membership and active membership. Interestingly, the country-level explanations fared much better with regard to membership than with regard to active participation. Apparently, these factors are more relevant for the decision to become a member of a voluntary association than for the decision to take an active role in these organizations.

Individual-level explanations concern both demographics and attitudes. In general, there is wide consensus about the impact of a few demographics. Education increases participation; males participate more than females, middle-aged citizens participate more than young and old citizens, the employed more than the unemployed, married people more than unmarried. As far as attitudes are concerned, social trust and postmaterial values appear to reinforce participation especially in new social movement associations.

Civil Society in South Africa

During the apartheid era, South Africa actually hosted two civil societies: a 'White' civil society that mediated between the White minority and the apartheid state, and a fully separated 'Black' civil society[1] that mobilized the Black majority in opposition to the apartheid state. The two associational configurations that formed these two societies were almost completely separated, as interracial organizing was made extremely difficult by the apartheid laws. In his description of the Polish society in the years of repression, Sztompka (1998) alluded to a similar process in Poland. Civil society in conspiracy, he called it, referring to the period that civil society was pushed underground. In South Africa, the end of apartheid changed all that. It led not only to a reconfiguration in which the two associational configurations were to merge, but also to a reorientation in which both were to fundamentally redefine their role vis-á-vis the state. One may wonder to what extent the two continue their separate existence instead of merging. It is certainly true that many of the associations that constituted the 'White' and the 'Black' civil society are still separated, that is to say, fully White or fully Black without much overlap or collaboration between the two. However, reorientation was inevitable.

The recent transition to democracy in South Africa requires the South Africans to assess critically the role civil society has played in their country. This is of particular importance given the central role that 'White' civil society structures have played in maintaining the apartheid state and 'Black' civil society structures in the struggle against it. One of the key challenges confronting the 'two civil societies' in South Africa since 1994 is to (re)define its role vis-à-vis the new state. For its part, the new state needs

---

[1] Here we are using 'Black' in the generic sense in which it was used in South Africa to denote all non-Whites.

to clarify its relationship with the 'two civil societies.' This mutual role clarification is particularly important because the present South African state is run by the former liberation movement (Klandermans, Roefs, & Olivier, 1998). To the 'White' civil society, this means that the state is now run by the people never trusted with any access to power and forcefully denied every influence in the decision-making process. Some Whites have responded by creating their own homeland, Orania, in what Sztompka (1998) called "ghettoization," building impenetrable boundaries to protect the group against an alien and threatening environment. Others have withdrawn in associations that have loosened their links with the state. Again others have begun to define citizenship in the new state. In the final analysis, if they do not want to become marginalized, 'White' CSOs have no choice but to connect to the new state. Some may choose to become racially integrated associations; others may stay predominantly White, but in order to take their role as CSOs they must develop working relations with the new state.

To the 'Black' civil society, the transition meant that the state is now run by their people. Large numbers of activists have moved into government since the 1994 election. This enhanced, of course, the influence of the 'Black' civil society, but left its organizations in a leadership crisis because many CSO leaders moved into government positions. It also presented the 'Black' civil society with new challenges. As the South African National NGO Coalition observed, 'Black' civil society organizations had to adopt new roles as participants in the policymaking process, partners in service delivery, and monitors of the new government's performance. This implies a shift in orientation, as the skills, structures, and modes of interaction involved in political resistance differ markedly from those needed in reconstruction and development. The new era calls for technical expertise instead of mass mobilization, long-term strategies instead of spontaneous actions, administrative capacity instead of resistance creativity, and positive policy input instead of negative critique (Sangoco, 1999). On the other hand, 'Black' CSOs run the risk of losing their autonomy and being co-opted and becoming part of the very state it has to monitor. In other words, whereas 'White' CSOs must tighten their ties with the new state, 'Black' CSOs face the opposite problem and must loosen their ties.

In terms of Schofer and Fourcade-Gourinchas' (2001) typology, the "old" South Africa fit into the *high statism/high corporateness* quadrant. The apartheid state was characterized by a highly authoritarian and centralized regime that used collective 'White' organizations as the main channel for political incorporation. Although the African National Congress (ANC) government continues to be centralized and the family of anti-apartheid organizations is closely linked to the new regime, the transition process has definitely opened up the regime and moved South Africa's national polity structure toward lower levels of statism and corporateness. From this development one would predict that South Africa is moving toward higher levels of associational involvement, both in 'old' and 'new' social movements.

At the same time, the literature on democratic transitions gives some reason for concern about civil society's ability to mobilize citizens— an ability of crucial importance for the development of sustainable democratic institutions. Drawing from experience in former communist countries and in Latin America, this literature (O'Donnell & Schmitter, 1986; see Ginsburg, 1996, and Greenstein, Heinrich, & Naidoo, 1998, for a discussion of the South African case) suggests that for societies that experience a transition from an authoritarian regime to a democracy, the new regime tends to demobilize the very movements and organizations that struggled to bring it into power. Others, on the other hand, argue that certainly in South Africa there is little evidence of such demobilization (Adler & Webster, 1995; Muthien & Olivier, 1999). These authors are supported by Foweraker and Landman (2000) who provide convincing evidence from a longitudinal study of the transitions in Brazil, Chile, Mexico, and Spain, showing that civil society organizations continue to play an important role under the new political circumstances. Rather than being a demobilizing force, these authors propose that a robust civil society constitutes an essential pillar of a mature liberal democracy.

Such findings corroborate one of the central tenets of the leading paradigm in social movement literature, namely, resource mobilization theory, which emphasizes the crucial importance of organizations and social networks for the generation of social movements (McAdam, McCarthy, & Zald, 1996). Since this assumption was first formulated (McCarthy & Zald, 1973), numerous studies have confirmed the argument, by documenting either the role of organizations and social networks in recruitment and mobilization, or the role of organizations in the strategic planning and timing of protest (Klandermans, 1989a, 1989b; but see Piven & Cloward, 1979, for a diverging view). Gerlach and Hine (1970) were among the first to draw attention to the loosely coupled network structure of social movements. A decade and a half later Neidhardt (1985) characterized social movements as networks of networks. Curtis and Zurcher (1973) coined the term *multiorganizational field* (further elaborated by Klandermans, 1989a, 1992) to account for the embeddedness of social movement organizations in the social networks of a community. All of this was developed to underscore the central tenet of resource mobilization theory—that the organizational and social networks in a society play a crucial role in sustaining the social movement sector—which in turn is considered a separate intermediary between a state and its citizens (Jenkins & Klandermans, 1995; see also Meyer & Tarrow, 1998).

We conceive of civil society as an essential link between citizens and the state, be it in support of or in opposition to the state. In this chapter, we investigate the involvement of the South African population in civil society and assess whether there is any sign of demobilization. We first describe the extent to which South Africans participated in civil society organizations between 1994 and 2000 and whether that participation changed over time. During those years, we asked our respondents whether they were active members of any of the listed civil society organizations. The answers to this question form the core of this chapter. Next, we explore the possible antecedents for differences in participation. Finally, we try to assess the role of civil society organizations in the new South Africa.

A Brief Overview on Methods

The data in this chapter stem from seven surveys conducted annually between February 1994 and March 2000. The first survey was held in February 1994, just before the first national democratic election in South Africa; the last survey was conducted 6 years later in March 2000, 9 months after the second national election in 1999. The surveys were always held at the same time of year—around February or March. Interviews were conducted among representative samples of the South African population. The realized samples totaled 2,286 in 1994, 2,226 in 1995, 2,228 in 1996, 2,220 in 1997, 2,227 in 1998, 2,210 in 1999, and 2,666 in 2000. Data were collected by means of face-to-face interviews in people's homes. The interviews were carried out by trained interviewers and conducted in English or Afrikaans or in the respondent's home language when needed. On average the interviews lasted 30 to 45 minutes. For this chapter, we used the questions on involvement in civil society organizations, trust in government, political interest and involvement (voting intention, campaigning), actual participation and preparedness to take part in peaceful protest, and patterns of identification.

Participation in Civil Society Organizations

The active involvement in civil society fluctuated over the years since 1994, as the two graphs in Figure 7.1 show. In all four population groups, active participation dropped considerably between 1994 and 1995 (with or without taking church organizations into account). Among the Blacks, participation continued to decline between 1995 and 1996; among the others, the level of participation stabilized or improved slightly. But from 1996 onwards, participation among black South Africans began to increase again and in 1998 almost reached the level of 1994. After 1999, it declined again somewhat. This pattern emerged whether or not participation in church organizations was taken into account.

Among the Coloureds and Whites, we witnessed an increase in participation between 1995 and 1999, although less spectacular than among the Blacks. The developments over time in these groups were remarkably similar, including a modest decline in the last year of our study. The Asians diverged from the general pattern. First of all, the level of participation among the Asians was the lowest of all four groups and, second, in their case participation only began to increase after 1997. However, these differences—both in regard to level of participation and in regard to its development over time—appeared to be predominantly due to membership in church organizations. Once church organizations were omitted, patterns of participation in civil society organizations among the Coloureds, Asians, and Whites were not only more similar but remained closer to the level of 1995, with some peaks in the intermittent years.

FIGURE 7.1

Participation in grassroots organizations.

a. with churches

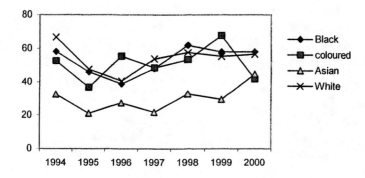

b. without churches

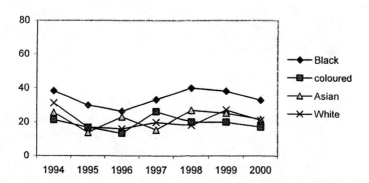

These figures suggest that after an initial decline between 1994 and 1995, participation in CSOs stabilized and, among the Blacks, even returned to levels close to those of 1994. As such they give an indication of people's embeddedness in civil society. The results pictured in Figure 7.1 are based on participation figures in the eight types of organizations that were included in our surveys from the very beginning. In the course of our study we included seven more types of organizations that were presumed to be relevant.[2] Table 7.1 presents participation in these 15 organizations as it developed over time.

---

[2] The analyses reported in Fig. 7.1 were conducted also for summary measures that included the remaining organizations. These analyses revealed the same patterns.

TABLE 7.1
Active Member in Grass Roots Organizations: Percentages

	1994	1995	1996	1997	1998	1999	2000
Political party	20.6	13.1	8.6	14.8	10.3	14.5	10.5
Trade union	7.7	6.1	5.3	7.1	7.8	11.1	9.5
Hawkers association	*	*	*	*	5.2	3.3	2.6
Land owners committee	*	2.1	1.9	2.4	5.0	5.2	2.7
Civic organization	6.5	4.3	3.4	4.5	6.8	6.0	4.9
Street block committee	8.8	5.2	4.2	5.8	7.2	7.3	6.7
Squatters or tenants committee	3.4	2.7	2.8	5.8	3.6	3.1	3.3
Anticrime group	*	*	*	*	9.7	7.1	7.5
Cultural organization	11.3	6.2	7.6	7.5	12.6	11.2	8.9
Youth organization	10.3	8.7	6.8	8.5	10.3	8.4	8.4
Women's organization	*	7.0	6.2	7.7	10.9	10.2	8.1
Educational organization	*	6.9	4.7	6.6	11.6	8.8	9.4
Environmental organization	*	*	*	*	*	6.1	3.3
Burial society or stokvel	*	*	*	*	21.1	24.8	23.6
Church organization	45.2	31.2	26.9	31.2	44.7	42.7	43.2

Note. Most organizations are comparable to their Northern equivalent, but some need clarification. Hawkers Associations are associations of street vendors; civic organizations are comparable to neighborhood organizations, and so are street block committees; anti-crime groups are comparable to neighborhood watch; stokvels are savings clubs where members rotate access to the money among its members on, say, a monthly basis; and church organizations are not churches per se but organizations related to churches.
*Not measured.

Active participation in political parties decreased significantly since 1994. About one in five of the respondents was an active member of a political party shortly before the founding election of 1994. This decreased overall to 1 in 10 in March 1998. In the run-up to the 1999 election this figure rose to 14.5%, but returned again a year later to the level of 1998. In 1994 active membership of political parties was highest among Africans (24%), followed by Whites (17%), and then Coloureds and Indians (5% each). As the level of participation in political parties was already low among the Coloureds and Asians, the downward trend reflected in the figures in Table 7.1 predominantly originated among the Black and White population. The decline since 1994 suggests that South Africans were disengaging from active politics.

Interestingly, after a modest decline in the first 3 years, participation in trade unions increased to a level higher than before. This trend could be witnessed among all four population groups. Moreover, participation in trade unions was about equally strong in all four groups. Obviously, trade unions continued to be significant players in South Africa's civil society. Two other types of organizations in the socioeconomic realm—hawker associations and landowner committees—drew their members predominantly from the Black population.

The four community-based organizations that were included in our surveys—civic organizations, street block committees, squatter or tenant committees, and anticrime groups—lost some ground in the years after the election in 1994, but were able to reclaim most of it between 1998 and 2000. With the exception of the anticrime groups, these were predominantly "Black" organizations. On average, participation levels among Black South Africans were three to four times higher than those among the other groups. The anticrime groups were the only exception, as in 2000 more White people (10%) were engaged in such groups than Black people (8%).

The five organizations in the sociocultural domain also managed to retain their active membership, whereas women's and educational organizations even showed some growth. On the whole, they all went through the same cycles as every CSO in South Africa: a decline in membership after the first election, an increase at the time of the second election, and some levelling off in the final year of our study. The racial distribution of membership over the five types of organizations showed some interesting variation. Unlike any other organizations, cultural organizations showed the largest membership among the Asian population (around 13% as compared to around 10%, 3%, and 7% for the Blacks, Coloureds, and Whites, respectively). Youth and women's organizations were about twice as large among the Black population (8% to 10%) than among the other population groups (3% to 5%). Initially this also held for educational and environmental organizations, but in 2000 Black, Asian, and White South Africans supported those organizations in approximately the same proportions (8% to 10% for educational organizations and 3% to 4% for environmental organizations). Only the Coloured population lagged behind (3% and 2%, respectively).

In 1998, we began to ask whether people were involved in burial societies and/or stokvels. These were essentially economic support organizations that existed primarily in Black communities (30% of the Blacks were involved in such organizations), although there were some in the Coloured communities as well (about 10% of the Coloureds were members of such organizations).

Finally, church organizations were by far the most important organizations in South Africa. Church organizations experienced the same cycle all civil society organizations went through. Active participation declined in the years between 1994 and 1997, but then recovered and reached approximately the same level as in 1994. This, at least, was the pattern we observed among the Black population. Among the Coloureds and Whites, the 1994 level was not reached again. Among both groups, the level of participation fluctuated considerably, but both were some 10% below the initial level. Church organizations were relatively unimportant among the Asian population, fluctuating between 10% and 15%.

In summary, although we witnessed a decline in active participation in civil society organizations immediately after the 1994 election, we found in the longer run little evidence of a demobilization of civil society in South Africa in the course of the transition process. Among the three minority groups (Coloureds, Asians, and Whites) levels of participation remained more or less stable after the initial decline; among the Black population we witnessed a strong increase. The net result of all the discussed trends was that in 2000 only 2% fewer South Africans participated in some civil society organization than in 1994 (56% compared to 58%). This is not to say that nothing changed. On the contrary, the profile of the citizens' involvement changed significantly. Political parties lost half of their active participants, trade unions and sociocultural organizations gained active participants, and community-based organizations consolidated their share of citizen participation. These trends might signal a depoliticization of civil society, but political parties do not hold a monopoly in policymaking, because other civil society organizations are involved in politics as well.

We proposed that the South African society has changed to lower levels of statism and corporateness. The accompanying reconfiguration of civil society, according to Schofer and Fourcade-Gourinchas (2001), would mean an increase in participation in CSOs, with an emphasis on 'new' or 'old' social movement associations depending on whether statism or corporateness would reduce more. Our findings suggest that in South Africa both 'old' and 'new' movement organizations have at least consolidated their positions and, in most cases during the last years of our study, expanded their share. Altogether participation in CSOs has grown after the initial decline following the election in 1994. In that respect the transition to democracy in South Africa seems to have triggered the same increase in associational involvement that Schofer and Fourcade-Gourinchas reported as a trend throughout the democratic world.

Determinants of Participation

It is clear from the previous section that people differed considerably in their levels of participation in various civil society organizations. What were the determinants of these differences? Obviously, the four population categories differed significantly in their membership patterns both quantitatively and qualitatively. But did such individual characteristics as social class, being unemployed, age, gender, education, and living in the center or periphery make a difference in addition to race? And what about patterns of identification? Did people who displayed different patterns of identification exhibit different patterns of participation? These are the questions that concern us in the second part of this chapter.

Race alone explained between 2% and 5% of the variance in participation in civil society organizations, depending on the combination of organizations included in the analyses.[3] The remaining individual characteristics added 3% to 4%, and patterns of identification added another percentage point to the variance explained. Altogether race, individual characteristics, and patterns of identification explained 7% to 8% of the variance in participation in grass roots organizations. With the exception of age, all characteristics contributed independently of the others. Living standard appeared to be the strongest determinant ($\beta = .15$), followed by level of education ($\beta = .12$) and unemployment ($\beta = -.07$). Gender and living

---

[3]We conducted regression analyses with summary measures based on participation in the 8 organizations that were included all the time, the 11 that were included since 1995, the 14 that were included since 1998, and the 15 that were included since 1999. All these regression analyses revealed the same pattern.

in the center or periphery were the weakest determinants (β = -.04 and β = .03, respectively). People were more embedded in civil society if they had a higher living standard, were better educated, were employed rather than unemployed, were male rather than female, and lived in the periphery rather than the center. In this respect, our findings seem to be comparable to those reported in the literature on involvement in voluntary associations (Curtis et al., 2001; Schofer & Fourcade-Gourinchas, 2001). Apparently, associational involvement obeys the same rules in South Africa as everywhere else.

As for identification patterns, people were more involved in civil society if they identified with some group in the South African community (β = .10). Obviously, involvement in civil society organizations is related to someone's social identity.

Individual Characteristics and Participation

The findings in the previous section were based on summary measures of participation. There is, however, reason to assume that individual characteristics such as those included in our study varied in their impact on participation in individual organizations. In this section, we unpack these global correlations and look into the more detailed links between membership in specific organizations and individual characteristics. In the next section, we do the same for identification patterns.

Social Class

People who were more embedded in civil society had a higher living standard. Did this hold for every organization or did organizations differ in this respect? In order to look more closely into the link with social class, we categorized our respondents into four groups on the basis of different living standards and compared levels of participation of the four groups. Indeed, living standard was linked to participation in all types of organizations, but not always equally strong, and perhaps more interesting, for all but one type of organization (churches), we found a curvilinear relationship, with the lowest and the highest classes participating less than the two middle classes. This implies that the linear beta coefficient underestimates the relationship between the two variables. In two cases, the differences were larger than average: membership of hawker associations and membership of burial societies or stokvels (eta = .16 and .25, respectively). In seven cases, etas were below average (.05 to .10): trade unions, cultural organizations, church organizations, women's organizations, educational organizations, landowner committees, and environmental organizations. The remaining etas ranked in between (.12 to .14): political parties, youth organizations, civic organizations, street block committees, and squatter and tenant committees. Church organizations were the only organizations that deviated from the general pattern, as they drew a smaller proportion from the lowest class, but equal proportions from the three others.

Unemployment

People who were unemployed were less likely to participate in grass roots organizations. However, when we unpacked the components of this global correlation, the relationship between unemployment and participation appeared to be dependent on the organization. Sometimes the unemployed were less involved, but sometimes they were more involved. This explains why the correlation with the overall measure of involvement was relatively low. The unemployed were less involved in trade unions, church organizations, and educational organizations (etas .10, .04, and .04, respectively), but more involved in youth and women's organizations, civics, street block and squatter/tenant committees, hawker associations, and burial societies and stokvels (etas between .03 and .06). Being unemployed or not did not make a difference for participation in political parties, cultural and environmental organizations, landowner committees, and anticrime groups.

Level of Education

Higher levels of education made it more likely for people to be involved in civil society. At the level of individual organizations, this held for seven of the organizations: political parties, trade unions, cultural, youth, church and educational organizations, and anticrime groups (etas ranging from .03 to .12). However, for seven other organizations the relationship was the opposite: civics, street block, squatter, tenant and landowner committees, hawker associations, and burial societies/stokvels (etas ranging from .03 to .18). This did, of course, lower the overall correlation between education and participation. Educational level did not influence involvement in environmental organizations.

Gender

Females were less involved in civil society organizations than males. On the whole, this appeared to be the case for most organizations (etas ranging from .03 to .11). There were three exceptions, however, which obviously lowered the global correlation between gender and involvement in civil society: Women were more involved in church organizations (eta = .06), women's organizations (eta = .23), and burial societies/stokvels (eta = .05). It is not surprising that women were more likely to be involved in women's organizations than men, nor should their stronger involvement in church organizations surprise us. Burial societies and stokvels are also more related to the social roles of females than to those of males.

Living in the Center or Periphery

People who lived in the periphery appeared to participate more in civil society organizations than people who lived in the center, but the correlation was weak. This is understandable in view of the fact that at the level of individual organizations the relation went in opposite directions for various organizations. Moreover, living in the center or periphery did not influence participation in trade unions, civics, street block, squatter/tenant and landowner committees, or youth, educational, and church organizations. Participation in political parties, cultural organizations, women's organizations, and burial societies/stokvels was more likely in the periphery than in the center (etas between .05 and .08), but participation in anticrime groups, hawker associations, and environmental organizations was more likely in the center (etas in the range of .07 to .10).

Individual characteristics obviously influenced participation in civil society organizations. With the exception of age, we found at an aggregated level the same correlates that Curtis et al. (2001) and Schofer and Fourcade-Gourinchas (2001) reported from their multination study. In South Africa, age did not have any impact on levels of participation, but social class, gender, employment, education, and living in the center or the periphery did. However, aggregated data are misleading, as the same individual characteristics appeared to encourage participation in some organizations, but discouraged participation in others. Indeed, after we had unpacked the global correlations, a more variegated picture emerged. As a consequence, global correlations tend to underestimate the strength of the relationship between individual characteristics and participation in CSOs.

Identification and Participation

People who identified with some group within the South African community participated more frequently in civil society organizations. Apparently, a sense of collective identity reinforces involvement in civil society organizations. This was, of course, to be expected. If people identify with other people with whom they share a place in society, they will be more likely to participate in organizations that relate to that place. This was indeed what we found. People with strong class identification were more likely to participate in labor unions, but also in hawker associations and burial societies or stokvels. Youth with a strong generational identification were more likely to participate in youth organizations. People who identify strongly with their neighborhood were more likely to participate in organizations such as civics, street block committees, and burial societies/stokvels. People with a strong political identification participated more frequently in political parties, and people with a strong religious identification were more likely to participate in church organizations. Women with a strong gender identification participated more often in women's organizations. Finally, people with a strong ethnic identification participated more frequently in political parties and church organizations, a finding that must be interpreted against the background that in South Africa both politics and religion are to a large extent ethnically demarcated. Of course, causality remains an open matter. Someone may become actively involved in associations because he or she identifies with the other members of the category, whereas, on the other hand, people involved in CSOs usually develop a feeling of we-ness, solidarity, and tolerance.

The Role of Civil Society Organizations

The previous sections bore evidence that civil society was not in decline. But did the role civil society plays in South Africa change?

Mediating Between Citizens and the State

One way of approaching this issue was to explore whether involvement in civil society organizations reinforced trust in government and stimulated involvement in politics. Therefore, we computed the correlations between trust in government, political interest, intention to vote, preparedness to participate in peaceful collective action and actual participation, on the one hand, and participation in grass roots organizations, on the other hand (Table 7.2). These correlations served as indicators of the mediating function of civil society organizations between citizens and the state.

The correlations in Table 7.2 are based on the combined data of the surveys since 1995. Because we were interested in the role of civil society in the new South Africa, we omitted the year 1994. Several observations can be made. The first is fairly straightforward. Participation in every civil society organization included in the survey strengthened trust in government, interest in politics, the intention to vote, the intention to participate in collective action, and actual participation in such action. That said, a few qualifications are to be made. Participation in church organizations was of limited weight. To be sure, the correlations were statistically significant, but they were very modest indeed. This is not surprising. Church organizations are—mostly although not necessarily—apolitical organizations. Thus one would not expect that participation in church organizations would strongly politicize people. Participation in political parties, on the other hand, generated the strongest correlations. This is not surprising either. Political parties are, after all, designed to mediate between citizens and the state. They are the specialists, so to speak. Yet, it is obvious that they were not holding a monopoly. On the contrary, a variety of organizations appeared to be active in the same market place. The correlations between level of involvement in these organizations and our indicators of political mediation fluctuated for all organizations more or less within the same latitude. These correlations basically tell us that involvement in civil society organizations increased involvement in the political domain, in the form of either more trust in government or higher levels of participation in both electoral and protest politics.

The correlations with the two indicators relating to protest politics (preparedness and reported participation) were on average higher than those relating to electoral politics. This finding suggests that participation in civil society organizations reinforced protest politics more than electoral politics. The finding that participation in grass roots organizations stimulated trust in government and political interest, on the other hand, is important because it underscores that the effect on participation in protest politics was rather a matter of being integrated in society than of being estranged from it.

On the whole, the observed correlations were much the same for the consecutive years of our study. Therefore, the correlations in Table 7.2 provide a good summary assessment of the mediating role of civil society organizations. There is, however, one significant exception to this rule. In the year 1999—the run-up to the second election—almost every correlation of participation in a civil society organization with trust in government

TABLE 7.2
The Role of Civil Society 1995-2000: Pearson correlations

	Trust in Government	Political Interest	Intention to Vote	Preparedness to Participate in Peaceful Action	Participated in Collective Action
Political party	.13	.23	.16	.21	.20
Trade union	.09	.17	.07	.19	.20
Hawkers association	.13	.15	.08	.16	.11
Land owners committee	.11	.16	.07	.14	.11
Civic organization	.14	.12	.10	.19	.16
Street block committee	.13	.10	.09	.17	.16
Squatters or tenants committee	.12	.09	.08	.18	.15
Anti-crime group	.11	.16	.06	.18	.18
Cultural organization	.06	.11	.06	.16	.13
Youth organization	.11	.14	.09	.20	.17
Women's organization	.10	.06	.06	.15	.09
Educational organization	.09	.15	.06	.19	.16
Environmental organization	.13	.13	.06	.12	.12
Burial society or stokvel[a]	.15	.08	.08	.13	.10
Church organization	.04	.04	.02	.04	.05

Note. [a]Stokvels are savings clubs where members rotate access to the money among its members on say a monthly basis (see, e.g., White, 1998).
All correlations are significant at $p < .01$.

doubled and then returned to a much lower level in 2000. We have mentioned already that in the years 1998 and 1999 the participation in grass roots organizations was higher than ever. Apparently, in the election year participation in those organizations also translated into higher levels of trust in government. The political-psychological dynamics behind this finding are not easy to define, but it appears that in the election year state and civil society were more intertwined.

The Old Versus the New State

Did the role of civil society change? To answer this question we compared the correlations in Table 7.2 with those for the year 1994—the last year of the old regime. As fewer organizations were included in our first survey we could only compare the seven organizations listed in Table 7.3.[4]

TABLE 7.3
The Role of Civil Society—Old and New: Pearson Correlations

	Trust in Government		Political Interest		Preparedness to Participate in Peaceful Action		Participated in Collective Action	
	1994	1995 >	1994	1995 >	1994	1995 >	1994	1995 >
Political party	-.09	.13	.24	.23	.30	.21	.25	.20
Trade union	-.04	.09	.15	.17	.19	.19	.15	.20
Cultural org.	.03	.06	.14	.11	.12	.16	.12	.13
Youth org.	-.08	.10	.14	.14	.22	.20	.19	.17
Civic org.	-.05	.14	.15	.12	.24	.19	.22	.16
Street block committee	-.07	.13	.14	.10	.23	.17	.21	.16
Church org.	.06	.04	.04	.04	.02	.04	.04	.05

The results with regard to trust in government immediately catch the eye. In 1994, with the exception of cultural and church organizations, people who were involved in civil society organizations trusted government less, whereas from 1995 onwards people who were involved in civil society organizations trusted government more. This reflects, of course, the change of power. It alludes to the fact that before that change took place, civil society mobilized against the state (Muthien & Olivier, 1999).

The results with regard to political interest were very much the same in 1994 and after 1994. Being involved in grass roots organizations increased interest in politics in the old and new South Africa alike.

The role of civil society organizations with regard to action mobilization seems to have changed, although not dramatically. Participation in political parties, civics, and street block committees stimulated preparedness to participate in collective action and actual participation in 1994 more than in the years after the change of power. On the other hand, participation in trade unions and in cultural organizations seem to have gone in the opposite direction. South Africans who were actively involved in those two types of organizations were more likely to be involved in collective action in the years after the change of regime than

---

[4] In samples of the size we are working with (2,286 in 1994 and over 14,000 in the years after 1994), correlations and differences between correlations of .03 are significant.

before. Youth organizations and church organizations retained their role in action mobilization, which was relatively important in the case of the former and negligible in the case of the latter.

The Transformation of Discontent Into Collective Action

Obviously, civil society organizations played a significant role in collective action mobilization. Klandermans (1997) argued that organizational networks are necessary conduits for the transformation of discontent into collective action. They support and constrain the social construction of collective identities and grievances, the politicization of collective identity, and the recruitment of participants. In the last section of this chapter, we test whether civil society organizations in South Africa actually played these roles. For that matter, we computed Pearson correlations between dissatisfaction, on the one hand, and preparedness to participate in peaceful action and actual participation in collective action, on the other hand, for people who were actively involved in civil society organizations and people who were not (Table 7.4).

TABLE 7.4
The Transformation of Discontent Into Collective Action: Pearson Correlations of Dissatisfaction With Action Preparedness and Participation by Involvement in Civil Society Organizations

	Preparedness to Participate in Peaceful Action		Participated in Collective Action	
	Not Involved	Actively Involved	Not Involved	Actively Involved
Political party	.06	.09	.02	.11
Trade union	.07	.10	.03	.10
Hawkers association	.06	.19	.01	.12
Land owners committee	.06	-.01	.02	-.01
Civic organization	.07	.04	.03	.12
Street block committee	.06	.14	.03	.13
Squatters or tenants committee	.03	.08	.01	.09
Anticrime group	.03	12	.00	.10
Cultural organization	.06	.16	.03	.09
Youth organization	.07	.05	.03	.11
Women's organization	.02	.10	.01	.04
Educational organization	.03	.08	.02	.00
Environmental organization	.04	.06	.01	.10
Burial society or stokvel[a]	.05	.09	.01	.00
Church organization	.05	.10	.02	.06

Note. [a]Stokvels are savings clubs where members rotate access to the money among its members on say a monthly basis (see, e.g., White, 1998).

A look at the findings with regard to actual participation reveals that participation in all but three types of organizations (landowner committees, educational organizations, and burial societies or stokvels) seems to have facilitated the transformation of grievances into actual participation in collective action. In the case of women's and church organizations, the differences between the correlations among the involved and noninvolved were relatively small, though significant, but for the others the differences ranged between .06 and .11.

Preparedness to participate in peaceful action revealed a more varied pattern. Among those who were not involved in CSOs small but usually significant correlations were found between discontent and action preparedness. The only exceptions were women's organizations. Among those who were actively involved, most correlations were significantly higher than among the noninvolved (differences ranging between .03 and .16). Landowner committees, civics, and youth and environmental organizations were the exceptions.

In summary

Involvement in civil society organizations did foster trust in government and involvement in politics. For obvious reasons, participation in political parties had the most influence and participation in church organizations the least. Participation in civil society organizations seemed to reinforce participation in protest politics more than participation in electoral politics. The role of civil society organizations changed significantly with the change of regime in 1994. Whereas in 1994 involvement in civil society made people trust government less, it made people trust government more after 1994, especially in 1999, the second election year. Civil society mobilized against the state before the change of power took place. With regard to the remaining indicators, we found no qualitative changes. Some organizations became less important for protest politics, others became more important. Finally, participation in civil society organizations helped people to translate discontent into collective action.

Conclusion

Civil society in the new South Africa continues to be vibrant and viable. Close to 60% of the South African population were actively involved in at least one of the organizations included in our study. Half of those participated in only one organization, usually a church organization. The remaining half participated in two or more organizations. Black South Africans were more involved in civil society organizations than any other population group. During the years of our study, 25% to 40% of the Blacks were involved in organizations other than churches as compared to 15% to 30% of the other populations groups. Whereas participation in grass roots organizations remained fairly stable among the Asians, Coloureds, and Whites, it declined significantly among the Blacks in the first years after the change of power, but recovered in the last few years. Apparently, it took some time for "Black civil society" to reorganize itself. After decades of mobilization against the state, "Black civil society" became the state. Thousands of officials left Black civil society organizations in order to move into government. The liberation movement literally took office (Klandermans et al., 1998).

Not only did substantial proportions of the populace participate in civil society organizations, but participation in these organizations also had a significant influence on people's assessment of government and on their interest and participation in politics. South Africans who were actively involved in civil society trusted government more, were more interested in politics, were more likely to vote in an election, and were more likely to participate in collective action. Obviously, such results leave the question of causality open. Indeed, the causal link between participation in civil society and political attitudes and behavior can go either way. However, if they were dissatisfied with some aspect of life, active participation in civil organizations made it more likely that they would turn that dissatisfaction into participation in collective action. In conclusion, there was very little evidence of demobilization, as civil society continued to mediate between citizens and the state. In fact, in the election year involvement in all types of associations increased—another demonstration of civil society's role between citizens and the state. We hold that the extent to which South Africans were embedded in civil society and the extent to which in the course of the transition process CSOs became involved in policymaking and in monitoring politics is part of the secret of the relatively peaceful and successful transition South Africa experiences.

Over the years, the configuration of civil society changed. Some organizations gained while others lost significance, the most important example of the latter being political parties. Not only did fewer people participate actively in political parties, but political parties also became less central in the mediation between citizens and the state. This process took place among the Blacks and Whites in particular; the Asians and Coloureds had always been less involved in politics and therefore had little to lose. In their introductory chapter in *The Politics of Social Protest: Comparative Perspectives on States and Social Movements*, Jenkins and Klandermans (1995) argued that social movement organizations are becoming increasingly important as an alternative to political parties in the process of mediation between citizens and the state. Meyer and Tarrow (1998) coined the phrase "social movement society" to refer to this phenomenon. South Africa seems to be no exception to that rule. Whereas fewer people participated in political parties, more people became actively involved in trade unions over the years. Community-based organizations and sociocultural organizations retained their position in the multiorganizational civil society. Among the latter type of organizations, women's organizations and educational organizations grew and became even more significant as intermediaries.

Active involvement in civil society reinforced participation in protest politics more than participation in electoral politics. This is not to say that civil society in the new South Africa mobilized against the state, as it did before the regime transition. In this respect, the comparison of 1994 with the years after 1994 was revealing. In 1994, active involvement in civil society meant both more participation in protest politics and less trust in government. After the change of power took place, involvement in civil society still meant more participation in protest politics; however, under the new regime it combined with more trust in government. These findings evidenced that, in addition to creating links between citizens and the state, civil society in South Africa began to play that other role Foweraker and Landman (2000) found so important, namely, ensuring accountability on the part of the state. In this context, protest is meant not to undermine or replace the regime, but to remind it to deliver the public goods it promised the people. Simon and Klandermans (2001) argued that rather than becoming estranged from the state, people who mobilize tend to identify with the larger community. Our findings with regard to patterns of identification support that assumption.

People's embeddedness in civil society appeared to be influenced by their place in society and patterns of identification related to that. People with a strong class identification were more likely to participate in labor unions, hawker associations, and burial societies; women with a strong gender identification were more likely to be actively involved in women's organizations; people who identified with their neighborhood were more often participating in community-based organizations such as civics and street block committees. People with a strong political identification were more actively involved in political parties, those with a strong religious identification in church organizations. Ethnic identification, finally, made it more likely that people would participate in political parties or church organizations. In other words, collective identity reinforced active involvement in civil society organizations. The more people identified with others who occupied the same place in society, the more likely they were to participate in organizations related to that place. Elsewhere, we have defined participation in an identity organization as the behavioral component of social identity (de Weerd & Klandermans, 1999). Indeed, such participation seems to be the behavioral expression of identification with a group or category. A strong subgroup identity combined with a strong national identity increased the likelihood that people would be actively involved in civil society. In fact, the two forms of identification (subgroup and superordinate national identity) reinforced each other. Obviously, the causality of this relation was unclear. A so-called dual identity may have generated higher levels of involvement in civil society, but the opposite causal path was equally plausible. A high level of involvement in civil society may have generated a strong dual identity. The most plausible assumption is that the two reinforced each other, because active involvement in civil society reinforced active participation in protest politics, which in turn bolstered collective identity.

References

Adler, G., & Webster, E. (1995). Challenging transition theory: The labour movement, radical reform and the transition in South Africa. *Politics and Society, 23*, 75.

Bothwell, R. (1998). Indicators of a healthy civil society. In John Burbridge (ed.) *Beyond Prince and Merchant: Citizen Participation and the Rise of Civil Society* (pp. 249-262). New York: Pact.

Camerer, L. (1992). *Civil society and democracy: The South African debate.* Paper presented at the Bi-annual Colloquium of the South African Political Science Association, Broederstroom, South Africa.

Curtis, J. E., Baer, D. E., & Grabb, E. G. (2001). Nations of joiners: Explaining voluntary association membership in democratic societies. *American Sociological Review, 66*, 783-805.

Curtis, R. L., & Zurcher, L. A. (1973). Stable resources of protest movements: The multi-organizational field. *Social Forces, 52*, 53-61.

de Weerd, M., & Klandermans, B. (1999). Group identification and social protest: Farmer's protest in the Netherlands. *European Journal of Social Psychology, 29,* 1073-1095.

Diamond, L. (1997). Civil society and democratic consolidation: Building a culture of democracy in a new South Africa. In R.A. Siddiqui (Ed.), *Subsaharan Africa in the 1990s: Challenges to democracy and development* (pp. 4-17). Westport: Preager.

Foweraker, J., & Landman, T. (2000). *Citizenship rights and social movements. A comparative and statistical analysis.* Oxford, England: Oxford University Press.

Gerlach, L. P., & Hine, V. G. (1970*). People, power, change: Movements of social transformation.* Indianapolis: Bobbs-Merill.

Ginsburg, D. (1996, February). *Transition theory and the labour movement.* Paper presented at the Social Movements conference in Durban, South Africa.

Greenstein, R., Heinrich, V., & Naidoo, K. (1998). *The state of civil society in South Africa: Past legacies, present realities, and future prospects.* Report by Community Agency for Social Enquiry (CASE) and the South African National NGO Coalition (SANGOCO).

Hyden, G. (1998). Building civil society at the turn of the millennium. In J. Burbidge (Ed.), *Beyond prince and merchant: Citizen participation and the rise of civil society* (pp. 17-46). New York: Pact.

Jenkins, J. C., & Klandermans, B. (1995). *The politics of social protest: Comparative perspectives on states and social movements.* Minneapolis/London: University of Minnesota Press/UCL Press.

Klandermans, B., Roefs, M., & Olivier, J. (1998). A movement takes office. In D. Meyer & S. Tarrow (Eds.), *The social movement society: Contentious politics for a new century* (pp. 173-194). Oxford: Rowland and Littlefield.

Klandermans, B. (1989a). Interorganizational networks. In B. Klandermans (Ed.), *Organizing for change: Social movement organizations in Europe and the United States, International Social Movement Research,* (Vol. 2, pp. 301-314). Greenwich, CT: JAI.

Klandermans, B. (1989b). Social movement organizations. In B. Klandermans (Ed.), *Organizing for change: Social movement organizations in Europe and the United States, International Social Movement Research,* (Vol. 2, pp. 1-20). Greenwich, CT: JAI.

Klandermans, B. (1992). The social construction of protest and multi-organizational fields. In A. Morris & C. Mueller (Eds.), *Frontiers in social movement theory* (pp. 77-103.). New Haven, CT: Yale University Press.

Klandermans, B. (1997). *The social psychology of protest.* Oxford: Blackwell.

Marais, H. (1998). *South Africa limits to change. The political economy of transition.* Cape Town: University of Cape Town Press.

McAdam, D., McCarthy, J. D., & Zald, M. N. (1996). *Comparative perspectives on social movements.* Cambridge, MA: Cambridge University Press.

McCarthy, J. D., & Zald, M. N. (1973). *The trend of social movements in America.* Morristown, NJ: General Learning Press.

Meyer, D., & Tarrow, S. (1998). *The social movement society: Contentious politics for a new century*. Boulder, CO: Rowman and Littlefield.

Mondak, J. (1998). Psychological approaches to social capital. *Political Psychology, 19*, 433-439.

Muthien, Y. G., & Olivier, J. (1999). The state and civil society: Implications for democracy in South Africa. *South African Review*, (No. 8.), Johannesburg, South Africa: Ravan.

Neidhardt, F. (1985). Einige Ideeen zu einer allgemeinen Theorie Sozialer Bewegungen [Some Ideas on a Theory of Social Movements]. In S. Hradil (Ed.), *Sozialstruktur in Umbruch* (pp. 193-204). Opladen, Germany: Leske Verlag und Budrich GmbH.

O'Donnell, G., & Schmitter, P. C. (1986). *Transitions from authoritarian rule: Tentative conclusions about uncertain democracies*. Baltimore: Johns Hopkins University Press.

Piven, F. F., & Cloward, R. A. (1979). *Poor people's movements: Why they succeed, how they fail*. New York: Vintage.

Sangoco. (1999). The state of civil society in South African.

Schmitter (1997). Bowling in the Bronx: The uncivil interstices between civil society and political society. In R. Fine & S. Rai (Eds.), *Civil society: Democratic perspectives* (pp. 94-114). Frane Cass: London.

Schofer, E., & Fourcade-Gourinchas, M. (2001).The Structurak contexts of civic engagement: Voluntary association membership in comparative perspective. *American Sociological Review, 66*, 806-828.

Simon, B., & Klandermans, B. (2001). Politicized collective identity: A social psychological analysis. *American Psychologist, 56*, 319-331.

Sztompka, P. (1998). Mistrusting civility: Predicament of a post-communist society. In J. C. Alexander (Ed.), *Real civil societies: Dilemmas of institutionalization* (pp. 191-210). London: Sage.

8

SOCIAL PARTICIPATION AND SOCIAL TRUST IN ADOLESCENCE: THE IMPORTANCE OF HETEROGENEOUS ENCOUNTERS

Constance Flanagan
Sukhdeep Gill
Leslie Gallay
The Pennsylvania State University

Trust is a unique attribute. It is both a dispositional aspect of individuals and a property of strong democracies. The lion's share of the literature has focused on the latter, perhaps because it has been the province of sociologists and political scientists. Our chapter approaches the topic from a different perspective, the point of view of human development. We look at the association between young people's participation in clubs, extracurricular activities, and community service, and their attitudes toward others in their communities and their fellow students at school. We argue two points: First, social isolation should be related to more negative views of others when compared to social participation either in clubs or community service, and second, engaging in community service has particular benefits for social trust. In contrast to "interest-based" organizations and activities that tend to pull a rather homogeneous group of individuals together, many community service activities offer opportunities to interact with others in the community that young people would otherwise not naturally encounter. We contend that group stereotypes are undermined in these encounters and that social trust is increased.

Trust is considered a fundamental underpinning of democratic polities and of civil society. In democracies, social order is not maintained by the state's coercive measures or even by legal constraints. Rather, rule by the people presumes that the people feel committed to a common or shared public good, requiring less need for personal vigilance or state surveillance measures. Instead, we can assume that, in general, others, like ourselves, are trustworthy, that is, people of good will who choose to do things that benefit rather than take advantage of fellow members of their community. In fact, theories in the political socialization tradition argued that the basis for political stability could be traced to the young child's belief that elected leaders were trustworthy, benevolent people who would make decisions with her best interests in mind

(Easton & Dennis, 1969). Social trust also strengthens civil society because it motivates and sustains cooperation. When we have a general faith in humanity, when we believe that people are typically not out for their own gain, we have less need for vigilance, less reason to worry about protecting our own competitive advantage. Instead, we can turn our attention to cooperating with fellow members of the community to preserve our common or public good.

From a psychological point of view, trust refers to our relationships with "others." They may be family, friends, acquaintances, strangers, or more abstract institutions such as the government. The essence of trust is an assumption that others have our best interests in mind, that they would choose to do things that help rather than harm us although they are free to choose otherwise. At an interpersonal level, with friends or family, such assumptions can be experientially grounded—confirmed or disconfirmed. In the case of the generalized "other," however, it is not clear why some individuals have a positive view of humanity while others are less willing to give people they do not know the benefit of the doubt (see Flanagan, 2003, for a discussion of the developmental roots of social trust).

Interpersonal trust that is based on close relationships is different from social trust. The distinction in the literature is that of thick versus thin trust. The former is rooted in and informed by regular contact with people we know, the latter a more expansive but less intense trust in people in general (Uslaner, 2002). The importance of the latter for democracy is that it extends the radius of humanity to which trust is applied (Putnam, 2000). Social trust taps a general view of humanity as either fair, helpful, and trustworthy, or out for their own advantage, as the following three survey items that tap this construct suggest:

Generally speaking, would you say that most people can be trusted or that you can't be too careful in dealing with people?

Would you say that most of the time people try to be helpful or that they are mostly just looking out for themselves?

Do you think that most people would try to take advantage of you if they got a chance or would they try to be fair?

Trends in Social Trust

Scholarly interest in the phenomenon of trust has increased of late due to concerns that Western societies may be experiencing a loss of trust that is particularly problematic in younger generations. Analyses of the General Social Survey indicate that the generation gap in beliefs that "most people are trustworthy, fair, and helpful" grew between 1985 and 1997 due to precipitous declines in such beliefs among the youngest cohorts (18- to 25-year-olds; Smith, in press). Like other adults today, the younger generation has less confidence in institutions such as the government or the press, but they are also more cynical about humanity in general (Smith, in press).

Why this is the case is not clear, although trends toward increasing materialism and self-interest may be implicated. Longitudinal analyses of data from the Monitoring the Future project show that declines in social trust among high school seniors can be traced to increasing commitments to materialist values over time (Rahn & Transue, 1998). What psychological dynamics may underlie this relationship? One possibility is the relationship between trust (of others) and our own trustworthiness in a context of competition for limited resources. That is, if accumulating material goods becomes a higher personal priority, we may be less likely to trust "others" who (like ourselves) must want to accrue more for themselves. They (like we) must be looking out for their competitive advantage. Thus, we should be vigilant about protecting our own. In this regard, it is worth noting that as economic disparities increase in a society, levels of social trust decline (Uslaner, 2002).

Experimental studies provide convergent evidence that competition for limited resources in a group decreases a sense of trust among the members (Dawes, van de Kragt, & Orbell, 1990). Developmental studies also suggest that trust is lower to the extent that winning or being superior to others in a particular domain is a core component of one's self-concept. For example, McGowan and McGowan (1991) found that high-school athletes who were starters for their teams were less likely to trust others when compared to their nonstarter teammates who presumably continued to play for reasons other than advancing themselves in the limelight.

Participation in Youth Organizations and Adult Civic Engagement

According to retrospective studies with adults, engagement during one's youth in extracurricular activities and community groups is related to the likelihood of being engaged in civic and political affairs in adulthood (Verba, Schlozman, & Brady, 1995; Youniss, McLellan, & Yates, 1997). With the exception of sports, adults who as young people were members of organizations like 4-H or stayed after school to work on the yearbook or participated in social movements during their college years are more likely than their peers who did not participate in such groups to vote, to attend community meetings, to be a member of the PTA, to be an officer in a community organization—in other words, to be engaged in and take responsibility for the affairs of their communities. Why?

In other work, we have argued that participation in such organizations develops an affinity for the community (Flanagan & Van Horn, 2003). Youth groups offer a chance to bond not only with peers but with an organization that has an identity in the community. Because their structure is informal, with group-based projects and young people in charge, these groups offer unique opportunities for youth to exercise rights and responsibilities in communities of membership. They allow members to identify with the group, have a voice in its collective decisions, and be held accountable to group processes and products.

However, because most of these nonformal groups are interest based, young people will be gaining this civic practice with peers who are similar to them. Empirical work indicates that the types of organizations in which one participates as a young person are related to the types of community organizations in which one is active as an adult (Van Horn, Flanagan, & Willits, 2002). From a developmental perspective, this makes sense if the exploration of interest-based activities is the route through which one consolidates identity. However, if the experiences of young people are to prepare them to participate as citizens in a diverse democracy, the policy question is, what kinds of participatory experiences do they need?

We contend that different kinds of participatory opportunities are important in the development and sustenance of trust. Our first point is that interest-based youth organizations such as community clubs or extracurricular activities at school provide excellent opportunities for developing the kind of "thick trust" that Putnam (2000) has described among people who get to know one another very well. Our second point is that community service offers unique opportunities for developing the "thin trust" (i.e., the generalized trust in others one does not know well), that is essential to democracies. It does so, we believe, by engaging youth with people who are different from them (whether in age, social background, culture, need, etc.). The learning that occurs in these encounters helps to undo stereotypes about others, for example, homeless people at a soup kitchen, the elderly at a nursing home, or children in a Head Start program.

Social Isolates Versus Socially Engaged Youth

Why might thick trust develop in interest-based youth groups? First, learning to trust others and being a trustworthy person are integral to the process of becoming a member of a peer group. These forms of social participation are opportunities to feel a sense of identification with and loyalty to the group and to gain an understanding of others based on real people. In contrast to families, where acceptance typically is assumed, trust among one's peers is earned by being reliable, by keeping promises, and by working together for the good of the relationship or the group. Young people demonstrate their loyalty to the group when they show up for a meeting or event or when they pitch in and do their share of the work load. The reciprocity between trustworthiness and trust is learned in peer groups. By fulfilling responsibilities to the group, young people show each other that they can be trusted to come through. And by learning about these same virtues in other members of the group, they develop social trust, that is, the belief that others will also work for the benefit of the group.

Why would these twin virtues of trustworthiness and trust be related to adult civic engagement and ultimately to the stability of a polity? One answer is that affective ties to the group and, by extension, the community, become integral to the young person's emerging identity. Extension of this identity into adulthood ultimately means that contributing to the community becomes, simply, the right thing to do. Typically, we consider the absence of such affective ties a problem for the individual and for the community as well. We refer to such youth as disaffected or alienated, as if they were strangers in their own society.

This brings us to the second reason that interest-based groups play a role in the development of trust, that is, that social participation, even in homogeneous interest-based groups is an opportunity to develop views of others based on real people, not stereotypes. In contrast to the malevolent images of "most others" found on entertainment television, we submit that youth who are involved in community groups, even relatively homogeneous ones, have regular encounters with real people who in general are fair, helpful, and not out for their own advantage. As a result, a positive view of others and a sense of trust is reinforced even when the others one encounters are similar to oneself. We know that both civic engagement and social trust are lower among adults who are social isolates and spend a lot of time watching television (Brehm & Rahn, 1997; Verba, Schlozman, & Brady, 1995). In addition, from time use studies we know that teenagers who are not involved in some type of organization are likely to spend significant amounts of their time alone, primarily watching entertainment TV (Larson, 2001). Although we are aware of no specific studies on social trust and TV viewing in children or adolescents, one study of 5th through 8th graders found an inverse relationship between interpersonal trust (a measure that included trust of parents, teachers, peers) and TV viewing (Ridley-Johnson, Chance, & Cooper, 1984).

Interest-Based Groups Versus Encounters With Diverse Others

Having outlined the benefits of social participation over isolation, we turn next to our second point—that is, that all social participation is not equal. Research with adults suggests that, whereas involvement in charitable organizations, community service, and groups with a diverse membership boosts trust, spending time in homogeneous or interest-based groups does not (Stolle, 1998; Uslaner, 2002).

Stated in terms of the relationship of social participation to democracy, we would argue that the individual's views about the polity may depend on how narrow or broad their experiences of the polity are. If one's experience of the community is narrowly defined, then those who can be trusted may also be narrowly defined. As Levi (1996) has pointed out in the literature on social capital, the distinction between trusting others who are similar to ourselves and extending that feeling to people we do not know is often murky. In fact, if group solidarity and internal bonds of trust exist at the expense of excluding others, one could argue that social capital in this form is a cost to democracy (Portes, 1998). To build a polity, trust must be extended beyond our closest associates or, to borrow from Dewey (1916), the relationships that members of a group have with other groups or networks of people must be "full and free" (p. 83).

Community Service

Social trust has not been a prominent variable in the research on community service or service learning. Yet, evidence from some programs shows a positive relationship between service learning and young people's attitudes towards cultural diversity and tolerance, and an inverse relationship with racial prejudice (Eyler & Giles, 1999; Melchior & Bailis, 2002), although such changes may be more likely for youth whose backgrounds place them at risk (Blyth, Saito, & Berkas, 1999) and for programs of sufficient duration (Myers-Lipton, 1994).

The process by which this occurs has received less attention. However, Yates and Youniss' (1997) study provides a compelling argument. They conducted a longitudinal study of high school students in a Catholic school who volunteered in a soup kitchen for the homeless as part of a class on social justice. Over time, the researchers found that the identities of some students changed as a result of their interactions with the homeless. This occurred in stages as students became aware of the humanity of homeless individuals, compared their own more privileged circumstances with the conditions that the homeless faced, and ultimately achieved a more transcendent identity. In our view, this speaks to the potential of community service projects for breaking down group stereotypes and for learning about and developing trust in others, especially if the projects put the young person in contact with people in need. Metz, McLellan, and Youniss (2003) found that, after a year of working in projects that served the needs of the poor, high school students were less likely to blame individuals for being poor and were more likely to see the systemic bases of poverty.

Hypotheses

Based on the literature on the positive relationship between participation in associational networks and social trust, we expected that youth who were social isolates would have lower levels of trust in others (measured as their positive views of people in their community and of fellow students at school) when compared to peers who participated either in clubs or in community volunteer work. Second, based on our belief that engagement in volunteer work exposes youth to a broader range of others than does engagement in interest-based clubs, we expected that youth who engaged in volunteer work would have higher levels of trust when compared to their peers who were only in clubs or were social isolates. Finally, within the group of youth who engaged in volunteer work, we expected to find higher levels of trust among those who were open to and learned from their volunteer experience when compared to peers who did volunteer work but felt that they learned nothing from the experience.

Methods

Sample

The data reported in this chapter were gathered as part of a project on youth intergroup relations and beliefs about social justice. Surveys were group administered in schools to an ethnically diverse sample of 12- to 18-year-olds (mean age of 15). The majority of the students were White, but approximately 300 students were from African American, Arab American, and Latino backgrounds. Schools were located in low-middle income communities that differed in their racial/ethnic mix. The analyses for this chapter are based on the responses of 1,031 youth.

Data Reduction and Analyses

We created a categorical variable based on adolescents' responses to two participation variables: a) whether they were involved in any community or school-based organizations or clubs, and b) whether they were engaged in any community service work. The resulting participation variable was coded (1) if the student was a member of clubs and volunteered ($N = 567$); (2) if the student volunteered but was not a member of any club ($N = 116$); (3) if the student was a member of a club but did not volunteer ($N = 211$); and (4) if the student did not participate in a club or in volunteer work ($N = 137$). In the first group, 269 young people participated in clubs both in the community and at school, 230 participated only at school, and 68 only in the community. In the third group, 40 participated both in community and in school-based groups, 136 participated only in school, and 35 only in the community.

The dependent variables were the youth's perceptions of the characteristics of fellow members of their communities and of their schools.

Items in each scale are listed in Tables 8.1 and 8.2. Coefficient alpha for each of the scales were acceptable (all scales above .71). Although these items are not the classic indicators, they do tap similar dimensions of social trust including the belief that people in general are fair, helpful to others, and committed to the collective well-being of their community. In addition, these measures overcome the methodological problem inherent in the classic items, that is, confusion about the referent the respondents are using for "most people." Our items tie the adolescents' perceptions of humanity to others in the actual environments in which youth are spending their time.

High scores on the first two community scales reflect youth's views that people in their communities are generally benevolent and pull together to resolve community problems. The third community scale addresses what has been referred to as the potential downside of social capital , that is, that strong internal bonds of trust in a community can be maintained by excluding newcomers (Portes, 1998). Thus, items in this scale tap adolescents' views that members of their community make newcomers, including people from different races and cultures, feel welcome. The last community measure focuses specifically on youth's views that the police are helpful and mete out justice fairly. These items have a more specific referent than the other scales. However, this referent is key to the role of trust in stabilizing polities. In political socialization literature, youth's attitudes toward the police are similar to their views about the state (Easton & Dennis, 1969).

TABLE 8.1
Adolescents' Views of "Others" in Their Communities

People are benevolent and trusting.
>   There are people I can ask for help when I need it.
>   People trust each other.
>   Most people try to make this a good place to live.
>   If someone has a problem, they can usually count on others to help them out.

Perception of collective efficacy.
>   Most people feel safe.
>   People pull together to help each other.
>   If there is a problem getting some service from the government, people could get the problem solved.
>   Every town has some problems. In general, people in my town work together to solve our problems.

People are open to newcomers.
>   When someone moves here, people are pretty nice to them.
>   People like to meet others from different races and cultures.
>   When someone moves here, people make them feel welcome.

The police are fair and helpful.
>   The police are fair to everyone.
>   Everyone can rely on the police to help them.

The two student scales tap dimensions of trust in the school context. Again, the youth's views of a generalized other are tied to a group, in this case, the student body at their school. The first scale reflects the view that most students are benevolent and committed to the good of the entire school community. The second reflects a climate of inclusion in which students feel trusted. Adolescents' sense of belonging or mattering in institutions such as schools has been consistently noted as a protective factor against a host of health risk behaviors (Resnick et al., 1997). Experimental studies have also shown that individuals are more willing to make personal sacrifices on behalf of a group when they feel a sense of solidarity with the group (Brewer & Gardner, 1996; Dawes et al., 1990).

Results and Discussion

Oneway analyses of variance were run with the four level participation variable as the independent variable and the seven scales measuring perceptions

TABLE 8.2
Adolescents' Views of Fellow Students at School

Student solidarity/pride
> Everyone tries to keep the school looking good.
> Most students seem to care about each other, even people they don't know well.
> Students feel like they're part of a community where people care about each other.
> Students feel like they're an important part of the school.
> Kids feel safe.
> Students feel proud to be a part of this school.

Student inclusion
> Students have a voice in what happens.
> Students are encouraged to express their opinions.
> Students can disagree with teachers as long as they are respectful.
> Students can disagree with each other as long as they are respectful.

of others in one's community and school as the dependent variables. Significant F-statistics were followed up with posthoc Scheffe tests. The results are presented in Table 8.3.

Social Isolates, Club Members, and Volunteers

Two conclusions are supported by these data. The first is that, as a general pattern, some level of participation is better than no participation. The adolescents who do not belong to or participate in any organization (the "neither" group in Table 8.3), whom we have labeled *social isolates*, have less positive views of others when compared to their peers in the other categories. However, based on the Scheffe test, this group was not significantly different on several dependent variables from the group who participated only in clubs. Even with this stringent test, however, the social isolates have less confidence in the police and are less likely to feel that students have a voice at school. This latter seems to be the most directly amenable to intervention because a major value of extracurricular activities and community-based youth organizations is the voice that students have in such groups (National Research Council & Institute of Medicine, 2002).

The second conclusion drawn from the data in Table 8.3 is that, generally, the more participation the better. Although not always statistically significant, this relationship is consistent across the dependent variables and generally linear. Those who both participate in clubs and do volunteer work have more positive views of fellow community members when compared to those who do volunteer work alone, a group which, in turn, is more positive than their peers who participate in clubs alone. This linear relationship between participation and trust also has been found in international comparisons in which, across seven countries, the greater the number of organizations in which a young person participated, the higher was his or her trust in others in the community (Buhl, 2001).

The Scheffe test is a stringent test of group contrasts. We argue that the overall pattern for trust in others in one's community supports the conclusions that (a) participating in some activity with others is better than isolation; (b) engaging in both clubs and volunteer work is better than either alone; and (c) if one had limited time and had to choose, opportunities to do community service may have greater potential for developing social trust when compared to interest-based clubs.

Finally, averaging across groups and comparing the degree to which young people have positive views of various aspects of their school and community climates, two dependent variables are lower overall: perceptions of a caring student climate at school and perceptions that the police are helpful and mete out justice fairly. Although we do not have independent observations to confirm the self-reports, these relatively low means on student solidarity are disconcerting insofar as other studies have shown that this aspect of a school's climate is positively related to young people's commitment to civic goals (Flanagan, Bowes, Jonsson, Csapo, & Sheblanova, 1998). Furthermore, if the perception of the generalized other among one's fellow students is somewhat misanthropic, one wonders whether this view might generalize to a misanthropic view of humanity. Because interventions to create more caring and trusting student climates have been successful (Battistich, Solomon, Watson, & Schaps, 1997), this may be a direction worth pursuing.

Second, the picture for trust in the police does not engender confidence. In the political socialization literature, attitudes towards the police are considered a good pulse on the younger generation's attitudes towards the state (Easton & Dennis, 1969). If this is so, there may be cause for concern. Not only do the results of our study reflect a relatively low endorsement that the police mete out justice fairly, but other work suggests that the breach in youth's relations with the police may be growing (Borrero, 2001).

What Do Young People Feel That They Learn From Engaging in Community Service?

We turn next to the second phase of our argument, that is, the potential of community service for learning about and de-stereotyping others. Adolescents in our study were asked, "Did you learn anything about yourself, about others, or about your community by doing this volunteer work?" Roughly 70% of those who volunteered said *yes*, 30% said *no*, and there were important differences between the two groups.

According to chi-square tests, there was a significant relationship between frequency of volunteering and learning from the experience: Whereas 37% of those who viewed volunteering as a learning experience had volunteered once a week for about a year, among those who did not learn from the experience, only 25% volunteered at least once a week. In contrast, 56% of those who learned and 70% of those who did not learn had volunteered only a few times. In other words, learning from one's participation in community

TABLE 8.3

Participation in Clubs and Community Service Work and Perceptions of "Others" in Community and School

	Clubs and Volunteer Work		Volunteer Work Only		Clubs Only		Neither		F statistic
	M	SD	M	SD	M	SD	M	SD	
				Community					
Benevolent	3.38[a]	.76	3.43[a]	.76	3.16[b]	.74	3.08[b]	.76	9.26
Open	3.35[a]	.77	3.41[a]	.80	3.22[ab]	.82	3.03[b]	.86	7.09
Efficacy	3.17[a]	.75	3.13[a]	.75	2.97[ab]	.81	2.83[b]	.74	8.44
Police are fair	2.89[a]	1.02	2.79[ab]	1.06	2.81[a]	1.08	2.48[b]	1.04	5.54
				Students at School					
Solidarity/care	2.81[a]	.80	2.85[a]	.78	2.70[ab]	.75	2.56[b]	.82	4.41
Inclusion/voice	3.55[a]	.86	3.52[a]	.91	3.51[a]	.82	3.22[b]	.93	5.18

Note. Means with different subscripts are significantly different based on Scheffe test.

service is related to how often one engages in service, a finding supported in other work on service learning (Billig, 2000; Melchior & Bailis, 2002).

We next ran the same set of dependent variables (perceptions of others in one's community and at school) for the two groups of youth who participated in community service, that is, participants who felt they learned something versus those who participated but said they did not learn anything. These results are presented in Table 8.4 and indicate that those youth who felt they learned something had more positive views of fellow students and members of their community when compared to their peers who volunteered but, in their own estimation, learned nothing from the experience.

TABLE 8.4
Learning From Community Service Work and Perceptions of "Others" in Community and School

	Learned		Did Not Learn		
	M	SD	M	SD	F statistic
Community Members					
Caring	3.43	.73	3.09	.74	24.89
Open	3.41	.73	3.12	.69	19.11
Effective	3.20	.72	2.94	.71	14.91
Police are Fair	2.95	.99	2.64	1.05	11.31
Students at School					
Solidarity	2.88	.75	2.61	.76	15.29
Democratic	3.67	.77	3.32	.88	23.91

These results remind us that what individuals bring to the community service experience plays a role in what they get out of it. One interpretation of these results is that the group who learned something from volunteering was more open-minded or had more positive views about others to begin with. Furthermore, their motivations for volunteering may have differed from their peers who did not learn from the experience. We know that adults who participate in volunteer organizations have different motivations for participating and that their length of service depends in part on whether the experience fulfills their needs (Omoto & Snyder, 1995). It is certainly possible that youth who say they learned from service work experienced a better match for what they expected to get from the experience. Alternatively, as others have noted, the specific content, that is, what the youth does as service, have everything to do with the outcome. Compared to functionary work, direct service with people in need is more likely to be related to the kinds of civic outcomes we would like to see (Metz et al., 2003).

What did young people feel that they learned from their community service experience? We put that question to the participants in our study who said they learned something. Examples of these open-ended responses are presented in Table 8.5 where we have organized responses into categories referring to what the student felt she or he learned (a) about him- or herself; (b) about others; and (c) about his or her relationship with others and the social contract that binds them. In the first category, youth noted that it felt good to be benevolent and that they became better persons in the process.

The second category, which we have called references to others, implies a change in the adolescent's attitudes toward or interactions with individuals in various social groups. For example, youth said they learned to get along with children, to respect the elderly, and to know and trust old people. These statements suggest that two changes may be going on in these encounters. The first involves a process of de-stereotyping. While meeting others in real concrete encounters through volunteer service, young people have the opportunity to, as one teen put it, "meet new people and learn that not all people are bad." Second, learning to get along with, know, trust, and respect others implies that the adolescent him- or herself is accommodating. This change is vital to democracy because resolving political issues requires citizens who are sensitive to the needs of others, open to alternative perspectives, and willing to compromise rather than only get their own way.

TABLE 8.5
Youths' Reflections on What They Learned From Participation in Community Service

About themselves
> Learned who I am and how people operate.
> Became a better person.
> I like helping and being around others.
> Feels good to help others—better than helping yourself.

About others
> Meet new people—Not all people are bad.
> Get along with children.
> Respect elderly.
> Got to know and to trust old people.

About relationships with others and the social contact that binds us together
> Learned that not everyone is as fortunate as I.
> People need and want help. Some need it just to get by.
> We all need help.
> Always give help because it will probably be there when you want it back.
> There are a lot of people who care and are willing to help.

Statements in the third category also capture what we have referred to as young people's understanding of the social contract. By this we mean their understanding of the conditions in which others in their society live and their beliefs about the obligations that members of a society owe one another. Some statements in this category reveal the young person's developing ideas about privilege and disadvantage and their appreciation of their own position of relative advantage vis-à-vis others. The recognition of the human condition they share with less advantaged others is part of the transformative process that Yates and Youniss (1997) contend young volunteers exposed to people in need go through. The youth's responses indicate not only that they recognize their relative position of privilege, but that they also realize that there may be occasions when they will be on the receiving end. The response "Always give help because it will probably be there when you want it back" suggests a view of the social contract that goes beyond charity. Not only the spirit of noblesse oblige should motivate us to help others but also the fact that we all benefit when an ethic of care binds a society of people together.

Finally, responses in this category reflect another means by which participation in community service might add to the collective stock of social trust, that is, by exposing young people to adults who care about others and devote their lives to the volunteer sector. One of the things youth in our study said that they learned was that "there are a lot of people who care," "there are a lot of people who are willing to help others." In the research on community service little attention is given to the fact that the leaders of voluntary organizations and the staff of human service agencies are typically people who give of themselves for the benefit of others in their communities. From a developmental point of view, these public servants, these models of good will, could be especially inspiring in the formative years. Whether or not young people will choose to do similar work as adults, they have gotten to know adults who do, which should enhance their views of the generalized other as helpful, fair, and trustworthy.

Conclusions

In her book *Democracy on Trial*, Elshtain (1995) notes "to be viable, a democracy depends on people with democratic dispositions who are prepared to work with those who are *different from themselves* towards shared ends and who have a commitment to civic goods that are not the possession of one person or one small group alone" (p. 2). We submit that the everyday opportunities the typical adolescent has for encounters with others are rather homogeneous. As a result of decreasing family size, age grading practices, social homogenization of neighborhoods, and school tracking, adolescents have fewer opportunities to interact with people who are different from them on a wide range of dimensions. This fact can have consequences for democracy.

In this regard, we believe there are two implications for youth programming and policy that one can take away from our study. First, social participation even in interest-based groups is better than isolation for the development of trust. Second, in addition to opportunities to participate in homogeneous groups, opportunities for more heterogeneous encounters and exchange are important means for adding to the stock of social trust that undergirds democracy. The opportunity to interact with people one would otherwise not get to know is a chance to learn about the basic benevolence of humanity.

Although participation in community-based organizations offers a number of potential civic benefits, the opportunities for young people to participate in such organizations are unevenly distributed across communities. In a recent analysis of the National Longitudinal Survey of Youth, Hart, Atkins, and Ford (1998) found that youth from more advantaged families are more likely to be involved in community clubs, teams, organizations, and service. They argue that socially advantaged communities have both the financial and social resources necessary to support such organizations. Because a larger pool of active adults is often available to serve as volunteers, adolescents in such communities are more likely to be reached by community-based organizations (Hart & Atkins, 2002). Not only are there fewer opportunities for structured social participation in poorer communities, but when programs do exist they are typically unpredictable and less sustainable than those in privileged communities.

We raise the issue of equity because, if opportunities for participation are unevenly distributed, this could result in an unequal distribution of social trust as well as other civic attitudes and competencies in younger generations. If youth in socially disadvantaged communities are not given the opportunity to contribute to their community, then the democratic foundations of these communities are weakened. In a perverse way, if these opportunities are unevenly distributed, community service programs themselves could be an early contributor to what Verba and his colleagues (Verba et al., 1995) have referred to as the political advantages that higher SES groups stockpile over their lifetimes.

It is not only opportunities for social connection and civic engagement but the types of opportunities to connect and engage that are important policy matters. Even when youth have adequate access to interest-based groups, these questions remain: Do they have opportunities to work with others who are different from themselves? Do they have practice in accommodating their own desires as they consider broader public needs? Do they have the opportunity to build networks of trust that extend beyond their local communities? The trends pointing to declines in social trust in younger generations are a cause for concern because of the role that trust plays in sustaining democracy and civil society. Given the increasingly normative expectation that community service should be integral to the education of American youth (Billig, 2000), the potential of these programs for increasing our collective stock of social trust should be explored.

ACKNOWLEDGMENTS

Support from the William T. Grant Foundation and the Carnegie Corporation of New York for the project described in this chapter is gratefully acknowledged.

References

Battistich, V., Solomon, D., Watson, M., & Schaps, E. (1997). Caring school communities. *Educational Psychologist, 32,* 137-151.

Billig, S. H. (2000). Research on K-12 school based service learning: The evidence builds. *Phi Delta Kappan, May,* 658-664.

Blyth, D. A., Saito, R., & Berkas, T. (1997). A quantitative study of the impact of service-learning programs. In A. S. Waterman, (Ed.), *Service-learning: Applications from the research* (pp. 39-56). Mahwah, NJ: Lawrence Erlbaum Associates.

Borrero, M. (2001). The widening mistrust between youth and police. *Families in Society, 82,* 399-408.

Brehm, J. & Rahn, W.M. (1997). Individual level evidence for the causes and consequences of social capital. *American Journal of Political Science, 41,* 888-1023.

Brewer, M. B., & Gardner, W. (1996). Who is this "we"? Levels of collective identity and self representations. *Journal of Personality and Social Psychology, 71,* 83-93.

Buhl, M. (2001, April). Involvement in free time activities and thoughts about society—Correlates and gender differences in seven nations. Paper presented at the biennial meetings of the Society for Research in Child Development, Minneapolis, MN.

Clary, E. G., & Snyder, M. (1999). The motivations to volunteer: Theoretical and practical considerations. *Current Directions in Psychological Science, 8,* 156-159.

Dawes, R. M., van de Kragt, A. J. C., & Orbell, J. (1990). Cooperation for the benefit of us—Not me, or my conscience. In J. J. Mansbridge (Ed.), *Beyond self-interest* (pp. 97-110). Chicago: University of Chicago Press.

Dewey, J. (1916). *Democracy and education: An introduction to the philosophy of education.* New York: The Free Press.

Easton, D., & Dennis, J. (1969). *Children in the political system.* New York: McGraw Hill.

Elshtain, J. B. (1995). *Democracy on trial.* New York: Basic Books.

Eyler, J., & Giles, D. E., Jr. (1999). *Where's the learning in service learning?* San Francisco: Jossey-Bass.

Flanagan, C. A. (2003). Trust, identity, and civic hope. *Applied Developmental Science, 7,* 164-170.

Flanagan, C., Bowes, J., Jonsson, B., Csapo, B., & Sheblanova, E. (1998). Ties that bind: Correlates of adolescents' civic commitments in seven countries. *Journal of Social Issues, 54,* 457 - 475.

Flanagan, C. A., & Van Horn, B. (2003). Youth civic development: A logical next step in community youth development. In F. A. Villarruel, D. F. Perkins, L. M. Borden, & J. G. Keith. *Community youth development: Practice, policy, and research* (pp. 273-296). Thousand Oaks, CA: Sage.

Hart, D., & Atkins, R. (2002). Civic competence in urban youth. *Applied Developmental Science, 6,* 227-236.

Hart, D., Atkins, R., & Ford, D. (1998). Urban America as a context for the development of moral identity in adolescence. *Journal of Social Issues, 54,* 513-530.

Larson, W. R. (2001). How U.S. children and adolescents spend time. *Current Directions in Psychological Science, 10,* 160-164.

Levi, M. (1996). Social and unsocial capital: A review essay on Robert Putnam's *Making democracy work. Politics & Society, 24,* 45-55.

McGowan, S. J., & McGowan, R. W. (1991). Trust and adolescent sports: Starters vs. nonstarters. *Perceptual and Motor Skills, 73,* 714.

Melchior, A., & Bailis, L. (2002). Impact of service-learning on civic attitudes and behaviors of middle and high school youth: Findings from three national evaluations. In A. Furco & S. Billig (Eds.), *Service-learning: The essence of the pedagogy* (pp. 201-221). Greenwich, CT: Information Age.

Metz, E., McLellan, J. A., & Youniss, J. (2003). Types of voluntary service and adolescents' civic development. *Journal of Adolescent Research, 18,* 188-203.

Metz, E., & Youniss, J. (2003). A demonstration that school-based required service does not deter—but heightens—volunteerism. *PS: Political Science and Politics, 36,* 281-286.

Myers-Lipton, S. (1994). *The effects of service-learning on college students' attitudes towards civic responsibility, international understanding, and racial prejudice.* Unpublished doctoral dissertation, University of Colorado, Boulder.

National Research Council & Institute of Medicine. (2002). *Community programs to promote youth development.* Washington, DC: National Academy Press.

Omoto, A. M., & Snyder, M. (1995). Sustained helping without obligation: Motivation, longevity of service, and perceived attitude change among AIDS volunteers. *Journal of Personality and Social Psychology, 68,* 671-686.

Portes, A. (1998). Social capital: Its origins and applications in modern sociology. *Annual Review of Sociology, 24,* 1-24.

Putnam, R. D. (2000). *Bowling alone: The collapse and revival of American community.* New York: Simon & Schuster.

Rahn, W. M., & Transue, J. E. (1998). Social trust and value change: The decline of social capital in American youth, 1976-1995. *Political Psychology, 19,* 545- 565.

Resnick, M. D., Bearman, P. S., Blum, R. W., Bauman, K. E., Harris, K. M., Jones, J., et al. (1997). Protecting adolescents from harm: Findings from the National Longitudinal Study on Adolescent Health. *JAMA, 278*(10), 823-832.

Ridley-Johnson, R., Chance, J. E., & Cooper, H. (1985). Correlates of children's television viewing: Expectancies, age, and sex. *Journal of Applied Developmental Psychology, 5,* 225-235.

Smith, T. (1997). Factors related to misanthropy in contemporary American society. *Social Science Research, 26,* 170-196.

Smith, T. (in press). The generation gap. In R. A. Settersten, Jr., F. F. Furstenburg, & R. G. Rumbaut, (Eds.), *On the frontier of adulthood: Theory, research, and public policy.* Chicago: University of Chicago Press.

Stolle, D. (1998). Bowling together, bowling alone: The development of generalized trust in voluntary associations. *Political Psychology, 19,* 497-525.

Uslaner, E. M. (2002). *The moral foundations of trust.* Cambridge, MA: Harvard University Press.

Van Horn, B., Flanagan, C. A., & Willits, F. K. (2002). *Youth, family and club experiences and adult civic engagement.* Manuscript submitted for publication.

Verba, S., Schlozman, K. L., & Brady, H. E. (1995*). Voice and equality: Civic voluntarism in American politics.* Cambridge, MA: Harvard University Press.

Yates, M., & Youniss, J. (1997). Community service and political-moral identity in adolescents. *Journal of Research on Adolescence, 6,* 271-284.

Youniss, J., McLellan, J. A., & Yates, M. (1997). What we know about engendering civic identity. *American Behavioral Scientist, 40,* 620-631.

9

DESIGNING INTERVENTIONS TO PROMOTE CIVIC ENGAGEMENT

Robert G. Bringle
Indiana University-Purdue University Indianapolis

Research on relationships and social networks supports the conclusion that there are mental health and physical health benefits that accrue from rich social connections and social participation (Piliavin, 2005). Other analyses lead to the conclusion that participation in social networks and communities is advantageous to the health of democracies, which, in turn, provides a basis for free enterprise and commerce (Putnam, 1995, 2000). In addition, the quality of life of individuals, in the most general sense, is tied to participation in social networks (Wright, 1999). This pattern of results provides a rationale for designing interventions to encourage, support, and enhance civic participation and for designing specific interventions for particular groups, including youth, retired persons, professional groups, and neighborhoods. This chapter focuses on *service learning*, which is a particular type of intervention that is designed to enhance educational outcomes and civic engagement among college students. There are many ways in which social psychology theory and research can contribute to and learn from the development of service learning as a purposive intervention to enhance cognitive and personal development, civic participation, volunteering, political participation, and intergroup relationships.

Service learning is defined as a "course-based, credit-bearing educational experience in which students (a) participate in an organized service activity that meets identified community needs and (b) reflect on the service activity in such a way as to gain further understanding of course content, a broader appreciation of the discipline, and an enhanced sense of civic responsibility" (Bringle & Hatcher, 1995, p. 112). Service learning is an academic enterprise. Although other forms of community service (e.g., volunteering) can have educational benefits, service learning deliberately integrates community service activities with stated educational objectives. This means that not just any community service activity is appropriate for a service learning class, but that the service activities must be selected for and coordinated with the educational objectives of the course. Furthermore, the community service activities should be meaningful not only for the student's educational outcome but also to the community. Thus, well-executed service learning classes represent an effective partnership between the campus and the community, with the instructor identifying service activities that are relevant to the educational agenda and community representatives ensuring that the students' community service is consistent with client and community interests (Enos & Troppe, 1996; Zlotkowski, 1999).

Service learning, then, is a course-based intervention with the dual purposes of (a) learning through service (i.e., enhancing educational outcomes through community service) and (b) learning to serve (i.e., enhancing the intentions and future behaviors of students to be engaged in their communities). Although service learning can occur in nonacademic settings and in K-12 settings, this discussion focuses on service learning in higher education. At Indiana University-Purdue University Indianapolis (IUPUI), which has 29,000 commuting students and a large representation of professional schools, service learning fits the mission of the institution, its urban setting, a tradition of practice-based instruction in communities, and the desire to develop a new model for higher education by making service an integral part of the campus culture.

Campus/Community Partnerships in Service Learning

High quality service learning classes demonstrate *reciprocity* between the campus and the community, with each giving and receiving. Developing good campus/community partnerships, particularly between service learning faculty and community-based agency personnel, is important for successful service learning experiences. Theory and research on relationships can prove useful for examining several aspects of campus/community partnerships (Bringle & Hatcher, 2002):

1. Relationship initiation: for example, having a clear mission and purpose, communicating what is sought and expected in a partnership, identifying rewarding partners, choosing partners from among the many potential partners, knowing what the other party values.
2. Relationship maintenance: for example, emphasizing the importance of fairness and equity, transforming motives from exchange (tit-for-tat) to a communal ("us") attitude, monitoring evidence of relationship development.
3. Relationship dissolution: for example, recognizing that length is not a good indicator of success, understanding how short-term relationships may be appropriate in some cases, terminating relationships without stress, guarding against exploitive relationships.

The analysis of relationship closeness by Berscheid, Snyder, and Omoto (1989) can be particularly useful in evaluating campus/community partnerships. They posit the following three characteristics as defining the degree of closeness: (a) frequency of interaction, (b) diversity of activities, and (c) interdependency. In evaluation of a 4-year HUD-sponsored Community Outreach Partnership Center that IUPUI operated in three Indianapolis neighborhoods, both university and community respondents acknowledged that, during the 4 years, the campus and community were interacting more frequently and doing more activities together, but that mutual influence had not yet been demonstrated. Furthermore, the respondents indicated that when there was influence, the campus was more likely to have influenced community affairs than vice versa (Muthiah & Reeser, 2000). These findings provided useful information for understanding how the relationship had changed over time and what needed to occur in the future to deepen the relationships between the campus and the neighborhoods.

Reflection in Service Learning

In addition to reciprocity between the educational goals and the community needs, high quality service learning includes deliberate, structured opportunities through which the student can connect the service experience to the academic course. These reflection activities can take a variety of forms, including journals, written assignments, group discussion, multimedia presentations, and reports to the community agency. Bringle and Hatcher (1999) posit that reflection activities should (a) clearly link the service experience to the course content and learning objectives; (b) be structured in terms of description, expectations, and the criteria for assessing the activity; (c) occur regularly during the semester so that students can develop the capacity to engage in deeper and broader examination of issues; (d) provide feedback from the instructor so that students learn how to improve their critical analysis and reflective practice; and (e) include the opportunity for students to explore, clarify, and alter their personal values. Bringle, Hatcher, Muthiah, and McIntosh (2001) conducted multiple regression analyses of data from service learning classes on seven campuses to evaluate the relative importance of regularity, structure, and clarification of values. Each of these three characteristics of reflection were significant predictors of the quality of the learning environment of the course: reflection that allowed clarification of values, cumulative $R = .58$; reflection that was regular, cumulative $R = .62$; and reflection that was structured, cumulative $R = .63$. The number of hours and the total pages of written reflection did not significantly predict the quality of the learning environment.

Social psychology offers interesting perspectives that are relevant to the role that written reflection plays in meeting educational, social, and personal goals of service learning. Pennebaker, Kiecolt-Glaser, and Glaser (1988) manipulated whether college students wrote about either traumatic experiences or superficial topics on 4 consecutive days. Those who wrote about the traumatic event, compared to the other group, had more favorable immune-system responses, less frequent health center visits, and higher subjective well-being. Similar effects about the benefits of writing have been found in many other studies on diverse groups ranging from grade-school children to nursing home residents. "Not only are there benefits to health, but also writing about emotional topics has been found to reduce anxiety and depression, improve grades in college, and . . . aid people in securing new jobs" (Pennebaker, 1990, p. 40).

Although Pennebaker's research focuses on writing about traumatic events, the results can be generalized to writing about other events that involve emotional content (e.g., empathetic responses to persons who are suffering). More relevant to the analysis of reflection in service learning, Pennebaker conducted analyses of essay content to determine if characteristics of the narratives were related to the writer's subsequent health and well-being. The most important factor that differentiated persons showing healthy improvements from those who did not was the ability to show marked improvement in their constructions of stories that contained causal thinking, insight, and self-reflection. These are attributes that educators may focus on as they construct reflection activities for students (Eyler, Giles, & Schmeide, 1996). Thus, reflection activities in service learning classes that are conducted regularly and promote both personally and academically meaningful exploration of experiences in service settings have the potential, if appropriately structured, to yield health and intellectual benefits to the student.

However, some risks may be associated with structuring reflection activities in a service learning course; instructors of service learning classes will need to keep these liabilities in mind. Batson, Fultz, Schoenrade, and Paduano (1987) conducted studies that examined critical self-reflection, which is an honest attempt to answer the question, "Why, *really*, am I doing good?" Batson and his colleagues (Batson et al., 1987) found that critical self-reflection caused a self-depreciating bias, which eroded the attribution that helping was done for altruistic reasons. The effect was particularly strong for those individuals who valued honest self-knowledge and those who were cognizant of the personal gain they would receive by helping others. All three of these conditions— reflection on motives, promoting self-knowledge, and personal gains for helping (e.g., course credit)—can exist in service learning courses. These results by Pennebaker (1990; Pennebaker et al., 1988) and Batson et al. illustrate the potential benefits and liabilities of written reflection, and subsequent research can clarify when, how, and why certain outcomes occur due to the nature of reflection in service learning classes.

What College Students Bring to Campus and Service Learning Classes

Recent surveys of college students demonstrate that a majority of entering students came to campus with prior experience in voluntary service, but that campuses failed to keep these students engaged at a similar rate during college (Sax & Astin, 1997). In order to study the motives and experiences that students bring to the college classroom, Bringle, Madjuka, Hatcher, and McIntosh (2002) conducted a survey of 550 entering IUPUI students. Because IUPUI has a large number of professional programs, we were interested in how professional students, and business majors in particular, might differ from other college students; the sample was analyzed according to the following groups:

prospective business majors, prospective professional school majors, and prospective liberal arts, science, and humanities majors. Consistent with past research by others, 25% of these entering students had not volunteered in the past 5 years. In addition, during the last year, 25% of the students had volunteered 20 hours or more (Bringle et al. 2002).

Motives

Given this prior experience, what different motives for volunteering do college student bring to campuses that can provide a basis from which educators can tailor experiences that match motives? The Volunteer Functions Inventory (VFI; Clary et al., 1998) provides a measure of six functions that are served through volunteer activity:

1. Values: the degree to which volunteering expresses altruistic and humanitarian concern for others.
2. Understanding: the degree to which volunteering provides opportunities for new learning experiences and to use knowledge, skills, and abilities.
3. Social: the degree to which volunteering allows the person to be with friends and receive the recognition of others.
4. Career: the degree to which volunteering promotes clarity about vocational choices.
5. Protective: the degree to which volunteering allows the person to avoid guilt and cope better with personal problems.
6. Enhancement: the degree to which volunteering promotes an individual's sense of personal growth and positive feelings.

Entering IUPUI students reported that the most salient reason for volunteering was *values* ($M = 5.44$ on a 7-point response scale), followed by *understanding* ($M = 4.91$), *enhancement* ($M = 4.38$), *career* ($M = 4.01$), *protection* ($M = 3.23$), and then *social* ($M = 3.02$; Bringle et al., 2002). These results suggest that students arrived with a strong intrinsic interest in helping others. Furthermore, these students reported that both cognitive and personal development were strong motives, stronger than the more pragmatic motives of furthering their career, reducing personal guilt, and making friends. In addition, when motives were examined by intended major (business vs. professional vs. humanities/arts/science), no differences existed among the motives of Understanding, Protective, Social, Career, or Enhancement. Both business majors ($M = 5.30$) and other professional majors ($M = 5.38$) scored lower than arts/sciences/humanities majors ($M = 5.63$) on Values; however, Values was still the strongest motive for volunteering for those two groups of students (Bringle et al., 2002).

Interest in Types of Service

Respondents were asked to indicate their level of interest in different types of service opportunities that colleges might make available. The most interest was indicated for one-time service activities (30% saying "very interested"), followed by service as an option in a course (28%) and paid community service (27%). International service (19%), service learning classes (12%), and long-term immersion community service (8%) had the least interest (Bringle et al., 2002). No differences were evident among majors for the different types of service, although business majors were less interested in immersion service than the other two groups.

Predicting Interest in Types of Service

In order to understand interest in enrolling in a service learning class, multiple regression analyses were conducted. The two significant predictors of interest in enrolling in a service learning class were Understanding and Values, the motives that are most central to the service and learning components of service learning (Bringle, Hatcher, & McIntosh, 1999).

Obstacles

Respondents were also asked to rate the importance of various obstacles. The most common reasons for not becoming involved were lack of time (89% indicated "very" or "somewhat" significant) and inflexibility of their schedule (75%), followed by lack of information about opportunities (57%). Most important to subsequent analyses and discussion, 42% indicated that lack of interest in volunteering was either "very" or "somewhat" significant (Bringle, Hatcher, & McIntosh, 1999).

Discussion

The results indicate that many, but not all, students had been active in volunteering prior to college, that they brought a well-developed motive base for volunteering to college, and that this characterization fit students from all majors, with minor exceptions. Thus, volunteering in the community has rather even appeal for all types of students and can be considered as a viable component across the curriculum. Values and Understanding, the two key aspects of a service learning class, were the only motives that were identified as related to interest in enrolling in service learning classes; these were the two strongest motives among entering students. This is important because Clary et al. (1998) contend that matching volunteers' motives to the capacity of a volunteer activity to satisfy particular volunteer needs is critical to sustaining involvement. However, college students, and particularly commuting students on our campus who work more than students at peer institutions, reported that time and schedule were major impediments to becoming involved in community service. Furthermore, these obstacles resulted in a lack of interest in volunteering for about one half of the entering students. This suggests that one of the best ways in which to involve students in community service is through the classroom because they have little time for extracurricular involvement.

Benefits of Service Learning

Does service learning, as an intervention, enhance students' commitment to civic involvement? Astin and Sax (1998; Sax & Astin, 1997) found, in a large 5-year, postgraduation follow-up survey, that outcomes associated with involvement in community service and service learning during the college years include gains in civic responsibility (e.g., future plans to volunteer, efficacy to change society, commitment to influence social values), gains in academic development (e.g., contact with faculty, aspirations for advanced degree), and gains in life skills (e.g., leadership skills, interpersonal skills, conflict resolution skills) when compared to nonparticipating students and covarying out pre-existing differences (Sax & Astin, 1997).

Furthermore, students who participate in service learning reported increased interaction with faculty and peers (Astin & Sax, 1998; Giles, Eyler, & Braxton, 1997), greater relevance of coursework to career clarification (Keen & Keen, 1998; Vogelgesang & Astin, 2000), stronger commitment to social responsibility and future volunteering (Astin & Sax, 1998; Gray et al., 1996; Markus, Howard, & King, 1993; Perry & Katula 2001), improved learning (Astin & Sax, 1998; Eyler & Giles, 1999; Markus et al., 1993), improved ability to think critically about complex problems (Batchelder & Root, 1994; Eyler & Giles, 1999), increased racial understanding and tolerance (Vogelgesang & Astin, 2000), and greater satisfaction with the learning experience (Gray et al., 1996) than undergraduates who do not participate in a service learning courses.

Our research on IUPUI students, who represent a broad cross-section of demographic characteristics, indicates that students enrolled in service learning courses reported significantly more favorable outcomes on several key dimensions of IUPUI's Principles of Undergraduate Learning (see Table 9.1), when compared to a random sample of returning students who responded to the same survey items.

Roles for Social Psychological Theory and Research

The psychological literature is strongly related to issues in designing and implementing effective service learning experiences for students. Specific examples of the application of psychological theories are contained in the AAHE psychology monograph (Bringle & Duffy, 1998) and the issue of *Journal of Social Issues* edited by Stukas and Dunlap (2002). This section illustrates some interesting applications.

TABLE 9.1
Means for Items on Which Service Learning Students Reported Significantly Greater Outcomes Than Returning Undergraduates in General

Items	Service Learning Students	Returning Students
In-depth understanding of course material	3.77	3.32
Ability to critically examine ideas and issues	3.86	3.20
Ability to relate knowledge with practice	4.09	3.29
Ability to express facts, ideas, etc., in writing	3.60	3.34
Speaking in a small group setting	3.67	3.22
Speaking to a large group	3.16	2.69
Ability to integrate knowledge from several fields	3.55	3.15
Ability to view events from different perspectives	3.87	2.97
Developing a sense of values and ethical standards	3.64	2.76
Ability to make sense of personal and social experiences	3.84	2.87
Understanding different people and traditions	3.79	2.87

Note. Each mean difference in a row is significant at $p < .05$.

Intergroup Contact Theory

Service learning typically involves college students in service settings in the nonprofit sector. The most frequent service activity is tutoring in K-12 schools, often inner-city schools, although college students work with many disenfranchised populations, including homeless, youth, victims of violence, sick and disabled persons, and elderly (Campus Compact, 2001). As such, students are in unfamiliar community settings and interact with persons with whom they differ on several characteristics (e.g., age, class, race, education) and for whom they may have prejudices and stereotypes. A promising educational outcome is that the service learning experience can have positive effects on their understanding and relationships to other groups in society.

The typical approach to diversity education focuses on changing attitudes, and thus beliefs and feelings, of students about other groups (Erickson & O'Connor, 2000). This approach reflects one of the most fundamental tenets of social psychology, which assumes that if one changes attitudes, beliefs, and feelings, then behavior will subsequently be altered. In contrast, service learning is based on the alternative causal sequence that changing behavior can result in changed attitudes. Thus, service learning places students in situations with others who are different and anticipates that their experiences are such that changes in attitudes will follow.

The intergroup contact theory can contribute to the design of service learning classes because each of its components (i.e., pursuit of common goals, equal status, contact that contradicts stereotypes, long-term contact, norms) has the potential (a) to be present in service learning and reduce prejudice ("Pro" in Table 9.2), or (b) to be absent ("Con") and strengthen prejudices, stereotypes, and discrimination (Erickson & O'Connor, 2000). This analysis demonstrates how social psychological research can guide the design of these educational experiences so that they produce the desired outcomes and avoid unintended results.

TABLE 9.2
Potential Effects of Intergroup Contact Variables on Service Learning

Pursuit of common goals
> Pro: Students and community have aligned interests.
> Con: Students and community have different interests.

Equal status
> Pro: Students and community work together as equals, both giving and taking.
> Con: Hierarchical relationships with power differences are established.

Contact contradicts stereotypes
> Pro: Contact results in increased familiarity, which results in perceptions of similarity.
> Con: Contact reinforces stereotypes.

Long-term contact
> Pro: Service learning provides regular contact and deep involvement.
> Con: Service learning provides short-term contact and shallow involvement.

Norms
> Pro: Service learning promotes interdependency, justice, and empathy.
> Con: Service learning promotes a charity model.

Attribution Theory

A second area in which social psychology can contribute to the practice of service learning is *attribution theory*. Bringle and Velo (1998) examined how engaging in community service produces numerous attributional tasks, including students making attributions about those they are helping, self-attributions about their motives for helping, attributions by recipients about why the students are helping, and attributions about why help is needed. Morton (1995) observes that campus-community relationships are too often rooted in charity rather than justice. Charity occurs when resources and surpluses are given from one community ("haves") to another community ("have nots"; see Nadler, 2002), whereas justice is demonstrated when resources are considered to be common property and shared accordingly. Traditionally, faculty rely on a charity model, rather than a justice model, when working with community partners (Morton, 1995). Harkavy and Puckett (1991) note that the expert model, which is frequently used by faculty members, is one in which the relationships are elitist, hierarchical, and unidimensional (also see Nadler, 2002) rather than collegial, participatory, cooperative, and democratic. The risk is that service learning may create hierarchical relationships that promote a charity model, power differentials, dependency, and counterproductive attributions by students and recipients. There is also a risk that students engaged in community service will make defensive attributions of blaming the victim, a response generated by a belief in the Just World Hypothesis.   However, exemplary service learning should promote a democratic, collaborative, reciprocal approach to the relationships that lessen these risks and that promote the use of nonstigmatizing attributions.

What Are the Consequences of Requiring Service in Service Learning Classes?

One approach to engaging students in community service is to work only with students who are motivated to be involved. Working with students who are committed to service has merit and deepening their experiences is a worthwhile goal.   However, working only with those motivated students is short-sighted and shirks our educational responsibility to foster change and development in all students. Rather than *achievement through selection* for a few students, we have a responsibility to produce *achievement through intervention* for as many students as is possible. Recall that our research found that the vast majority of our college students were not inclined to enroll in a service learning class.

As educators create learning environments to instill and develop philanthropic motives and voluntary action, they face the paradox of how to structure experiences that produce the desired goals. Requiring service is one structural element of service learning courses that is frequently used to engage students in educationally meaningful service learning. However, requiring service contributes to controlling conditions that could undermine intrinsic motivation. Does it?

Stukas, Snyder, and Clary (1999) reported the results of a field study and a laboratory experiment on the effects of mandatory service. The field study focused on business students in a one-credit, tuition-free course through which they satisfied a 40-hour community service requirement. The second study by Stukas and colleagues was a laboratory study in which students were either required or induced to tape books for the blind, the latter being the choice condition. In both studies, they found a main effect (Table 9.3), indicating that requiring service resulted in lower motivation. In addition, there was an interaction, but the nature of the interaction was different for the two studies (see second and fourth rows of Table 9.3).

We conducted three studies that looked at the effects of required service.

Study 1

End-of-semester surveys for service learning classes at IUPUI were given to 267 students in 3-credit hour service learning classes.   The questionnaires had multiple-item measures of outcomes that are typically identified as goals in service learning classes: active learning, community in the classroom, attitudes toward service, leadership, academic persistence, career clarification, and course satisfaction (all with acceptable coefficient alphas; Bringle, Hatcher, & McIntosh, 1999).

TABLE 9.3
Summary of Research Results

	Stukas, Clary, & Snyder		IUPUI		
	Study 1	Study 2	Study 1	Study 2	Study 3
Requiring service lowered intention	Yes	Yes	Yes	No	Yes
Effect of noncontrolling intervention for extrinsically motivated students	No effect	Increased motivation	Increased motivation	No test	No test
Choice maintains motivation for experienced students	Yes	Yes	No test	No test	Yes
Controlling intervention adversely affects motivated students	Yes	Yes (?)	No test	No test	No

A comparison of outcomes for courses that required community service versus those that offered service learning as an option in the course found that students in optional service reported higher outcomes on all variables including civic responsibility, with the exception of leadership. There was no information on prior history of community service or motivation for community service; therefore, only the main effect could be examined in this study, not the interaction. The number of hours of community service in the service learning class did not interact with required versus optional on any of the outcome measures.

Study 2

Seventy-eight students enrolled in service learning classes at IUPUI completed a questionnaire with multi-item measures of the same outcomes as in the previous study (Bringle, Hatcher, & McIntosh, 1999). ANOVAs found no significant differences between students reporting required versus optional community service on active learning, community in the classroom, attitudes toward service, leadership, academic persistence, career clarification, and course satisfaction. In addition, there were no differences on any of the same variables for whether or not the students had prior knowledge that service was part of the course, suggesting that self-selection of students into service learning classes did not play a role.

Study 3

This study was an improvement on the previous two studies because it examined a broader range of courses on multiple campuses and collected additional information about the students and the courses (Bringle, Hatcher, Muthiah, & McIntosh, 2001). Questionnaires were distributed to 471 students enrolled in service learning classes on eight campuses. Questionnaires were distributed at the beginning and the end of the semester. The questionnaire at the beginning of the semester obtained background information on the students. To control for pre-existing differences between groups, the following variables from the questionnaire administered at the beginning of the semester were entered as covariates in all analyses: gender, age, high school GPA, first semester in college, anticipated semester GPA, credit hours enrolled this semester, level of service involvement in the past 4 years, level of parents' service involvement over past 4 years, father's educational level, mother's educational level, evidence of civic responsibility, and importance of graduating from this campus.

When the covariates were not entered, no significant difference was evident for required versus optional. A MANOVA with covariates found that in courses requiring service learning (vs. optional service learning), more interaction with peers, more relevance to future careers of students, and *less* civic responsibility was reported by students. Because one of the covariates was a measure of civic responsibility at the beginning of the semester and because Stukas et al. (1999) found an interaction, a median split on pretest civic responsibility was made and the data were reanalyzed as a 2 x 2 ANOVA with require/optional as one factor and low/high pretest civic responsibility as the other factor. There was a significant interaction, and simple effects tests suggested that for those students with *little* inclination toward civic responsibility, required community service was associated with significantly lower civic responsibility at the end of the semester when compared to optional community service.

Discussion of Research Results on Required Service

The outcomes from these five research studies present a puzzle because of the variations in results on key research questions for which there is information. Stukas and associates (Stukas et al., 1999) present results indicating that (a) required service was associated with lower civic responsibility than optional service (Study 1), and (b) required service eroded interest for those with a history of service (Study 1); but this was not clear in Study 2 (see Table 9.3). Although Stukas et al.'s research may still be relevant to service learning, this research was not focused on service learning because: (a) there was no course;

(b) there were no reflection activities, or at least reflection activities that satisfy the criteria of being regular, structured, bridging service and learning, allowing feedback, and clarifying goals (Bringle & Hatcher, 1999); and (c) there is no evidence of reciprocity with the community, although this might have been present in some cases. Results from our three studies found, consistent with Stukas et al.'s research, that optional service was associated with higher civic responsibility. However, unlike Stukas et al.'s results, we also found no differences associated with required service, and required service was associated with lowered civic responsibility only for those students with a history of lack of interest in community service (not those intrinsically motivated).

What is central to an analysis of the discrepancies in these findings is the degree to which all the different conditions that are present in service learning classes are perceived as *controlling* by students with differing motives. Rewards and requiring service can increase the perception of external regulation. However, rewards and required service can also produce opportunities for feedback that supports perceptions of competence. Research shows that to make rewards less controlling and more informational requires (a) minimizing the use of authoritarian style, (b) acknowledging good performance but not using rewards to strengthen or control behavior, (c) providing choices about how to do the task, and (d) emphasizing the interesting and challenging aspects of the task (Deci, Koestner, & Ryan, 1999; Deci & Ryan, 2000). The same is true of information and verbal feedback: It can be controlling, especially when it is expected, or it can facilitate growth, when it is unexpected and informative about competence. Thus, all of the research results may be accurate and their differences might be understood in terms of other qualities of the students' experiences that were not measured.

Role of Motivations

In addition to learning, service learning aims to have students demonstrate internalization of civic skills in a manner that is integrated with their sense of self. Deci and Ryan's Self-Determination Theory (SDT) provides a framework for examining the internalization of motivation (Deci et al., 1999; Deci & Ryan, 2000). They posit a continuum of different types of motivation:

1. *Amotivation*: The activity is not interesting, there are no skills that lead to the behavior, or the behavior will not lead to a desirable outcome.
2. *External Regulation*: Behaviors are performed to meet external demands or to obtain an external reward; behaviors are externally regulated. Thus, for this type of motivation, extrinsic rewards can modify responses and control behavior. However, what are the consequences of arranging these contingencies after the contingencies are discontinued? At the most general level, behavior is more likely to cease when the contingencies have been continuous and predictable, and is less likely to cease when the contingencies have been intermittent and less predictable.

3. *Introjected Regulation*: Behaviors are performed to avoid guilt, or to enhance the ego and feelings of self-worth. There may be some internal regulation, but the behavior is not an integrated part of the self.
4. *Identification*: Behavior is performed because the person identifies with its importance; for example, it is personally relevant, leads to other goals that are valued. Regulation is somewhat more internal than the previous types of motivation.
5. *Integrated Regulation*: Behaviors are fully assimilated with the self-concept and are consistent with other values and needs, but are still done because of their relationship to other outcomes.
6. *Intrinsic Motivation*: Behaviors are self-determined, fully integrated, and inherently satisfying.

Deci and Ryan note that, although this is a continuum, it is not necessarily a developmental continuum (Deci et al., 1999; Deci & Ryan, 2000). For example, one does not necessarily achieve growth and there is no necessary sequence to movement. Thus, a person can start anywhere and move in either direction.

Recall that our results showed marked variability in student interest for different kinds of service. If college students are well distributed across this motivational continuum, then educators need to consider different strategies for motivating students at different points on the continuum. For example, students may be *unmotivated* to participate in community service; if so, the only way in which they will be motivated is by external rewards, instrumental value, and external requirements. However, even if external motivation produces the targeted behavior, given the importance of internalization, the critical issue for educators concerns how to promote the growth of autonomous regulation of civic engagement for unmotivated students. Furthermore, educators want to ensure that students for whom community service is internally motivated or motivated by a mix of internal and external forces are nurtured toward the enhancement of self-determined behavior that is fully integrated and inherently satisfying. And, educators do not want to create circumstances that undermine intrinsic motivation.

One of the central propositions of SDT is that *external, controlling conditions only undermine the intrinsic motivation of those students who are intrinsically motivated*. Deci and Ryan (Deci et al., 1999; Deci & Ryan, 2000) differentiate several aspects of tangible rewards that can potentially undermine intrinsic motivation: (a) whether or not it is expected, (b) whether or not it is task contingent, and, (c) if it is task contingent, whether or not it is engagement contingent, completion contingent, or performance contingent.

So, what promotes and facilitates internalization of motivation? Verbal support is positively related to intrinsic motivation. Thus, encouraging, supporting, praising intrinsically motivated persons may be more important than whether or not they are required to do service. Why are verbal rewards so central to enhancing and maintaining intrinsic motivation? According to Deci and Ryan (Deci et al., 1999; Deci & Ryan, 2000), there are three factors that lead to internalization:

1. *Relatedness*: Developing a sense of belongingness and connectedness to other persons, groups, and society.
2. *Competence*: Developing an understanding of the activity and goal, and seeing that they have the relevant skills to succeed and sense satisfaction.
3. *Autonomy*: Controlling environments can promote relatedness and competence, and yield introjected motivation. However, grasping the meaning and worth of the goal, according to self-determination theory, only occurs when autonomy is present.

This theoretical analysis suggests that it is appropriate, even necessary, to provide external inducements and controlling conditions in order to involve unmotivated students in community service. The problem with extrinsic and tangible rewards is not that they can increase the target behavior, but that they can produce behavioral compliance without internal change. If so, then removing external controlling conditions will lead to a lower likelihood of the behavior continuing. Thus, if one of our goals as educators is to produce a transformation of motives from extrinsic to intrinsic, then service learning classes that require service must find ways to promote relatedness, competence, and autonomy.

Concerning relatedness, one of the more reliable findings from research (e.g., Eyler & Giles, 1999) is that service learning produces higher levels of student-student and student-faculty interaction than traditional classes, which should allow students to develop social connections. Connections to community service providers and to persons served would also be a basis for transforming motives from extrinsic to intrinsic.

In well-designed service learning courses, instructors select service sites that are (a) matched to the skill levels of the students, and (b) provide opportunities, either through training or service experiences, to develop a sense of efficacy, fulfillment, and helping substantively on an issue. Thus, service learning should promote feelings of competency even when students are required to engage in the service.

Finally, service learning instructors should design courses that promote perceptions of choice and autonomy among students. Does this mean that community service should never be required? According to SDT, autonomy does not have to be present throughout the entire experience for all students. If students are not motivated, then competence and relatedness can move their motivation toward integration. Autonomy is most important for completing the move to integration, not necessarily for starting the movement. Furthermore, different types of choices can influence the perception of autonomy. The difficulty is that *requiring* community service in a service learning class may be perceived by students as an option (student can choose to drop the class or switch sections). Similarly, *voluntary* or optional service in a class may be perceived by students as not being an option, depending on the attractiveness of the alternative choice.

How does this analysis help develop an understanding of the conflicting research results about required versus optional service in service learning classes in Table 9.3? SDT provides a useful conceptual framework for a more refined analysis of the role of required service in service learning. Subsequent research can clarify the role of these other constructs in SDT and, hopefully, provide more clarity than past research on how they are related to students' motives for future civic engagement. In addition, this analysis suggests additional issues for research on this question. First, the independent variable (required vs. optional) is quite gross and may mask important heterogeneity in these service learning classes on other characteristics that influence relatedness, competency, and autonomy. Second, numerous factors may promote the perception of choice and freedom in a course that requires community service. For example, students may have choice over placement sites, types of clients that they serve, types of volunteer activities at placement sites, and the type of reflection activities that they use to connect service and learning. Third, there may be other factors in a service learning class that matter more to the development of philanthropic tendencies in these courses, such as fostering an ethic for service, establishing norms that support engaging in service, and presenting a clear educational rationale for the service component of the course. Finally, the conflicting results may be due to students with different motivational sets being in classes with characteristics that are appropriate and inappropriate to the goal of increasing intrinsic motivation for service. For example, these classes may vary on the use of deadlines, threats, and surveillance, which are known to inhibit the development of intrinsic motivation (Deci et al., 1999; Deci & Ryan, 2000).

In order to evaluate the possibility that other course characteristics may be more important than whether or not the service is required, a stepwise multiple regression analysis was conducted on the data from Study 3 with students' civic responsibility at the end of the semester as the dependent variable and the following predictors: quality of the learning experience, characteristics of the service learning course, and required versus optional (Bringle et al., 2001). The most important predictor of attitudes of civic responsibility was the quality of the learning environment. Thus, when students have positive educational experiences in the community, they are more likely to be intrinsically motivated for community service in the future. The second predictor was the degree to which academic content was integrated with the community service. Again, the quality of the educational experience promotes future intentions for civic engagement. Required/optional was the next significant predictor. These results support the conclusion that other course characteristics are more important than whether or not service is required.

Conclusion

Service learning is an evolving intervention to promote civic engagement that is directed at college students, many of whom will assume important leadership roles in commerce, government, and the nonprofit sector. Service learning is particularly significant to higher education because of the role that service learning is playing in (a) transforming the nature of teaching and learning by adding breadth to the learning objectives across the curriculum, (b) involving students with faculty in civic engagement, (c) deepening the relationships of campuses to their communities, and (d) contributing to a broader agenda of the scholarship of engagement that includes teaching, research, and professional service in and with the community (Bringle, Games, & Malloy, 1999). Thus, service learning is one manifestation of the challenge that Boyer (1997) presented to higher education when he noted,

> the academy must become a more vigorous partner in the search for answers to our most pressing social, civic, economic, and moral problems, and must reaffirm its historic commitment to what I call the scholarship of engagement (p. 11).

The theory and research that have been presented are only a sample of topics that illustrate how social psychology can provide important input into the design of service learning courses (see Bringle & Duffy, 1998; Stukas & Dunlap, 2002). These examples demonstrate the potential risks and benefits that service learning can have on attributions, attitudes and prejudices, and campus/community partnerships. They also illustrate how designing service learning courses shapes the outcomes depending on choices made by the instructor about the nature of reflection activities, whether or not service is required, verbal support, feedback, relatedness, competency, and autonomy.

In addition, this discussion illustrates how service learning provides a powerful test bed that is both convenient and appropriate for evaluating these and many other hypotheses about increasing civic involvement among students. Studying service learning within the framework of social psychology can lead to improvements in instructional practice and contribute to social psychological theory.

The potential contribution of service learning to developing habits of community involvement in students is also important to their character and their role in democratic processes. The severity of this issue is illustrated through (a) the lack of political interest among college students in spite of rising rates of volunteering (Astin, 1999), and (b) descriptions of critical decreases in social capital, which is viewed as the bedrock of democratic processes (Putnam, 2000). What can be done to ensure that college students are prepared to be active citizens? Service learning may be one of the best solutions for ensuring the democratic well-being of a country (Astin, 1999). This is well illustrated in the Community-Higher Education-Service Partnership (CHESP) project in South Africa (Lazarus, 2001). With the first democratic election in 1994, the challenge facing South Africa no longer lies at the policy level, but at implementing new policies and a democratic government. CHESP is a national initiative that is directed at undoing the tragedy of apartheid and at implementing a working democracy. CHESP is piloting service learning in six South African universities with the goal of expanding it to all universities. The ultimate aim of CHESP is the reconstruction and development of South African civil society through the development of socially accountable models for higher education, research, community service, and development. Proposed in a white paper after the democratic elections, the Department of Education chose service learning as the most important change in higher education to promote intergroup understanding and develop democratic skills among college students. The significance of CHESP is that the stakes are so high for South Africa and that service learning is the method of choice. The work of CHESP provides a strong reminder of the significance that engaging college students in educationally meaningful service can play, not only in their education but also in their communities and their nation.

ACKNOWLEDGMENTS

I would like to thank Julie Hatcher and Richard Muthiah for assistance in preparing this chapter and Indiana Campus Compact and the Indiana University Center on Philanthropy for grants to support some of the research reported.

References

Astin, A. W. (1999). Promoting leadership, service, and democracy: What higher education can do. In R. G. Bringle, R. Games, & E. A. Malloy (Eds.), *Colleges and universities as citizens* (pp. 31-47). Needham Heights, MA: Allyn & Bacon.

Astin, A. W., & Sax, L. J. (1998). How undergraduates are affected by service participation. *Journal of College Student Development, 39*, 251-263.

Batchelder, T. H., & Root, S. (1994). Effects of an undergraduate program to integrate academic learning and service: Cognitive, prosocial cognitive, and identity outcomes. *Journal of Adolescence, 17*, 341-355.

Batson, C. D., Fultz, J., Schoenrade, P. A., & Paduano, A. (1987). Critical self-reflection and self-perceived altruism: When self-reward fails. *Journal of Personality and Social Psychology, 45*, 706-718.

Berscheid, E., Snyder, M., & Omoto, A. M. (1989). The Relationship Closeness Inventory: Assessing the closeness of interpersonal relationships. *Journal of Personality and Social Psychology, 57*, 792-807.

Boyer, E. L. (1997). The scholarship of engagement. *Journal of Public Service and Outreach, 1*(1), 11-20.

Bringle, R. G., & Duffy, D. K. (Eds.) (1998). *With service in mind: Concepts and models for service-learning in psychology.* Washington, DC: American Association for Higher Education.

Bringle, R. G., Games, R., & Malloy, E. A. (1999). *Colleges and universities as citizens.* Boston: Allyn & Bacon.

Bringle, R. G., & Hatcher, J. A. (1995). A service-learning curriculum for faculty. *Michigan Journal of Community Service Learning, 2,* 112-122.

Bringle, R. G., & Hatcher, J. A. (1999, Summer). Reflection is service-learning: Making meaning of experience. *Educational Horizons,* 179-185.

Bringle, R. G., & Hatcher, J. A. (2002). Campus-community partnerships: The terms of engagement. *Journal of Social Issues, 58,* 503-516.

Bringle, R. G., Hatcher, J. A., & McIntosh, R. (1999, October). *Student involvement in service and service learning.* Paper presented at the Association for Research on Nonprofit Organizations and Voluntary Action, Washington, DC.

Bringle, R. G., Hatcher, J. A., Muthiah, R., & McIntosh, R. (2001, October). *The case for required service in service-learning classes: A multi-campus study of service-learning.* Paper presented at the First Annual International Conference on Service-Learning Research, Berkeley, CA.

Bringle, R. G., Madjuka, R. J., Hatcher, J. A., & McIntosh, R. (2002). *Motives for service among entering college students: Implications for business education.* Manuscript in preparation.

Bringle, R. G., & Velo, P. M. (1998). Attributions about misery. In R. G. Bringle & D.K. Duffy (Eds.), *With service in mind: Concepts and models for service-learning in psychology* (pp. 51-67). Washington, DC: American Association for Higher Education.

Campus Compact. (2001). *Annual service statistics 2000.* Providence, RI: Author.

Clary, E. G., Snyder, M., Ridge, R. D., Copeland, J., Stukas, A. A., Haugen, J., & Miene, P. (1998). Understanding and assessing the motivations of volunteers: A functional approach. *Journal of Personality and Social Psychology, 74,* 1516-1530.

Deci, E. L., Koestner, R., & Ryan, R. M. (1999). A meta-analytic review of experiments examining the effects of extrinsic rewards on intrinsic motivation. *Psychological Bulletin, 125,* 627-668.

Deci, E. L., & Ryan, R. M. (2000). The "what" and "why" of goal pursuits: Human needs and the self-determination of behavior. *Psychological Inquiry, 11,* 227-268.

Enos, S. L., & Troppe, M. L. (1996). Service-learning in the curriculum. In B. Jacoby & Associates (Eds.), *Service-learning in higher education: Concepts and practices* (pp. 156-181). San Francisco: Jossey-Bass.

Erickson, J. A., & O'Connor, S. E. (2000). Service-learning: Does it promote or reduce prejudice? In C. O'Grady (Ed.), *Integrating service learning and multicultural education in colleges and universities* (pp. 59-70). Mahwah, NJ: Lawrence Erlbaum Associates.

Eyler, J., & Giles, D. E., Jr. (1999). *Where's the learning in service-learning?* San Francisco: Jossey-Bass.

Eyler, J., Giles, D. E. Jr., & Schmiede, A. (1996). *A practitioner's guide to reflection in service-learning.* Nashville, TN: Vanderbilt University, Corporation for National Service.

Giles, D. E., Jr., Eyler, J., & Braxton, J. (1997). The impact of service-learning on college students. *Michigan Journal of Community Service Learning, 4,* 5-15.

Gray, M. J., Feschwind, S., Ondaatje, E. H., Robyn, A., Klein, S., Sax, L.J., Astin, A. W., & Astin, H. S. (1996). *Evaluation of Learn and Serve America: Higher Education: First year report* (Vol. 1). Los Angeles: Rand Corporation.

Hatcher, J. A., Bringle, R. G., & Muthiah, R. (2001, October). *The critical role of reflection in service learning: A multi-campus study of service learning.* Paper presented at the First Annual International Conference on Service-Learning Research, Berkeley, CA.

Harkavy, I., & Puckett, J. (1991). Toward effective university-public school partnerships: An analysis of a contemporary model. *Teachers College Record, 92,* 556-581.

Keen, C., & Keen, J. (1998). *Bonner student impact survey.* Bonner Foundation.

Lazarus, J. (2001, October). *Development of a national service-learning research programme: The South African experience.* Paper presented at the First Annual Conference on Service-Learning Research, Berkeley, CA.

Markus, G. B., Howard, J. P. F., & King, D. C. (1993). Integrating community service and classroom instruction enhances learning: Results from an experiment. *Educational Evaluation and Policy Analysis, 15,* 410-419.

Morton, K. (1995). The irony of service: Charity, project, and social change in service-learning. *Michigan Journal of Community Service Learning, 2,* 19-32.

Muthiah, N. R., & Reeser, D. M. (2000). *IUPUI-WESCO COPC evaluation report.* Indianapolis, IN: Center for Service and Learning.

Nadler, A. (2002). Inter-group helping relations as power relations: Helping relations as affirming or challenging inter-group hierarchy. *Journal of Social Issues, 58,* 487-502

Pennebaker, J. W. (1990). *Opening up: The healing power of expressing emotions.* New York: Guilford.

Pennebaker, J. W., Kiecolt-Glaser, J., & Glaser, R. (1988). Disclosure of traumas and immune function: Health implications for psychotherapy. *Journal of Consulting and Clinical Psychology, 56*(2), 239-245.

Perry, J., & Katula, M. (2001). Does service affect citizenship? *Administration and Society, 32,* 332-367.

Piliavin, J. A. (2005). *Doing well by doing good: Health consequences of social participation.* Claremont Symposium on Applied Social Psychology: Process of Community Change and Social Action (pp. 29-50). Mahwah, NJ: Lawrence Erlbaum Associates.

Putnam, R. D. (1995). Bowling alone: America's declining social capital. *Journal of Democracy, 6,* 65-78.

Putnam, R. D. (2000). *Bowling alone: The collapse and revival of American community.* New York: Simon & Schuster.

Sax, L. J., & Astin, A. W. (1997). The benefits of service: Evidence from undergraduates. *Educational Record, 78*(3/4), 25-32.

Stukas, A. A., & Dunlap, M. R. (2002). Community involvement: Theoretical approaches and educational initiatives. *Journal of Social Issues, 58,* 411-427.

Stukas, A. A., Snyder, M., & Clary, E. G. (1999). The effects of "mandatory volunteerism" on intentions to volunteer. *Psychological Science, 10*(1), 59-64.

Vogelgesang, L. J., & Astin, A. W. (2000). Comparing the effects of service-learning and community service. *Michigan Journal of Community Service Learning, 7,* 25-34.

Wright, D. E. (1999). *Personal relationships.* Mountain View, CA: Mayfield.

Zlotkowski, H. (1999). Pedagogy and engagement. In R. Bringle, R. Games, & E. Malloy (Eds.), *Colleges and universities as citizens* (pp. 96-120). Boston: Allyn & Bacon.

ABOUT THE CONTRIBUTORS

Robert G. Bringle, PhD, is the Chancellor's Professor of Psychology and Philanthropic Studies and the Director of the Center for Service and Learning at Indiana University–Purdue University Indianapolis (IUPUI). Dr. Bringle has been involved in the implementation and evaluation of educational programs and is recognized for his research on jealousy in close relationships. His interests also include institutionalizing service learning and civic engagement. He is editor of *With Service in Mind: Concepts and Models for Service-Learning in Psychology* (with Duffy) and *Colleges and Universities as Citizens* (with Games & Malloy). Dr. Bringle was awarded the Ehrlich Award for Service Learning from Campus Compact and the Hiltunen Award from Indiana Campus Compact. He is a member of the Campus Compact Consulting Corps and the National Review Board for the Scholarship of Engagement, and a consultant on the Community-Higher Education-Service Partnership project in South Africa.

Matthew J. Chinman is an Associate Behavioral Scientist at the RAND Corporation and Health Science Specialist at the West Los Angeles VA Mental Illness Research, Education, and Clinical Center. Before that, he was an assistant professor in the Department of Psychiatry, Yale School of Medicine, and the Director of Program Evaluation Services at The Consultation Center in New Haven, Connecticut, where he coordinated several evaluations and needs assessments for nonprofit agencies in the Greater New Haven and surrounding areas. He is a co-author of the manual *Getting to Outcomes 1999: Methods and Tools for Planning, Evaluation, and Accountability*, prepared by the National Center for the Advancement of Prevention. He is currently the principal investigator of a grant from the Centers for Disease Control and Prevention to examine how the Getting to Outcomes system helps to bridge the gap between science and practice in substance abuse prevention. Dr. Chinman has published on such topics as program evaluation methodology, empowerment evaluation, adolescent empowerment, and coalition functioning.

Mark H. Davis is Professor of Psychology at Eckerd College in St. Petersburg, Florida. He is the author of over 40 articles and chapters in the area of social psychology, as well as a book, *Empathy: A Social Psychological Approach*. He has served as editor of *Annual Editions: Social Psychology* and as a consulting editor for the *Journal of Personality and Social Psychology*. His research interests include empathy, helping behavior, and interpersonal conflict. He received his PhD in psychology from the University of Texas at Austin, and his BA in psychology and political science from the University of Iowa.

Rafael M. Diaz is by training a social worker (MSW, New York University, 1977) and a developmental psychologist (PhD, Yale University, 1982). He completed a 2-year postdoctoral traineeship in epidemiology, biostatistics, and prevention science at The Center for AIDS Prevention Studies (CAPS), University of California San Francisco (UCSF, 1992-1994). After 13 years as a Professor of Psychology and Education at the University of New Mexico and Stanford University, he joined the faculty at CAPS/UCSF for 7 years, conducting research on Latino gay men and HIV. Recently he was appointed Professor of Ethnic Studies at San Francisco State University (SFSU), where he has assumed the position of Director of the César Chávez Institute (CCI). Guided by principles of community participatory research, the CCI conducts research programs pertaining to the impact of social oppression on the health, education, and well-being of disenfranchised communities in the United States.

Constance Flanagan, PhD, is a professor of youth civic development in the Department of Agricultural and Extension Education at Pennsylvania State University. Her program of work, "Adolescents and the Social Contract," concerns the factors in families, schools, and communities that promote civic values and competencies in young people, a topic she has investigated with different racial/ethnic groups in the United States as well as in comparative work across countries. Flanagan is a William T. Grant Scholar and a member of the MacArthur Network on the Transition to Adulthood. She is on the editorial boards of four journals and on the advisory boards of Health!Rocks, the Social Science Research Council's Youth and Globalization in the 21st Century, and CIRCLE.

Leslie S. Gallay, PhD, is Research Associate and Project Manager for the Social Responsibility and Prevention Project at the Social Science Research Institute at Pennsylvania State University. He also lectures on comparative international health in the Department of Health Policy and Administration at Penn State University. His research interests include comparative health systems, the social ecology of health, the cultural and social aspects of health promotion and prevention, and importance of human environments in improving health. Dr. Gallay is currently involved in studying the importance of schools, families, and friends as allies in preventing risk behaviors among American adolescents.

Sukhdeep Gill, PhD, is Associate Director of Early Childhood Programs at the Prevention Research Center and Assistant Professor of Human Development and Family Studies at Penn State York. Her research interests include program evaluation, needs of women and children, and diverse and at-risk populations. Dr. Gill is currently involved in the evaluation of community-based early preventive intervention programs, including Early Head Start, New Parent Support Program, and Healthy Families America. Her work focuses on process evaluation for continuous improvement in program implementation quality as well as outcome evaluations to study program effectiveness.

Robert M. Goodman, PhD, MPH, MA, is a Professor at the Graduate School of Public Health, University of Pittsburgh. Formerly he was the Usdin Family Professor in Community Health Sciences at the Tulane University School of Public Health and Tropical Medicine. He directed the Center for Community Research at The Wake Forest University School of Medicine, and was a faculty member at the University of North Carolina and University of South Carolina Schools of Public Health. He has been the principal investigator and evaluator on projects for The Centers for Disease Control and Prevention (CDC), The National Cancer Institute, The Centers for Substance Abuse Prevention, The Children's Defense Fund, and several state health departments. Dr. Goodman has written extensively on issues concerning community health development, community capacity, community coalitions, evaluation methods, organizational development, and the institutionalization of health programs.

Bert Klandermans is Professor of Applied Social Psychology and Dean of the Faculty of Social Science at Free University, Amsterdam, The Netherlands. He has published widely on mobilization and participation in social movements. He is the author of *The Social Psychology of Protest* (University of Minnesota Press). He edited various thematic collections on social movements research, most recently *Methods of Social Movement Research* with Suzanne Staggenborg (University of Minnesota Press). Currently, he is involved in studies of social and political participation in South Africa, activism at the extreme right, and political participation among migrants. His review chapter, "Collective Political Action," appeared in the *Handbook of Political Psychology*.

Anna Malsch, MA, is a doctoral candidate in social psychology at Claremont Graduate University (CGU). She holds a masters degree in Organizational Behavior and Program Evaluation from CGU. She has conducted research and evaluation in community organizations providing health care for victims of domestic violence, community-based computer learning for disenfranchised youth, and HIV/AIDS prevention services. She has research interests in psychological sense of community, volunteerism, civic and community engagement, social participation, and health and well-being. She is currently working on several research projects on topics such as psychological sense of community among people affected by HIV/AIDS, compassionate acts and community involvement of older adults, and the relationship between psychological sense of global community and prosocial behavior that extends beyond traditional geographical boundaries.

Johan Olivier holds BA and BA (Hons) degrees from the University of Pretoria. He pursued his graduate studies at the University of South Africa (MA) and Cornell University (PhD). He was employed by the Human Sciences Research Council in Pretoria, South Africa. He is currently a management/research consultant and is involved in assignments for the South African Government, government agencies, and donors. He taught by invitation at the University of Cape Town, University of Pretoria, and Stanford University. He has authored/co-authored more than 60 publications in the areas of social change, democratization, and political stability.

Allen M. Omoto, PhD, is a Professor of Psychology at the Claremont Graduate University in Claremont, CA. He is a social psychologist whose research interests include the social and psychological aspects of volunteerism, interpersonal relationships, HIV disease, and lesbian, gay, and bisexual issues. He has an ongoing program of research on volunteerism and helping relationships, including multiyear studies that have been supported by federal and private foundation grants. He also has extensive public policy experience. He helped found and administer a community-based AIDS service organization, and he worked in the U.S. Congress as the American Psychological Association's inaugural William A. Bailey AIDS Policy Congressional Fellow.

Jane Allyn Piliavin, PhD is a professor in the Department of Sociology at the University of Wisconsin-Madison. She received her BA in Psychology from the University of Rochester (1958), and her PhD in Social Psychology from Stanford University (1962). She has held positions at the University of California-Berkeley, Mills College, and the University of Pennsylvania. She has co-authored four books: *Adolescent Prejudice* (with Glock, Wuthnow, & Spencer, 1975); *Emergency Intervention* (with Dovidio, Gaertner, & Clark, 1981), *Giving Blood: The Development of an Altruistic Identity* (with Callero, 1991); and *The Psychology of Helping and Altruism: Problems and Puzzles* (with Schroeder, Penner, & Dovidio, 1995). Her current research involves the effects of volunteering on mental and physical health.

Jesus Ramirez-Valles is an Associate Professor in Community Health Sciences at The University of Illinois-Chicago School of Public Health. He obtained his masters in public health and his doctoral degree from the University of Michigan. His teaching and research interests are in health education and promotion and the sociology of health. Particularly, his research includes community mobilization for health, youth health, gender and race in health promotion, and HIV/AIDS and substance use prevention. He conducts qualitative and quantitative research in both the United States and Latin America.

Marlene Roefs is a research specialist in the unit Democracy and Governance of the Human Sciences Research Council in South Africa. Prior to rejoining the HSRC, Dr. Roefs assisted in capacity building for the Local Government Programme of the UNDP, and worked for the Institute for a Democratic South Africa. She earned her doctorate in Social Psychology at the Free University of Amsterdam. She co-authored the book *The State of the People: Citizens, Civil Society and Governance in South Africa, 1994-2000* (2001) and has published internationally. Her research foci include intergovernmental relations, development of local governance, urban renewal, citizenship, and public participation.

Abraham Wandersman is a Professor of Psychology at the University of South Carolina. He is a co-author of Prevention Plus III and a co-editor of the seminal book on empowerment evaluation, *Empowerment Evaluation: Knowledge and Tools for Self-Assessment and Accountability*. He is a co-author of the manual *Getting to Outcomes 1999: Methods and Tools for Planning, Evaluation, and Accountability*, prepared for the National Center for the Advancement of Prevention. He has been funded by a variety of sources that range from private foundations to large government agencies like National Institute of Mental Health, National Institute of Drug Abuse, and the Center for Substance Abuse Prevention. Dr. Wandersman has over 100 publications on topics such as community participation, community-based coalition, public perceptions of environmental risks, and empowerment evaluation. He has served on 20 national task forces and committees, 8 University committees, and 10 professional associations, including 6 divisions of the American Psychological Association.

John Wilson is currently a professor of sociology at Duke University. He received his DPhil from the University of Oxford. He is the author of numerous articles on volunteering, including a chapter in the *Annual Review of Sociology* (2000).

NAME INDEX

SUBJECT INDEX